THE RUGBY LEAGUE WORLD CUP

THE RUGBY LEAGUE WORLD CUP

An illustrated history of Rugby's oldest global tournament

LEAGUE
Publications Ltd

ACKNOWLEDGEMENTS

For many years the Rugby League World Cup has been under-appreciated. The absence of a definitive history of the tournament, which was inaugurated in 1954, has long rankled among Rugby League supporters. At League Publications we thought it was about time to provide the game and the sporting world with a written record of rugby's oldest world cup.

Such a mammoth task would not have been possible without the knowledge and the love of the game of Harry Edgar, who wrote the histories of the tournament, and of Malcolm Andrews, who laboured long and hard to compile the statistical records for the book.

For the story of the 2000 World Cup we are also in the debt of League Express match reporters Raymond Fletcher, Mike Latham, Graham Clay, Tony Hannan, Mike Rylance, Phil Caplan, Gareth Walker, Martin Butcher, Steve Mascord and Neil Fissler. Thanks too to League Publications staff photographers Vicky Matthers and Andy Howard and the Varley Picture Agency; to League Publications' chief designer Danny Spencer and his oppo' Vicky Matthers for designing the book. And to Tim Hanson for his invaluable assistance in checking the statistics.

And lastly, thankyou to the great players, past and present, who have made us all into committed devotees of the wonderful sport of Rugby League.

Tim Butcher

First published in Great Britain in 2000 by
League Publications Ltd
Wellington House
Briggate
Brighouse
West Yorkshire HD6 1DN

Copyright © League Publications Ltd

A CIP catalogue record for this book is available from the British Library
ISBN 1-901347-08-7

Designed and Typeset by League Publications Limited
Printed by ColourBooks Ltd, Dublin, Eire

CONTENTS

INTRODUCTION

We owe it to the French.

If it hadn't been for the foresight of that imaginative race, and in particular one M Paul Barrière, the idea of a Rugby League World Cup would have remained just that - merely a pipe-dream.

The concept of a World Cup, of course, had its 'can't do' opponents back in the 1950s; administrators, sound people with the future of the game at heart, who couldn't see the merit or the potential of Rugby League as a world game.

Plenty of those people still abound within the sport, and at various times in its history since the first World Cup in 1954 arguments have raged as to whether Rugby League should even bother with such a tournament.

Perhaps that was why for many years the Rugby League World Cup was restricted to four nations – France, Great Britain, New Zealand and Australia, with England and Wales given brief appearances in the 1975 competition.

Papua New Guinea joined the party in 1985, but it wasn't until the 1995 World Cup, the centrepiece of the English Centenary celebrations, that Rugby League finally took the bull by the horns, with ten nations enjoying a wonderful three weeks in unseasonably balmy October English weather.

By the year 2000 the Rugby League World Cup had expanded to 16 teams, confirming Barrière's vision of League as a truly global sport.

The expanded competition gave the World Cup organisers the opportunity to showcase the game in every part of the United Kingdom, in Ireland, and in France.

How satisfying must it have been for Paul Barrière to see his beloved France qualify for the quarter-finals of the 2000 World Cup with their win in front of a capacity crowd in Carcassonne, on the same day the Treizistes unveiled a statue of their World Cup legend Puig-Aubert.

'Pipette' is just one of the legends that live on in Rugby League, and many have been made in the twelve World Cup tournaments that have been played since the inaugural competition in 1954.

There's the story of how a Scotsman, Dave Valentine, was the first to lift the great old trophy, resurrected for the 2000 competition, captaining a side of British no-hopers who weren't even allowed to take their coach with them to the first World Cup in France.

Did you know that the star of the 1957 World Cup was almost prevented from representing the Kangaroos by his club committee out in the Queensland bush?

Introduction

What of the Rugby League playing Roman Catholic priest from Newcastle who featured in the infamous battle of Headingley in 1970 that led to calls for Rugby League to be banned from TV screens to protect the nation's youth?

Recall how the late Clive Sullivan effectively won the World Cup for Great Britain - for the third and last time – by racing 70 metres for a stunning try in Lyon. His son Anthony would later play in two World Cups for Wales.

And remember how the Emperor Wally Lewis helped win the 1988 World Cup for Australia despite suffering a broken arm in the final.

Of such stuff legends are born. Wendell Sailor's two tries, and Mat Rogers' six goals in the 2000 final, and Ryan Girdler's World Cup record 46 point haul against Russia, are just some of the feats that will also be talked about in years to come.

The 2000 Rugby League World Cup had the misfortune to be held in Britain at a time of unprecedented disruption. Britain suffered more rainfall in the month of November than it has done since records began. Many parts of the country were cut off by floods, and the railway system remained in chaos throughout the duration of the World Cup and beyond, because of flooding and fears about passenger safety.

Added to that, the sport of Rugby League was subjected to what seemed to many like a campaign to undermine its appeal in just about every section of the media.

But even that combination couldn't stop the 12th Rugby League World Cup going ahead, and producing some memorable moments to join all those that have gone before.

And in Australia's victory over New Zealand, that secured their sixth consecutive World title, we surely witnessed one of the great performances seen in any sport for a long, long time.

We hope you enjoy this, the first comprehensive record of rugby's oldest World Cup tournament. We hope it leaves you with the hope held by Paul Barrière back in 1953, when he was attempting to persuade the rest of the Rugby League world to think global: "It appears to us...that the time has now come to organise a World Cup series – indeed we feel it indispensable."

Let's hope that the spirit of Paul Barrière will always win the day.

1
WORLD CUP 2000

THE FINAL

AUSTRALIA 40 ....**NEW ZEALAND 12**

Played at Old Trafford, Manchester, England, Saturday 25 November 2000

Australia's dominance of world Rugby League was irrefutable after the magnificent Kangaroos secured their sixth successive World Cup title with a record-breaking seven-try victory over the Kiwis.

The Kangaroos have held the World Cup since 1975 and have won the trophy nine times out of a possible twelve since it was inaugurated in 1954.

Man-of-the-match Wendell Sailor equalled the record for tries in a final with a decisive brace in four minutes, after the Kiwis had fought back to trail only 12-18 midway through the second half.

Mat Rogers, with six goals and twelve points, set new records for a final and Australia's winning margin surpassed their previous record 25-12 score-line against New Zealand in 1988, the Kiwis' only previous final appearance.

Sailor, with ten tries, and Rogers, with 27 goals and 70 points, also topped the World Cup 2000 scoring charts between them.

The unstoppable Kangaroos - hot favourites at the start of the competition - dominated the final quarter, amassing 22 points in the last 14 minutes.

But it was the monster defensive effort demanded from the Kiwis in the first half that won the game for the Kangaroos.

Kiwi coach, Frank Endacott, who stepped down from the post he had held since 1994 after the final, was pleased with the efforts of his side.

And Australian counterpart Chris Anderson dubbed the win: "as good a team performance as you could ask for under pressure."

Skipper Brad Fittler, Brett Kimmorley, Andrew Johns and Scott Hill all rivalled the magnificent Sailor for the man-of-the-match accolade and combined to give the Kangaroos so many midfield options.

Kimmorley's kicking game was superb and his ability to take the ball to the line and release his runners was never better demonstrated. Fittler, too, capped a memorable day with a fine try while Johns justified his switch to hooker with astute distribution. Hill's ability to join the line and combine with Fittler and Kimmorley was crucial.

Of the younger players, centre Matthew Gidley capped a magnificent personal tournament, while Trent Barrett looked another superstar in the making.

Adam MacDougall and Wendell Sailor hold aloft the World Cup

History was with the Kangaroos, the Kiwis having won only one of 15 previous meetings between the sides in the World Cup. New Zealand had also been defeated 0-52 in the Anzac Test the previous April.   When the sides last met in a World Cup game, the semi-final back in 1995, Australia won 30-20 after extra-time.

Fittler and Johns were the only survivors from the Kangaroos side on duty that day with Richie Barnett, Stacey Jones, Henry Paul, Quentin Pongia, Stephen Kearney and Ruben Wiki for the Kiwis.

The world champions dominated right from the opening stages with Kimmorley dictating their attacks and soon demonstrating his vast repertoire of attacking kicks.

The Kiwis' first attack took eleven minutes to mount but Sailor calmly knocked away Jones' kick with a foot in the dead-ball area to set up a 20-metre tap.

The forward battle was as tough and unrelenting as forecast but the Kangaroos looked to have made the breakthrough when Sailor blasted over in the right corner but the video referee ruled that Stephen Kearney's despairing tackle had succeeded in preventing Sailor from grounding the ball.

But the Kangaroos were not to be denied three minutes later when Sailor drilled the ball through and Gidley just got a hand to it before it went dead. The video referee gave his assent and Rogers converted from the touch-line.

It was the only score of the first half but Kimmorley began the second in the same dominant form and, after another testing kick, Nigel Vagana was trapped behind his own line by a magnificent Rogers tackle from dummy-half. From the resulting drop-out the Kangaroos engineered their second converted try as Johns and Fittler combined to send Nathan Hindmarsh stretching over on the left for a converted try.

But the crowd came to life as the Kiwis mounted their revival, Vainikolo grabbing his ninth try of the World Cup after Matt Rua had challenged Lockyer to

Jones' high, angled kick to the left, Henry Paul adding the conversion after the video referee had again been called upon.

Within three minutes the Kangaroos restored their 12-point advantage when Kimmorley, dummied to the right before cutting through to unselfishly provide the supporting Darren Lockyer with a run-in on the inside.

But the Kiwis were back in the game when centre Tonie Carroll received from Henry Paul and twice eluded Adam MacDougall - in for Ryan Girdler, injured the previous week - on a blockbusting 30-metre run for a try that Henry Paul converted.

With Bradford's Robbie Paul brought off the bench, the Kiwis spied their chance and Sailor, rescuing his side after Jones and Kearney combined to almost send Vainikolo in, knocked-on ten metres from his own line.

But the Kiwis were unable to take advantage of the opportunity and the Kangaroos took over after, first, Henry Paul had knocked on at dummy-half and then Carroll couldn't hold a pass, both in attacking positions.

The decisive try came in the 66th minute when Gidley took out three defenders with an exquisite inside pass and Sailor twisted over in Robbie Paul's last ditch tackle, Rogers again negotiating the tricky goal attempt.

Henry Paul compounded the Kiwis' misery by kicking-off directly into touch and, three minutes later, the Australians were home and dry as Johns, Lockyer and Gidley laid on Sailor's second.

Fittler, stepping inside the cover from Lockyer's pass in his own inimitable way, and Barrett, with a magnificent 60-metre effort from Fittler's pass, added further converted tries in the dying minutes.

The weather gods had relented for the game but, after the presentations by Britain's Olympic legend Steve Redgrave had been completed, the rain returned.

The crowds were sent on their way home with a drenching to remind them of the horrific weather that had plagued the 2000 World Cup.

AUSTRALIA: 1 Darren Lockyer (Brisbane Broncos); 5 Wendell Sailor (Brisbane Broncos); 4 Matthew Gidley (Newcastle Knights); 3 Adam MacDougall (Newcastle Knights); 2 Mat Rogers (Cronulla Sharks); 6 Brad Fittler (C) (Sydney City Roosters); 7 Brett Kimmorley (Melbourne Storm); 8 Shane Webcke (Brisbane Broncos); 9 Andrew Johns (Newcastle Knights); 10 Robbie Kearns (Melbourne Storm); 11 Gorden Tallis (Brisbane Broncos); 12 Bryan Fletcher (Sydney City Roosters); 13 Scott Hill (Melbourne Storm). *Subs (all used):* 17 Jason Stevens (Cronulla Sharks) for Webcke (13); 16 Darren Britt (Canterbury Bulldogs) for Kearns (20); 15 Nathan Hindmarsh (Parramatta Eels) for Fletcher (20); Fletcher for Tallis (27); Webcke for Stevens (57); Tallis for Fletcher (62); 14 Trent Barrett (St George-Illawarra Dragons) for MacDougall (64); Kearns for Hindmarsh (78)
Tries: Gidley (26), Hindmarsh (46), Lockyer (53), Sailor (66, 69), Fittler (74), Barrett (76); **Goals:** Rogers 6

NEW ZEALAND: 1 Richie Barnett (C) (Sydney City Roosters); 2 Nigel Vagana (Auckland Warriors); 3 Tonie Carroll (Brisbane Broncos); 4 Willie Talau (Canterbury Bulldogs); 5 Lesley Vainikolo (Canberra Raiders); 6 Henry Paul (Bradford Bulls); 7 Stacey Jones (Auckland Warriors); 8 Craig Smith (St George-Illawarra Dragons); 9 Richard Swain (Melbourne Storm); 10 Quentin Pongia (Sydney City Roosters); 11 Matt Rua (Melbourne Storm); 12 Stephen Kearney (Melbourne Storm); 13 Ruben Wiki (Canberra Raiders). *Subs (all played):* 16 Nathan Cayless (Parramatta Eels) for Smith (14); 15 Joe Vagana (Auckland Warriors) for Pongia (14); 17 Logan Swann (Auckland Warriors) for Rua (20); Pongia for J Vagana (31); Smith for Cayless (31); Rua for Wiki (41); 14 Robbie Paul (Bradford Bulls) for Swain (58); J Vagana for Smith (58); Cayless for Pongia (58); Wiki for Kearney (70); Smith for J Vagana (75); Pongia for Cayless (75).
Tries: Vainikolo (50), Carroll (57); **Goals:** H Paul 2

Penalty count: 3-3; **Half-time:** 6-0; **Referee:** Stuart Cummings (England) **Attendance:** 44,329

Men of the Match
Australia: Wendell Sailor; *New Zealand:* Stephen Kearney

ROAD TO THE FINAL

GROUP ONE

ENGLAND 2 ....AUSTRALIA 22

Played at Twickenham, Saturday 28th October 2000

ENGLAND were well beaten, but it was not the massacre many feared, in the game that effectively decided who would win group one.

Australia's Dream Team was held in check for most of the game, before scoring two tries towards the end of this historic first ever Rugby League match at rugby union headquarters.

But it was still an emphatic defeat, and the only time an all-England side has conceded more points in 12 matches against Australia was when they lost 25-0 a few days after the 1975 World Cup in a game which was not a full international. Lacking match fitness after playing just a couple of easy matches – against PNG (82-0) and New Zealand Residents (108-0) – in the previous two months, Australia showed only flashes of the form that made them such red-hot favourites.

The slippery conditions also slowed them down, and their flat attacking formation suited England, who were very much in their faces.

ENGLAND: 1 Kris Radlinski (Wigan Warriors); 2 Leon Pryce (Bradford Bulls); 3 Scott Naylor (Bradford Bulls); 4 Keith Senior (Leeds Rhinos); 5 Chev Walker (Leeds Rhinos); 6 Tony Smith (Wigan Warriors); 7 Sean Long (St Helens); 8 Harvey Howard (Brisbane Broncos); 9 Paul Rowley (Halifax Blue Sox); 10 Stuart Fielden (Bradford Bulls); 11 Adrian Morley (Leeds Rhinos); 12 Mike Forshaw (Bradford Bulls); 13 Andrew Farrell (C) (Wigan Warriors). *Subs (all used):* 14 Paul Wellens (St Helens); 15 Kevin Sinfield (Leeds Rhinos); 16 Darren Fleary (Leeds Rhinos); 17 Paul Anderson (Bradford Bulls).
Goal: Farrell
On report: Tony Smith (20) – high tackle, no case to answer

AUSTRALIA: 1 Darren Lockyer (Brisbane Broncos); 2 Mat Rogers (Cronulla); 3 Ryan Girdler (Penrith Panthers); 4 Matthew Gidley (Newcastle Knights); 5 Wendell Sailor (Brisbane Broncos); 6 Brad Fittler (C) (Sydney City); 7 Brett Kimmorley (Melbourne Storm); 8 Shane Webcke (Brisbane Broncos); 9 Andrew Johns (Newcastle Knights); 10 Robbie Kearns (Melbourne Storm); 11 Gorden Tallis (Brisbane Broncos); 12 Bryan Fletcher (Sydney City); 13 Scott Hill (Melbourne Storm). *Subs (all used):* 14 Adam MacDougall (Newcastle Knights); 15 Jason Croker (Canberra Raiders); 16 Darren Britt (Sydney Bulldogs); 17 Jason Stevens (Cronulla).
Tries: Sailor (4, 79), Gidley (32), MacDougall (66); **Goals:** Rogers 3

Penalties: Eng 9-8; **Half-time:** 2-8; **Referee:** David Pakieto (New Zealand)
Attendance: 33,758
Men of the Match
England: Sean Long; *Australia:* Brett Kimmorley

Australia's biggest threat came from their smallest player, scrum-half Brett Kimmorley, who ruled midfield all night. It was Kimmorley's keen eye and perfectly-placed kick that led to Australia's first try after only four minutes.

Spotting acres of space on England's left wing he plopped a kick over near the flag to leave Wendell Sailor with plenty of time to pick up the ball and stroll round

14

**Australian captain Brad Fittler looks for support under pressure from
England duo Darren Fleary and Keith Senior**

for the touchdown. Later in the half Kimmorley linked with Brad Fittler to send
Matthew Gidley sliding over.

It was still only 10-2, after Australia had opted for a pressure-easing penalty
well into the second half, when a break by Kimmorley set up the position from which
Adam MacDougall scored the try that really finished off England.

Rogers' goal made it 16-2, and England did well not to concede another try until the
last minute, when Australia flashed the ball out for Sailor to grab his second.

Australia's winning margin would have been greater but for two first-half video
rulings going against them. Girdler was penalised for a double movement, and
Fittler was adjudged to have knocked on when following up another neat kick by
Kimmorley.

The nearest England went to scoring a try was when Sean Long made a break
and was obstructed. The referee allowed play to go on, however, and Paul Rowley
hacked towards the corner, where Leon Pryce gathered before being bundled into
touch as his inside pass went to ground.

Stuart Spruce was a late English withdrawal because of illness, 18 year old Chev
Walker making a confident full international debut, along with other youngsters
Pryce, Kevin Sinfield and Paul Wellens.

FIJI 38...RUSSIA 12

Played at Craven Park, Barrow, Sunday 29th October 2000

The inquisitive rolled up to Craven Park on the first Sunday of the tournament and were rewarded with some splendid entertainment and confirmation that Russia really could play Rugby League. They gave Fiji a run for their money in what was a very enjoyable match.

Unfortunately for Russia they were bedevilled by handling errors throughout and completed only one set of six in the entire first half. As skipper and front-rower Ian Rubin - who had only joined up with his teammates in England - remarked later: "I was very impressed with the Russian team. It was a good performance all round - it was just our inexperience which proved to be costly.

"Russia can and will be a force in world Rugby League."

The Fijians were much steadier and found enough possession to show their full range of running and handling skills with Tabua Cakacaka at prop and Sam Marayawa in the second row starring up front.

"I was very happy with our recent training," enthused Fiji coach Don Furner, the former Kangaroo boss.

"And there was a lift in enthusiasm with Lote (Brisbane winger Tuqiri) joining the team. It was an excellent effort in defence as well as attack."

To their credit, Russia hung in with little possession, but demonstrated some strong defence.

Roosters prop Rubin was outstanding for them but others to impress were scrum-half Igor Gavriline, fullback Robert Iliassov and wingmen Mikhail Mitrofanov and Maxim Romanov.

Tuqiri was a class act throughout. He found a nice angle to run on to a flat pass for the opening try.

Fiji's Lote Tuqiri scores the opening try against Russia at Craven Park, Barrow

Russia's Igor Gavriline picks his way through the Fiji defence

Later, when he put in a chip-over, his winger Semi Tadulala gathered on the full, Joe Tamani linked and released Tuqiri with a terrific inside pass for a superb second. In between Marayawa broke and Jone Kuruduadua got on the end of another great movement.

Tuqiri proved that he could defend as well in the 15th minute.

Fiji probed up the right but the ball went loose. Iliassov snapped it up to race 80 metres only for Tuqiri to get back and make a sensational try-saving tackle. By half-time Russia had steadied the ship and produced six points when Iliassov ducked over from dummy-half.

The Bears needed the early score in the second stanza, but again poor ball control handed the initiative to Fiji. Loose forward Atunaisa Vunivalu came into the game with a bang, using his pace and strength to grab a second-half hat-trick, before Waisale Sovatabua put the icing on Fiji's cake with a last-second interception.

The Islanders had begun the singing well before the final hooter. But Russia had been competitive throughout and proved themselves to be worthy members of the World Cup Party.

FIJI: 1 Lote Tuqiri (C) (Brisbane Broncos); 2 Jone Kuruduadua (Bellingen-Dorrigo); 3 Waisale Sovatabua (Huddersfield-Sheffield Giants); 4 Eparama Navale (Northern Eagles); 5 Semi Tadulala (Brisbane Wests); 6 Stephen Smith (Otahuhu); 7 Kalaveti Naisoro Tuiabayaba (Bounty Rum Crushers); 8 Tabua Cakacaka (Cootamundra); 9 Fred Robarts (Te Atatu); 10 Eluale Vakatawa (Tumbarumba); 11 Josese Tamani (Cabramatta); 12 Samu Marayawa (Ourimbah); 13 Atunaisa Vunivalu (Serua Dragons). *Subs (all used):* 14 Farasiko Tokarei (Nadi Steelers); 15 Josefa Lasagavibau (Nadera Panthers); 16 Amani Takayawa (Nadi Steelers); 17 Peceli Vuniyayawa (Queanbeyan). **Tries:** Tuqiri (5, 23), Kuruduadua (17), Vunivalu (42,58,61), Sovatabua (80); **Goals:** Tuqiri 5

RUSSIA: 1 Robert Iliassov (Kazan Arrows); 2 Mikhail Mitrofanov (Kazan Arrows); 3 Matthew Donovan (Western Suburbs); 4 Craig Cygler (Cairns Brothers); 5 Maxim Romanov (Kazan Arrows); 6 Andre Olar (Toulouse); 7 Igor Gavriline (Lokomotiv Moscow); 8 Ian Rubin (C) (Sydney City); 9 Alexander Lysenkov (Lokomotiv Moscow); 10 Robert Campbell (Redcliffe); 11 Petr Sokolov (Lokomotiv Moscow); 12 Aaron Findlay (Bulldogs); 13 Joel Rullis (Western Suburbs). *Subs (all used):* 14 Pavel Kalachkine (Kazan Arrows); 15 Victor Netchaev (Lokomotiv Moscow); 16 Igor Jiltsov (Lokomotiv Moscow); 17 Vadim Postnikov (Lokomotiv Moscow). **Tries:** Iliassov (37), Rullis (46); **Goals:** Jiltsov, Mitrofanov

Penalties: Fiji 5-11; **Half-time:** 16-6; **Referee:** Russell Smith (England) **Attendance:** 2,187 **Men of the Match** *Fiji:* Atunaisa Vunivalu; *Russia:* Ian Rubin

AUSTRALIA 66 ....FIJI 8

Played at Gateshead International Stadium, Wednesday 1st November 2000

Mat Rogers broke Andrew Johns' Australian Test record when he scored 34 points in Australia's second game. His four tries and nine goals were amassed in the 66-8 disposal of a courageous Fiji, with skipper Lote Tuqiri again the star.

As it turned out, it was a mark which would last only until the following Saturday night. The three days in which he was the highest-scoring Australian international were three turbulent days for the 24 year old. The day after the Gateshead game, he had learnt his daughter had been admitted to hospital with a potentially serious illness.

Officials went as far as making plans for him to return home but, thankfully, the situation eased and he remained with the team.

Rogers must have been willing to admit that he had a rival for the limelight at what was formerly the Thunderdome. Tuqiri was outstanding, scoring a try and setting one up in an amazing individual display.

The try Fijian prop Tabua Cakacaka scored, after Tuqiri made a long break in the 24th minute, was the first scored against Australia in 252 minutes of football, or almost 12 months.

It was November 5 the previous year when it happened, when Nigel Vagana put New Zealand temporarily in front with eight minutes to go in the Tri-Nations final at Ericsson Stadium.

Cakacaka's try did not put the Fijians in front but it was celebrated as if it won them a grand final - as was Tuqiri's individual effort in the 52nd minute.

AUSTRALIA: 1 Darren Lockyer (Brisbane Broncos); 2 Mat Rogers (Cronulla); 3 Ryan Girdler (Penrith Panthers); 4 Matthew Gidley (Newcastle Knights); 5 Adam MacDougall (Newcastle Knights); 6 Trent Barrett (St George-Illawarra Dragons); 7 Andrew Johns (Newcastle Knights); 8 Jason Stevens (Cronulla); 9 Craig Gower (Penrith Panthers); 10 Michael Vella (Parramatta Eels); 11 Ben Kennedy (Parramatta Eels); 12 Nathan Hindmarsh (Parramatta Eels); 13 Brad Fittler (C) (Sydney City). *Subs (all used):* 14 Scott Hill (Melbourne Storm); 15 Jason Croker (Canberra Raiders); 16 Robbie Kearns (Melbourne Storm); 17 Shane Webcke (Brisbane Broncos).
Tries: Rogers (6, 21,65,78), Kennedy (11,62), Girdler (35, 42), Barrett (13), Hindmarsh (16), MacDougall (30), Gidley (50); **Goals:** Rogers 9

FIJI: 1 Lote Tuqiri (C) (Brisbane Broncos); 2 Jone Kuruduadua (Bellingen-Dorrigo); 3 Waisale Sovatabua (Huddersfield-Sheffield Giants); 4 Eparama Navale (Northern Eagles); 5 Semi Tadulala (Brisbane Wests); 6 Stephen Smith (Otahuhu); 7 Kalaveti Naisoro Tuiabayaba (Bounty Rum Crushers); 8 Tabua Cakacaka (Cootamundra); 9 Fred Robarts (Te Atatu); 10 Etuate Vakatawa (Tumbarumba); 11 Josese Tamani (Cabramatta); 12 Sam Marayawa (Ourimbah); 13 Atunaisa Vunivalu (Serua Dragons). *Subs (all used):* 14 Farasiko Tokarei (Nadi Steelers); 15 Mesake Navugona (Bounty Rum Crushers); 16 Amani Takayawa (Nadi Steelers); 17 Peceli Wawavanua (Wallangarra).
Tries: Cakacaka (24), Tuqiri (52)

Penalties: Aus 4-1; **Half-time:** 38-4; **Referee:** Robert Connolly (England); **Attendance:** 4,197
Men of the Match
Australia: Mat Rogers; *Fiji:* Lote Tuqiri

The game was only six minutes old when Rogers scored his first try, in the left corner, which he duly converted. Tries to second-rower Ben Kennedy and stand-off Trent Barrett followed reasonably quickly, with forward Nathan Hindmarsh capitalising on a jinking run from half-back Andrew Johns to make it 22-0 after 16 minutes.

Centre Girdler re-gathered a Johns kick for Rogers to score his second but then came the Cakacaka bombshell, which left the Australians standing in their own in-goal, hands on hips, as if it was they who trailed by 24.

Mat Rogers kicks one of his nine goals on the way to his 34 point haul

Their picnic soon resumed, however, with winger Adam MacDougall and Penrith's Girdler scoring before the break to make it 38-4 at half-time.

Girdler and centre Matthew Gidley scored after the break, with Newcastle's Johns failing in his cameo goal-kicking appearance after clubmate Gidley's touchdown.

Then Tuqiri scored a well-taken four-pointer, after St George Illawarra's Barrett knocked on and Fiji won the scrum, halfback Kalaveti Naisoro throwing the final pass.

Kennedy and Rogers - twice - then completed the Australian try scoring.

19

ENGLAND 76 ....RUSSIA 4

Played at Knowsley Road, St Helens, Wednesday 1st November 2000

ENGLAND ran up a record against Russia - who were given 80 start on the handicap margin – beating their previous best of 73-6 against France in 1996

England, without six players who played against Australia, struggled early in the game despite taking a 30-2 interval lead, and looked a lot sharper when Sean Long replaced Andy Farrell at stand-off.

Farrell had been one of England's best players, creating two tries and kicking five goals. He wore the number 13 shirt, despite playing stand-off, because they could not find a number 6 strip to fit.

ENGLAND: 1 Paul Wellens (St Helens); 2 Leon Pryce (Bradford Bulls); 3 Chev Walker (Leeds Rhinos); 4 Keith Senior (Leeds Rhinos); 5 Darren Rogers (Castleford Tigers); 13 Andrew Farrell (C) (Wigan Warriors) ; 7 Paul Deacon (Bradford Bulls); 8 Francis Stephenson (Wakefield Trinity Wildcats); 9 Paul Rowley (Halifax Blue Sox); 10 Darren Fleary (Leeds Rhinos); 11 Jamie Peacock (Bradford Bulls); 12 Andy Hay (Leeds Rhinos); 6 Kevin Sinfield (Leeds Rhinos). *Subs (all used):* 14 Sean Long (St Helens); 15 Stuart Spruce (Bradford Bulls); 16 Stuart Fielden (Bradford Bulls); 17 Harvey Howard (Brisbane Broncos).
Tries: Sinfield (10,40,78), Rowley (12,52), Peacock (45, 54), Long (59,76), Hay (14), Walker (30), Pryce (41), Stephenson (67), Deacon (72); **Goals:** Farrell 5, Long 5

RUSSIA: 1 Robert Iliassov (Kazan Arrows); 2 Mikhail Mitrofanov (Kazan Arrows); 3 Andrei Doumalkine (Locomotiv Moscow); 4 Craig Cygler (Cairns Brothers); 5 Maxim Romanov (Kazan Arrows); 6 Andre Olar (Toulouse); 7 Igor Gavriline (Locomotiv Moscow); 8 Ian Rubin (C) (Sydney City); 9 Alexander Lysenkov (Locomotiv Moscow); 10 Robert Campbell (Redcliffe); 11 Petr Sokolov (Locomotiv Moscow); 12 Aaron Findlay (Canterbury Bulldogs); 13 Joel Rullis (Western Suburbs). *Subs (all used):* 14 Paval Kalachkine (Kazan Arrows); 15 Victor Netchaev (Locomotiv Moscow); 16 Igor Jiltsov (Locomotiv Moscow); 17 Vadim Postnikov (Locomotiv Moscow)
Goals: Mitrofanov 2

Penalties: Eng 4-7; **Half-time:** 30-2;
Referee: Bill Shrimpton (New Zealand); **Attendance:** 5,736
Men of the Match
England: Paul Rowley; *Russia:* Ian Rubin

Long added pace to England's midfield, highlighting his performance with the night's best solo try. It was a classic piece of stand-off play as he sped away from a scrum 40 metres out. The Saints star scored another and had a hand in six more. Add five goals and it amounted to a very useful 40 minutes.

Kevin Sinfield led the tryscoring with a hat-trick, but England hooker Paul Rowley deservedly took the man of the match award with an all-action two-try display.

Like England against Australia, Russia never looked like scoring a try. The only way they were going to score was from goals and they accepted that when Mikhail Mitrofanov kicked a penalty to make it 24-2 and a second to pull them back to 54-4.

There was no lack of effort, though, with Alexander Lysenkov heading their tackle count with 22 and captain Ian Rubin setting a great example up front.

England's Francis Stephenson on the charge against Russia

ENGLAND 66...FIJI 10

Played at Headingley, Leeds, Saturday 4th November

Another emphatic defeat of game but outclassed opposition left England coach John Kear with plenty of selection posers.

Paul Rowley had been the official man of the match against Russia in midweek, but he was replaced at hooker by Tony Smith, who took the same award against Fiji. The new half-back pairing of Sean Long and Paul Deacon also combined well.

Second-rower Jamie Peacock followed up his two tries against Russia with another three - all the result of good support play and powerful finishing.

Smith was involved in half-a-dozen of England's 12 tries and retained his renowned support play to finish off a

The Fijian defence holds up England's Jamie Peacock

break by Deacon to go in for one himself. Long was also involved in several tries and half-back partner Deacon kept things ticking over smoothly.

England had far too much football intelligence for the Fijians, Andy Farrell equalling two England records with nine goals and 22 points, including a clever solo try when he dummied through in classic style.

The spectators were equally thrilled with the exciting running of Fiji captain Lote Tuqiri. From his first brilliant kick and run raid in the opening minutes to his breakaway 75th minute try, the tall fullback looked every inch one of the most outstanding players of the competition.

The crowd showed their appreciation as the Fijians took a lap of honour, their World Cup at an end.

ENGLAND: 1 Stuart Spruce (Bradford Bulls); 2 Paul Wellens (St Helens); 3 Scott Naylor (Bradford Bulls); 4 Kris Radlinski (Wigan Warriors); 5 Darren Rogers (Castleford Tigers); 6 Sean Long (St Helens); 7 Paul Deacon (Bradford Bulls); 8 Francis Stephenson (Wakefield Trinity Wildcats); 9 Tony Smith (Wigan Warriors); 10 Paul Anderson (Bradford Bulls); 11 Jamie Peacock (Bradford Bulls); 12 Andy Hay (Leeds Rhinos); 13 Andrew Farrell (C) (Wigan Warriors). *Subs (all used):* 14 Kevin Sinfield (Leeds Rhinos); 15 Chev Walker (Leeds Rhinos); 16 Stuart Fielden (Bradford Bulls); 17 Harvey Howard (Brisbane Broncos). **Tries:** Peacock (17,39,78), Wellens (10,47), Rogers (35,58), Hay (5), Smith (61), Farrell (68), Naylor (26), Radlinski (31); **Goals:** Farrell 9

FIJI: 1 Lote Tuqiri (C) (Brisbane Broncos); 2 Niko Vakararawa (Lismore Workers); 3 Seteriki Rakabula (Bounty Rum Crushers); 4 Eparama Navale (Northern Eagles); 5 Jimi Bolakoro (Bounty Rum Crushers); 6 Waisale Sovatabua (Huddersfield-Sheffield Giants); 7 Kalaveti Naisoro Tuiabayaba (Bounty Rum Crushers); 8 Etuate Vakatama (Tumbarumba); 9 Fred Robart (Te Atatu); 10 Tabua Cakacaka (Coolamundra); 11 Peceli Wawavanua (Wallangarra); 12 Samu Marayawa (Ourimbah); 13 Atunaisa Vunivalu (Serua Dragons). *Subs (all used):* 14 Farasiko Tokarei (Nadi Steelers); 15 Josefa Lasagavibau (Nadera Panthers); 16 Roger Matakamikamica (Whitsunday); 17 Peceli Vuniyayawa (Queanbeyan). **Tries:** Navale (21), Tuqiri (75); **Goals:** Vunivalu

Penalties: Eng 14-3; **Half-time:** 40-4; **Referee:** Thierry Alibert (France)
Attendance: 10,052
Men of the Match
England: Jamie Peacock; *Fiji:* Lote Tuqiri

AUSTRALIA 110 ....RUSSIA 4

Played at The Boulevard, Hull, Saturday, 4th November 2000

The records tumbled again at The Boulevard as the world champions ruthlessly piled up the points against Russia, Ryan Girdler leading the way with three tries and 17 goals from 19 attempts.

The 28 year old Penrith centre set a new world record for goals in an international match but fell two short of Hazem El Masri's 48-point record for Lebanon against Morocco last year when the previous record international score, 104-0, was established.

Winger Wendell Sailor also equalled the Australian and World Cup record with four tries.

The ink was hardly dry in the record books after Tasesa Lavea's 12 goals for the Kiwis against the Cook Islands on the previous Thursday, but Girdler surpassed that with ease and his 46-point tally was also a record for a World Cup game.

Girdler's two misses at goal came in succession as he failed to add conversions to the Australians' sixth and seventh tries of the evening, the first attempt hitting a post, but he then went on to kick 12 goals in succession.

The tone for a one-sided evening was set as early as the fourth minute when half-backs Brett Kimmorley and Trent Barrett set up Girdler for the opening.

The Russians had already earned the admiration of the small

AUSTRALIA: 1 Adam MacDougall (Newcastle Knights); 5 Wendell Sailor (Brisbane Broncos); 4 Matthew Gidley (Newcastle Knights); 3 Ryan Girdler (Penrith Panthers); 2 Jason Croker (Canberra Raiders); 6 Trent Barrett (St George-Illawarra Dragons); 7 Brett Kimmorley (Melbourne Storm); 8 Shane Webcke (Brisbane Broncos); 9 Andrew Johns (Newcastle Knights); 10 Robbie Kearns (Melbourne Storm); 11 Gorden Tallis (C) (Brisbane Broncos); 12 Bryan Fletcher (Sydney City); 13 Scott Hill (Melbourne Storm). *Subs (all used):* 14 Craig Gower (Penrith Panthers); 15 Nathan Hindmarsh (Parramatta Eels); 16 Michael Vella (Parramatta Eels); 17 Ben Kennedy (Newcastle Knights).
Tries: Girdler (4, 33, 68), MacDougall (7), Sailor (10, 38, 46, 79), Barrett (16, 40), Fletcher (24), Webcke (30), Tallis (50), Croker (52, 55), Hindmarsh (59, 76), Johns (74), Gidley (80): **Goals:** Girdler 17

RUSSIA: 1 Mikhail Mitrofanov (Kazan Arrows); 5 Rinat Chamsoutdinov (Kazan Arrows); 3 Maxim Romanov (Kazan Arrows); 4 Robert Iliassov (Kazan Arrows); 2 Matthew Donovan (Western Suburbs); 6 Andre Olar (Toulouse); 7 Igor Gavriline (Locomotiv Moscow); 8 Ian Rubin (C) (Sydney City); 9 Alexander Lysenkov (Locomotiv Moscow); 10 Robert Campbell (Redcliffe); 11 Kirillin Koulemine (Locomotiv Moscow); 12 Roustem Garifoulline (Kazan Arrows); 13 Joel Rullis (Western Suburbs). *Subs (all used):* 14 Pavel Kalachkine (Kazan Arrows); 15 Michael Giorgas (Logan City); 16 Andrei Kuchumov (Moscow Magicians); 17 Viatcheslav Artachine (Kazan Arrows).
Try: Donovan (19)

Penalties: Aus 5-1; **Half-time:** 50-4; **Referee:** Stuart Cummings (England) **Attendance:** 3,044
Men of the Match
Australia: Ryan Girdler; *Russia:* Ian Rubin

crowd with some brave tackling and adventurous attacking moves and they got their reward with a try, ironically made in Australia.

After Western Suburbs winger Matthew Donovan, who qualified for Russia through his grandparents, went close with a darting inside run, prop Robert Campbell took Igor Gavriline's pass and drilled a low kick to the left corner. Donovan gleefully pounced for the score that was allowed after referee Stuart Cummings went to the screen.

The Russian skipper, Ian Rubin of Sydney Roosters, said: "The England and Australia games were both very hard but Australia blew us off everywhere, up the

Australia's Adam MacDougall and Trent Barrett put a stop to this Russian attack

middle and out wide. But it has been a good week and everyone has enjoyed it and we have made a lot of new friends."

The group of 50-strong Russian supporters in the stand kept up a ceaseless encouragement to the end.

"First of all, I am very happy to have had my team play here," said Russian coach, Evgeni Klebanov, putting the World Cup into perspective. "They have been to a very good school but this is a very harsh school. It is the first time they have played at such a level and now we know where we want to go. It is very important that we have as many international games as possible because that is the only way we will develop."

GROUP TWO

WALES 38 ....COOK ISLANDS 6
Played at Racecourse Ground, Wrexham, Sunday 29th October 2000

WALES began their World Cup campaign with a six-try defeat of the Cook Islands, dominating after the break to score 32-unopposed points in the second half on the back of an outstanding hat-trick from Kris Tassell.

The Salford centre, who was born in Mount Isa in Queensland but whose grandfather was born in Pontypridd, sparked the Welsh revival with a superb finish just after the interval. But due to a late change in numbers, he heard the PA announcer credit all three of his tries to Jason Critchley.

On another rain-swept, bitterly cold night, Wales struggled for fluency against some committed tackling from the Cooks in a scrappy first half and were disappointed to go in at the interval on level terms, 6-6.

The Welsh had three survivors from the side that played at Old Trafford in the semi-final five years ago in skipper Harris, Anthony Sullivan and Keiron Cunningham. The Cooks had two remaining players, Craig Bowen and Jason Temu, from the side that impressed in winning the Emerging Nations World Cup in 1995.

WALES: 1 Paul Atcheson (St Helens); 2 Paul Sterling (Leeds Rhinos); 4 Jason Critchley (unattached); 3 Kris Tassell (Salford City Reds); 5 Anthony Sullivan (St Helens); 6 Iestyn Harris (C) (Leeds Rhinos); 7 Lee Briers (Warrington Wolves); 8 Anthony Farrell (Leeds Rhinos); 9 Keiron Cunningham (St Helens); 10 Dave Whittle (Leigh Centurions); 11 Justin Morgan (Canberra Raiders); 12 Mick Jenkins (Hull FC); 13 Dean Busby (Warrington Wolves). *Subs (all used):* 14 Ian Watson (Swinton Lions); 15 Wes Davies (Wigan Warriors); 16 Paul Highton (Salford City Reds); 17 Garreth Carvell (Leeds Rhinos).
Tries: Briers (6), Tassell (43, 70, 76), Jenkins (56), Cunningham (68); **Goals:** Harris 7

COOK ISLANDS: 1 Richard Piakura (Ngatangiia/Matavera); 2 Tangiia Tongia (Canterbury Bulls); 3 Steve Berryman (Wainuimata); 4 Kevin Iro (C) (St Helens); 5 Karl Temata (Hibiscus Coast Raiders); 6 Craig Bowen (Brisbane Wests); 7 Leroy Joe (Hull KR); 8 George Tuakura (Mangere East); 9 Zane Clarke (Cessnock Goannas); 10 Jason Temu (Newcastle Knights); 11 Patrick Kuru (Tumbarumba); 12 Tyrone Pau (Ponsonby Ponies); 13 Anthony Samuel (Workington Town). *Subs (all used):* 14 Michael Andersson (Caloundra); 15 Peter Lewis (Auckland Warriors); 16 Tere Glassie (Newtown Jets); 17 Adam Cook (Wynnum Manly).
Try: Temata (22); **Goal:** Piakura
On report: George Tuakura (60) - high tackle (found no case to answer)

Penalties: Wales 13-5; **Half-time:** 6-6; **Referee:** Thierry Alibert (France)
Attendance: 5,060
Men of the Match
Wales: Kris Tassell; *Cook Islands:* Jason Temu

The Welsh got a perfect start when Cunningham's tackle dislodged the ball from Karl Temata's icy hands to set up a scrum. After Anthony Farrell drove in close to the line, Lee Briers received from Cunningham at the ruck and dummied to pass

Justin Morgan (11) congratulates Lee Briers on scoring against the Cook Islands

outside before slicing through to score. Harris added the angled conversion for a 6-0 lead.

But the Cooks fought back as Anthony Samuel and skipper Kevin Iro combined down the left, Temata finishing with aplomb to go over despite the attempts to cover from Sterling and Paul Atcheson. Richard Piakura landed a superbly struck conversion from the touchline.

But when Harris's superb pass created room for Tassell down the left channel and the Australian finished incisively from 25 metres - Harris landed the touchline conversion for a 12-6 lead - Wales were on their way.

Harris extended the advantage with a penalty on 52 minutes and then took on the close-range Cooks defence and offloaded brilliantly for Mick Jenkins to score by the posts. Harris's fourth goal put Wales 20-6 to the good.

Cooks were frustrated when Patrick Kuru had a try ruled out by the video referee and with that their last hopes disappeared. Wales moved further ahead when Cunningham fought his way over from acting half-back after Jenkins had almost wriggled through, Harris tagging on his fifth goal.

On the back of an 8-0 penalty count in the second half, Wales were in control of the game and Tassell completed a successful evening with two late tries to complete his hat-trick.

NEW ZEALAND 64 ....LEBANON 0

Played at Kingsholm, Gloucester, Sunday 29th October 2000

THE KIWIS opened their World Cup account in impressive style with a comprehensive 12-try romp over Lebanon.

Making light of the atrocious conditions, with incessant heavy rain and a howling wind being the dominant factors, New Zealand's strength in two-try centres Willie Talau and Tonie Carroll, the power of second-rowers Logan Swann and Stephen Kearney and the ceaseless, intelligent probing of Stacey Jones, was too much for the gallant Cedars in their debut on the big stage.

NEW ZEALAND: 1 Richie Barnett (C) (Sydney Roosters); 2 Lesley Vainikolo (Canberra Raiders); 3 Tonie Carroll (Brisbane Broncos); 4 Willie Talau (Sydney Bulldogs); 5 Brian Jellick (N Queensland Cowboys); 6 Henry Paul (Bradford Bulls); 7 Stacey Jones (Auckland Warriors); 8 Craig Smith (St George-Illawarra Dragons); 9 Richard Swain (Melbourne Storm); 10 Quentin Pongia (Sydney Roosters); 11 Logan Swann (Auckland Warriors); 12 Stephen Kearney (Melbourne Storm); 13 Ruben Wiki (Canberra Raiders). *Subs (all used):* 14 Joe Vagana (Auckland Warriors); 15 Robbie Paul (Bradford Bulls); 16 Matt Rua (Melbourne Storm); 17 Nathan Cayless (Parramatta Eels).
Tries: Talau (11,69), Barnett (15,46), Carroll (23,52), Jellick (34), Vainikolo (37,66), Swann (60), Jones (76,78); **Goals:** H Paul 2, Jones 6

LEBANON: 1 Hazem El Masri (Sydney Bulldogs); 2 Najjarin Bilal (St George-Illawarra Dragons); 3 George Katrib (Sydney Bulldogs); 4 Travis Touma (Sydney Bulls); 5 Hassan Saleh (Canterbury Bulldogs); 6 Jason Stanton (Sydney Bulls); 7 Paul Khoury (Sydney Bulldogs); 8 Darren Maroon (C) (Sydney Bulls); 9 Anthony Semrani (Sydney Bulldogs); 10 Moneh Elahmad (Cabramatta); 11 Sami Chamoun (Sydney Bulls); 12 Michael Coorey (Balmain); 13 Joe Lichaa (Sydney Roosters). *Subs (all used):* 14 Christopher Salem (St Gaudens); 15 Charlie Nohra (The Oaks); 16 Kandy Tamer (Sydney Bulls); 17 Samer El Masri (Sydney Roosters).

Penalties: NZ 7-4; **Half-time:** 26-0; **Referee:** Bill Harrigan (Australia)
Attendance: 2,496
Men of the Match
New Zealand: Richie Barnett; *Lebanon:* Sami Chamoun

Lebanon – with several of their players suffering from mild hypothermia by the end of the game - were magnificently led by second-rower Sami Chamoun, Anthony Semrani and Hazem El Masri, but in the end they fell to the bigger, more experienced side.

No way through the Lebanon defence this time for New Zealand's Henry Paul

The Lebanese refusal to give in to their more illustrious opponents brought them accolades and friends, whilst the competition's second favourites produced some touches of outstanding quality, particularly from inspiring captain Richie Barnett – playing his first game since an horrific facial injury suffered in the Anzac Test the previous April.

For the opening eight minutes the Cedars' heroic, totally committed defence saw them pin the Kiwis back in their own half but their enthusiasm, although admirable, expended too much energy to remain effective.

New Zealand patiently weathered the storm and, with Henry Paul's pace beginning to carve openings, they decisively and ruthlessly took all the chances that came their way after Stacey Jones's searing burst from the base of the scrum provided the opening score for powerhouse centre Talau in the tenth minute.

NEW ZEALAND 84 .... COOK ISLANDS 10

Played at Madejski Stadium, Reading, Thursday 2nd November 2000

All thoughts of hypothermia were put aside as New Zealand rained tries in the Royal County on the Thursday evening.

The Kiwis ran in 15 in total as the Cook Islands defence burst its banks quicker than some of England's rain-swollen rivers.

Frank Endacott's team came close to breaking every record in the book as they proved too strong for the Cooks, winners of the 1995 Emerging Nations Tournament.

They fell just two points short of Australia's record score against South Africa at Gateshead five years ago, while Tasesa Lavea personally grabbed 32 points on his debut to establish a new Kiwi Test record.

The Melbourne Storm stand-off kicked twelve goals, beating the previous mark of Henry Paul, the man he was replacing, and scored two tries to take the man of the match award.

New Zealand's Tony Puletua looks for support against the Cook Islands

For the 20-year-old Lavea, it was a new goals-in-a-World Cup match record that was to stand for only two days.

NEW ZEALAND: 1 Richie Barnett (C) (Sydney Roosters); 2 Nigel Vagana (Auckland Warriors); 3 Richie Blackmore (Leeds Rhinos); 4 David Vaealiki (Parramatta Eels); 5 Lesley Vainikolo (Canberra Raiders); 6 Tasesa Lavea (Melbourne Storm); 7 Robbie Paul (Bradford Bulls); 8 Joe Vagana (Auckland Warriors); 9 Richard Swain (Melbourne Storm); 10 Nathan Cayless (Parramatta Eels); 11 Ali Lauiti'iti (Auckland Warriors); 12 Tony Puletua (Penrith Panthers); 13 Ruben Wiki (Canberra Raiders). *Subs (all used):* 14 Stacey Jones (Auckland Warriors); 15 Craig Smith (St George-Illawarra); 16 Quentin Pongia (Sydney Roosters); 17 Stephen Kearney (Melbourne Storm).
Tries: Barnett (3,65), Vagana (42), Vaealiki (52,79), Vainikolo (48), Lavea (21,24), Robbie Paul (11,16), Cayless (55), Lauitiiti (27), Puletua (36), Wiki (14), Pongia (78); **Goals:** Lavea 12

COOK ISLANDS: 1 Richard Piakura (Ngatangiia/Matavera); 2 Tangiia Tongia (Canterbury Bulls); 3 Peter Lewis (Auckland Warriors); 4 Kevin Iro (C) (St Helens); 5 Karl Temata (Hibiscus Coast Raiders); 6 Leroy Joe (Hull KR); 7 Michael Andersson (Caloundra); 8 George Tuakura (Mangere East); 9 Zane Clarke (Cessnock Goannas); 10 Jason Temu (Newcastle Knights); 11 Anthony Samuel (Workington Town); 12 Tere Glassie (Newtown Jets); 13 Meti Noovao (Burleigh Bears). *Subs (all used):* 14 Craig Bowen (Brisbane Wests); 15 Vaine Kino (Sydney Bulls); 16 Patrick Kuru (Tumbarumba); 17 Sonny Shepherd (Ngatangiia)
Tries: Noovao (33), Iro (74); **Goal:** Piakura

Penalties: NZ 2-4; **Half-time:** 48-4; **Referee:** Tim Mander (Australia)
Attendance: 3,982
Men of the Match
New Zealand: Tasesa Lavea; *Cook Islands:* Jason Temu

The Kiwis took their foot off the gas for long periods of the second half, otherwise the score might have been in three figures.

But the crowd took the Cooks to their hearts and were delighted with tries from Meti Noovao and Kevin Iro.

And the biggest cheer of the evening was reserved for Richard Piakura's successful kick from the touchline after he had earlier missed an easy chance from in front of the posts.

27

WALES 24 ....LEBANON 22

Played at Stradey Park, Llanelli, Thursday 2 November 2000

A virtuoso performance by the brilliant Iestyn Harris ensured Wales' qualification for the last eight.

Harris beat Lebanon virtually off his own bat, scoring two tries and having a decisive hand in the other three while adding two goals, rising above the vile, cold and wet conditions and the lack of sense of occasion.

The Cedars looked thoroughly out of sorts in the opening half-hour, giving Harris far too much respect as the Welsh set the platform for a seemingly comfortable win as they built an 18-0 lead.

But in the end Wales were thankful for Wes Davies's converted try midway through the second half that just gave them enough breathing space in the face of a stirring Lebanese revival.

At the start the Lebanese appeared transfixed by Harris's genius

Harris shrugged off a clutch of defenders to score a close-range try before combining with Briers and Jason Critchley to send Paul Sterling over on the right.

After Mick Jenkins was held up over the line on his back, Harris scored his second try as he used Jenkins as a foil before his jinking run created room for Cunningham to score the fourth try, that Harris converted.

Time ran out for the Cedars, who outscored their hosts by four tries to one in the final 45.

John Elias's side grew in confidence after centre Michael Coorey scored their first try of the tournament from a scrum five minutes before half-time and they came out for the second half a far different proposition.

With full-back Hazem El Masri a constant danger and Sami Chamoun and Ray Daher catching the eye in the back row, Lebanon dominated possession on the back of six successive penalty awards either side of the interval.

WALES: 1 Paul Atcheson (St Helens); 2 Paul Sterling (Leeds Rhinos); 4 Jason Critchley (unattached); 3 Kris Tassell (Salford City Reds); 5 Anthony Sullivan (St Helens); 6 Iestyn Harris (C) (Leeds Rhinos) ; 7 Lee Briers (Warrington Wolves); 8 Anthony Farrell (Leeds Rhinos); 9 Keiron Cunningham (St Helens); 10 Dave Whittle (Leigh Centurions); 11 Mick Jenkins (Hull FC); 12 Justin Morgan (Canberra Raiders); 13 Dean Busby (Warrington Wolves). *Subs (all used):* 14 Wes Davies (Wigan Warriors); 15 Chris Morley (Sheffield Eagles); 16 Paul Highton (Salford City Reds); 17 Garreth Carvell (Hull FC)
Tries: Harris (7, 19), Sterling (13), Cunningham (28), Davies (62);
Goals: Harris 2

LEBANON: 1 Hazem El Masri (C) (Canterbury Bulldogs); 2 Samer El Masri (Sydney Roosters); 4 Hassan Saleh (Canterbury Bulldogs); 3 Michael Coorey (Balmain); 5 Mohammed (Wally) Abbas (Canterbury Bulldogs); 6 Fady El Chab (Sydney Bulls); 7 Paul Khoury (Canterbury Bulldogs); 8 Darren Maroon (Sydney Bulls); 9 Anthony Semrani (Canterbury Bulldogs); 10 Moneh Elahmad (Cabramatta); 11 Sami Chamoun (Sydney Bulls); 12 Eben Goddard (St George-Illawarra Dragons); 13 Raymond Daher (Cabramatta). *Subs (all used):* 14 Christopher Salem (St Gaudens); 15 Joe Lichaa (Sydney Roosters); 16 Travis Touma (Sydney Bulls); 17 Kandy Tamer (Sydney Bulls).
Tries: Coorey (35), S El Masri (43), Saleh (78, 80); **Goals:** H El Masri 3

Penalties: Wales 8-11; **Half-time:** 18-6;
Referee: David Pakieto (New Zealand); **Attendance:** 1,497
Men of the Match
Wales: Iestyn Harris; *Lebanon:* Sami Chamoun

Samer El Masri raced over for a second try after hacking ahead a loose ball after Anthony Farrell's offload went to ground.

At 18-10 Wales were rocking and it took a piece of Harris magic to give them

Wales hooker Keiron Cunningham hit by the Lebanese defence

breathing space. The Welsh skipper ran across the face of the right-sided Lebanese defence before cutting between two defenders and supplying Davies with a smart inside pass for the game-breaker.

Harris was denied a well-deserved hat-trick when he just failed to reach Lee Briers' raking kick behind the line.

But the Cedars finished in style as centre Hassan Saleh grabbed a brace of tries in the last two minutes. But the hooter sounded as soon as Hazem El Masri kicked his third conversion.

COOK ISLANDS 22 ....LEBANON 22

Played at Millennium Stadium, Cardiff, Sunday 5 November 2000

A superb fightback by the gallant Lebanese, 22-10 down with four minutes to go, having been 18-4 behind at the break, ensured the honours were deservedly shared in the Cardiff curtain-raiser.

The game made history as the first international to be played 'indoors', the sliding roof being closed before kick-off to keep out the torrential rain.

It was a fine end to the tournament for the two nations, who went back to their countries to spread the League gospel.

It seemed, when Steve Berryman collected his second try and 12th point in the 74th minute, that the Cooks had weathered a Lebanese storm.

But Richard Piakura, who had earlier kicked magnificently from the touchline, missed a relatively easy conversion and left the door slightly ajar.

From the short kick-off Lebanon won a quickly taken penalty and Sami Chamoun, rated by many the most courageous forward in the tournament, sent in prolific try-scorer Hassan Saleh.

From the restart he was then baulked when chipping over - a tactic that cost the Islanders dear - and though George Katrib was dumped near the line by Michael Andersson, the ball spilled for Hazem El Masri to burrow through two defenders, his conversion levelling the scores.

COOK ISLANDS: 1 Richard Piakura (Ngatangiia/Matavera); 2 Tiri Toa (Manukau); 3 Peter Lewis (Auckland Warriors); 4 Kevin Iro (C) (St Helens); 5 Karl Temata (Hibiscus Coast Raiders); 6 Craig Bowen (Brisbane Wests); 7 Leroy Joe (Hull KR); 8 George Tuakura (Mangere East); 9 Zane Clarke (Cessnock Goannas); 10 Jason Temu (Newcastle Knights); 11 Anthony Samuel (Workington Town); 12 Tyrone Pau (Ponsonby Ponies); 13 Steve Berryman (Wainuiomata). *Subs (all used):* 14 Michael Andersson (Caloundra); 15 Sonny Shepherd (Ngatangiia); 16 Raymond Ruapuro (Tupapa Marrarenga); 17 Adam Cook (Wynnum Manly).
Tries: Joe (7), Berryman (23,74), Toa (36); **Goals:** Berryman 2, Piakura

LEBANON: 1 Muhamed Chahal (Sydney Bulls); 2 Mohammed (Wally) Abbas (Canterbury Bulldogs); 3 Hassan Saleh (Canterbury Bulldogs); 4 Hazem El Masri (C) (Canterbury Bulldogs); 5 Travis Touma (Sydney Bulls); 6 Jason Stanton (Sydney Bulls); 7 Samer El Masri (Sydney Roosters); 8 Darren Maroon (Sydney Bulls); 9 Nedol Saleh (Western Suburbs); 10 Sami Chamoun (Sydney Bulls); 11 Chris Salem (St Gaudens); 12 Kandy Tamer (Sydney Bulls); 13 Raymond Daher (Cabramatta). *Subs (all used):* 14 Paul Khoury (Canterbury Bulldogs); 15 Joe Lichaa (Sydney Roosters); 16 George Katrib (Bulldogs); 17 Charlie Nohra (The Oaks).
Tries: Touma (19), H El Masri (42,78), H Saleh (76); **Goals:** H El Masri 3

Penalties: Cooks 10-12; **Half-time:** 18-4;
Referee: Bill Shrimpton (New Zealand); **Attendance:** 5,500
Men of the Match
Cook Islands: George Tuakura; *Lebanon:* Hasem El Masri

"It's been a real pleasure," said Cedars skipper Hazem El Masri, who had guided a side with an average age of 21. "We made a real commitment to each other to leave on a positive note."

In many respects this game summed up the spirit of an expanded world tournament.

Despite having nothing but their futures to play for, both sides produced a match of pace, flow and determination in historic, rarefied indoor surroundings, that lent a surreal air to the proceedings.

The Cooks' bigger pack, well led by Zane Clark, generally gave them more momentum and direction until they faded in the later stages, whilst the willingness

**Cook Islands prop George Tuakura battles for possession with
Lebanon's Hazem El Masri**

of the Lebanese to continually move the ball, made them entertaining to watch, but initially prone to losing possession in crucial areas.

An 18-4 interval lead should have been enough for the Cooks, as coach Stan Martin acknowledged.

"Our changing room feels like it's a loss, but we went in as underdogs and showed that we could play Rugby League," was his reaction after the game.

"We need to get some indiscipline out of our game, but at one stage we held out for nearly 60 tackles and in the last ten minutes fitness levels got us again.

"In the end the draw was probably a fair result."

31

WALES 18 ....NEW ZEALAND 58

Played at the Millennium Stadium, Cardiff, Sunday 5 November 2000

Making their debut at the Millennium Stadium, the Welsh were enthusiastically roared on by a 17,000-plus crowd, and the majority went home happy in the knowledge that their League Dragons had fallen to one of the strongest Kiwi sides of recent times.

Given the amount of withdrawals and injuries that led to pre-tournament predictions that they wouldn't win a game, Wales' rag, tag and bob-tail side had done remarkably well.

The inspirational Keiron Cunningham and leading try-scorer Kris Tassell were missing, there was a hooker (Mick Jenkins) in the back row and a centre pairing of a current rugby union player – Jason Critchley - and a young former union player with just three months of reserve-grade Rugby League experience behind him, in Hefin O'Hare.

But Wales started brightly, and the noisy crowd enthusiastically cheered a double tackle on Richie Barnett that trapped the Kiwi full-back in his in-goal area following a deft chip from Iestyn Harris.

The Kiwis soon found their rhythm though, as Lesley Vainikolo, Willie Talau and Henry Paul all crossed before the first of Wales' three tries. O'Hare, on his debut, made the initial break down the right before straightening and sending Anthony Sullivan sprinting down the touchline, and Lee Briers eagerly supported for the inside ball and the sprint under the posts.

Harris added the extra points, and the patriotic crowd shook the roof with the biggest cheer of the day.

But they were quickly silenced when Barnett slid over in a three-man tackle, and Paul's goal made it 24-6 with half-time rapidly approaching. And there was still time for the Kiwis to stretch their lead and kill the game as a contest with a Ruben Wiki try right on the interval.

**Lee Briers, Iestyn Harris, Ian Watson and Paul Sterling celebrate Wales'
opening try against the Kiwis at the Millennium Stadium**

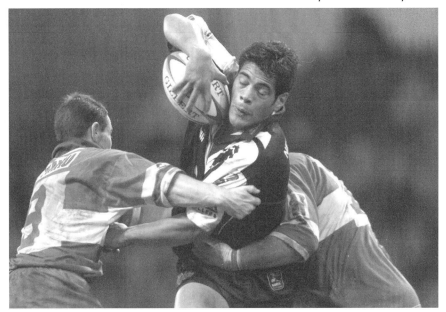

New Zealand's Stephen Kearney on the charge against Wales

Wales enjoyed the majority of possession for the third quarter, until Barnett returned a Sullivan kick and sent Vainikolo crashing through on a 70-metre sprint.

Carroll added another to bring up the 40 mark. From the re-start, substitute Ali Lauiti'iti's fresh legs romped over from 40 metres, despite Davies's despairing tackle; Barnett went over for his second and Tasesa Lavea, on for Henry Paul, popped over the goal to post the half century.

But Wales stuck to their task, and were rewarded with a second try when Harris stepped round Talau and put Atcheson through a gap from 15 metres. Then Chris Smith's searing break won the position for Harris to almost crash over and, when the ball came loose in the tackle on the line, Anthony Farrell pounced on the ball to claim a try.

It brought some respectability to the score, but the Kiwis had the final say with further tries from Joe Vagana and, in the final minute, Vainikolo, his third.

WALES: 1 Wes Davies (Wigan Warriors); 2 Paul Sterling (Leeds Rhinos); 3 Hefin O'Hare (Leeds Rhinos); 4 Jason Critchley (unattached); 5 Anthony Sullivan (St Helens); 6 Iestyn Harris (C) (Leeds Rhinos); 7 Lee Briers (Warrington Wolves); 8 Anthony Farrell (Leeds Rhinos); 9 Ian Watson (Swinton Lions); 10 Dave Whittle (Leigh Centurions); 11 Mick Jenkins (Hull FC); 12 Justin Morgan (Canberra Raiders); 13 Chris Morley (Sheffield Eagles). *Subs (all used):* 14 Barry Eaton (Dewsbury Rams); 15 Paul Atcheson (St Helens); 16 Paul Highton (Salford City Reds); 17 Chris Smith (St Helens).
Tries: Briers (31), Atcheson (70), Farrell (74); **Goals:** Harris 3

NEW ZEALAND: 1 Richard Barnett (C) (Sydney Roosters); 2 Nigel Vagana (Auckland Warriors); 3 Tonie Carroll (Brisbane Broncos); 4 Willie Talau (Canterbury Bulldogs); 5 Lesley Vainikolo (Canberra Raiders); 6 Henry Paul (Bradford Bulls); 7 Stacey Jones (Auckland Warriors); 8 Craig Smith (St George-Illawarra Dragons); 9 Richard Swain (Melbourne Storm); 10 Nathan Cayless (Parramatta Eels); 11 Matt Rua (Melbourne Storm); 12 Stephen Kearney (Melbourne Storm); 13 Ruben Wiki (Canberra Raiders). *Subs (all used):* 14 Tasesa Lavea (Melbourne Storm); 15 Joe Vagana (Auckland Warriors); 16 Tony Puletua (Penrith Panthers); 17 Ali Lauti'iti (Auckland Warriors)
Tries: Vainikolo (9, 51, 79), Talau (22), Paul (26), Barnett (36, 67), Wiki (40), Carroll (62), Lautiiti (64), Vagana (77); **Goals:** H Paul 5, Lavea 2

Penalties: 5-5; **Half-time:** 6-30; **Referee:** Russell Smith (England)
Attendance: 17,612
Men of the Match
Wales: Lee Briers; *Kiwis:* Henry Paul

GROUP THREE

FRANCE 20 ....PAPUA NEW GUINEA 23
Played at Charlety Stadium, Paris, Saturday 28 October 2000

The Kumuls overturned a 16-0 deficit to spoil their hosts' party and claim a valuable first win in the opening match of the opening day double header in Paris.

PNG captain and scrum-half Adrian Lam delivered a superb performance to take his side to victory, against the run of play, scoring a solo try out of the top drawer and dropping a goal that dented French hopes.

France were well organised and were growing in confidence as they led 12-0 at half-time and went further ahead after the break.

PNG, by contrast, had relied on their talented individuals, in particular Lam, Stanley Gene and Marcus Bai.

Banquet put Patrice Benausse over after Frederic Teixido had offloaded and the Toulouse winger went close twice more at the same corner. Then, on the other flank, Yacine Dekkiche skirted round the PNG defence direct from a scrum to touch down for France's second.

For a brief period it was much the same after the re-start.

Laurent Carrasco and Laurent Frayssinous combined to carve out a huge gap in the middle of the field which ended, four passes later, with the energetic prop Rachid Hechiche backing up to cross in the corner.

It could easily have been 20-0 just three minutes later after the PNG defence made a mess of Devecchi's bomb and Dekkiche touched down only to have the

FRANCE: 1 Freddie Banquet (Villeneuve); 2 Yacine Dekkiche (Avignon); 3 Arnaud Dulac (St Gaudens); 4 Jean-Emmanuel Cassin (Toulouse); 5 Patrice Benausse (Toulouse); 6 Laurent Frayssinous (Villeneuve); 7 Fabien Devecchi (C) (Avignon); 8 Rachid Hechiche (Lyon); 9 Vincent Wulf (Villeneuve); 10 Frederic Teixido (Limoux); 11 Jerome Guisset (Warrington Wolves); 12 Gael Tallec (Halifax Blue Sox); 13 Pascal Jampy (UTC). *Subs (all used):* 14 Abderazak El Khalouki; 15 Laurent Carrasco (Villeneuve); 16 Jason Sands (Limoux); 17 David Despin (Villeneuve).
Tries: Benausse (14), Dekkiche (27), Hechiche (46, 80); **Goals:** Banquet 2

PAPUA NEW GUINEA: 1 David Buko (Wagga Wagga); 2 John Wilshere (Brisbane Easts); 3 Eddie Aila (Brisbane Souths); 4 Alfred Songoro (Mackay Souths); 5 Marcus Bai (Melbourne Storm); 6 Stanley Gene (Hull FC); 7 Adrian Lam (C) (Sydney Roosters); 8 Raymond Karl (Enga Mioks); 9 Michael Marum (Port Moresby Vipers); 10 Lucas Solbat (Rabaul Gurias); 11 Duncan Naawi (Redcliffe); 12 Bruce Mamando (N Queensland Cowboys); 13 Tom O'Reilly (Oldham). *Subs (all used):* 14 Mark Mom (Brisbane Easts); 15 Alex Krewanty (Sydney Bulls); 16 Andrew Norman (Burdekin Roosters); 17 Michael Mondo (Yanco).
Tries: Bai (53), Krewanty (56), Buko (70), Lam (77);
Goals: Buko, Wilshere 2; **Field goal:** Lam

Penalties: Fra 6-10; **Half-time:** 12-0; **Referee:** Steve Ganson (England)
Attendance: 7,498
Men of the Match
France: Freddie Banquet; *PNG:* Adrian Lam

Jubilant PNG skipper Adrian Lam celebrates his side's win over France

score disallowed for interference.

Melbourne's Bai signalled PNG's comeback, first being held five metres short of the line and then going over for the Kumuls' first try after 53 minutes of play.

Three minutes later, Gene's break, followed by Lam's kick over the top, caught the French defence napping and substitute Alex Krewanty dived in to score PNG's second.

At 16-10 France were under siege. Their big lead had gone to their heads and now it was disappearing fast. Dekkiche and Frayssinous, within seconds of each other, threw out extravagant passes when something much simpler might have brought results. Then Banquet failed with a drop-goal attempt.

PNG were putting their game together. Lam's pass sent Gene on a 30-metre run, before the stand-off delayed his pass for David Buko to score under the posts. With ten minutes left, Wilshere converted to equalise at 16-all. Then Lam sold two dummies to cross the line without a hand laid on him to give his side the lead for the first time three minutes from time.

Two minutes later he was there again to drop the goal from which there would be no return for the French.

Frantic French pressure did lead to Jampy's inside pass to Hechiche who crashed over for his second try, but too late.

SOUTH AFRICA 18 ....TONGA 66

Played at Charlety Stadium, Paris, Saturday 28 October 2000

The way Tonga trampled all over South Africa's Rhinos set French alarm bells ringing.

As if self-destructing against Papua New Guinea had not been bad enough, les Bleus now had to prepare for a do-or-die encounter in Carcassonne the following Wednesday afternoon.

Three-try Bradford Bulls hero Tevita Vaikona led the rout in the second match of a Group Three double header. And it took just five minutes for the big fellow - playing at centre for his country - to get on the scoreboard, when he crashed over at the side of the posts, winger Fifita Moala converting.

When veteran Duane Mann followed Vaikona over the try-line just two minutes later, with Moala again adding the extras, most of the three or four thousand who had hung around for the second match settled back for a rout.

To their great credit, however, South Africa battled back.

Johannesburg full-back Tim O'Shea fired over a penalty, and then Pretoria Bulls stand-off Conrad Breytenbach went in for a 17th minute try that reduced the arrears to 12-6.

In fact, two minutes was all the time the Tongans needed to re-stretch their lead, via Vaikona's second try and another Moala goal.

And with captain Martin Masella covering just about every blade of grass on the pitch, and Phil Howlett playing out of his skin in an unfamiliar stand-off position, more tries inevitably followed.

Halifax Blue Sox star Jamie Bloem converted consolation tries from centre Leon Barnard and winger Brian Best. But that only emphasised the South Africans' fighting spirit in an ultimately hopeless cause.

Sean Skelton of South Africa surrounded by the Tongan defence

**Tonga's Talite Liava'a gets the ball awau under pressure from
South Africa's Sean Skelton**

Though obviously disappointed, coach South Africa coach Paul Matete was philosophical in defeat.

"Naive is a good word for South African Rugby League at the moment," he said.

Despite such a one-sided scoreline, there were some bright spots for the Rhinos.

Canberra's Sean Rutgerson was a tower of strength in the second row and worked his guts out for the whole 80 minutes.

And, as ever, there was their inspirational, not to mention emotional, skipper Bloem.

But 13 tries reflected the power and the pace of the Tongans, who looked inevitable qualifiers after this imperious performance. With the wily Duane Mann at the helm and some huge forwards – none more so than the giant back-rower Willie Mason – the physical match of any side in the tournament, the French were facing a humiliating early exit from the competition that meant so much for the future of their sport.

SOUTH AFRICA: 1 Tim O'Shea (Johannesburg); 2 Brian Best (Centurion Lions); 3 Leon Barnard (Centurion Lions); 4 Mark Johnson (Salford City Reds); 5 Archer Dames (Pretoria Bulls); 6 Conrad Breytenbach (Pretoria Bulls); 7 Jamie Bloem (C) (Halifax Blue Sox); 8 Jaco Booysen (Centurion Lions); 9 Sean Skelton (Marist, Aus); 10 Eugene Powell (Johannesburg Scorpions); 11 Sean Rutgerson (Canberra Raiders); 12 Quinton de Villiers (Pretoria Bulls); 13 Hercules Erasmus (Centurion Lions). *Subs (all used):* 14 Justin Jennings (Pretoria Bulls); 15 Corne Nel (Pretoria Bulls); 16 Hendrik Mulder (Centurion Lions); 17 Francois Cloete (Pretoria Bulls).
Tries: Breytenbach (17), Barnard (60), Best (70); **Goals:** O'Shea, Bloem 2

TONGA: 1 Paul Koloi (South Mackay); 2 Fifita Moala (Melbourne Storm); 3 Tevita Vaikona (Bradford Bulls); 4 Greg Wolfgramm (Canberra Raiders); 5 Lipina Kaufusi (Wests Magpies); 6 Phil Howlett (N Queensland Cowboys); 7 Willie Wolfgramm (Queanbeyan); 8 Martin Masella (C) (Wakefield Trinity Wildcats); 9 Esau Mann (Otahuhu); 10 Talite Liava'a (Auckland Warriors); 11 Willie Mason (Sydney Bulldogs); 12 Andrew Lomu (Sydney Roosters); 13 Duane Mann (Glenora). *Subs (all used):* 14 David Fisi'iahi (Eastern Tornadoes); 15 Willie Manu (Wests Magpies); 16 Nelson Lomi (Sydney Roosters); 17 Brent Kite (Canberra Raiders)
Tries: Vaikona (5, 19, 46), W Wolfgramm (54), D Mann (7, 75), Liava'a (26), Masella (36), Moala (40), E Mann (44), Lomi (51), L Kaufusi (63), Mason (80); **Goals:** Moala 6, D Mann

Penalties: SA 4-8; **Half-time:** 6-30;
Referee: Darren Hopewell (New Zealand); **Attendance:** 7,498
Men of the Match
South Africa: Sean Rutgerson; *Tonga:* Tevita Vaikona

FRANCE 28 ....TONGA 8

Played at Stade Albert Domec, Carcassonne, Wednesday 1 November 2000

They came to praise an all-time Rugby League great and went away singing the praises of 17 modern-day French gladiators.

After their heartbreaking last-gasp defeat to Papua New Guinea in Paris, few gave France a chance against a Tonga side still bristling with confidence after their 66-18 annihilation of South Africa.

But, on a gloriously sunny Wednesday afternoon in Carcassonne, France confounded the doubters and stunned a near-capacity crowd with a style of, by turns, exhilarating and controlled football not seen from a French side in years.

Puig Aubert's statue - unveiled that very morning before an audience of VIPs - now sits proudly at one end of the Stade Albert Domec, and both sets of players produced a display which did the Gallic spirit of "Pipette" great justice.

Where they had buckled in the face of an opposition comeback at the Charlety Stadium, this time they held on and actually pulled away from a highly competent Tonga side with two breathtaking late tries from Jean-Marc Garcia and Pascal Jampy.

A noisy, musical crowd, sky-divers, packed terraces, Olympic champions symbolically kicking the game off, all combined to create the sort of atmosphere that World Cups are made for.

At last the treizistes had been given the chance to see their chosen sport get its share of the media spotlight.

From the moment that Freddie Banquet crossed for France's first try after 26 minutes - to wipe out an eleventh minute 4-0 lead to the Tongans established by centre David Fisi'iahi - Gilles Dumas' men had made a start on re-establishing the national credibility of rugby a treize.

Banquet converted both his own effort and St Gaudens winger Claude Sirvent's four-pointer four minutes before the break, from an outrageously long Fabien Devecchi pass, to give France a deserved 12-4 lead while Tongan sub Nelson Lomi was in the sin bin for a flop.

The alarm bells began ringing again when Fisi'iahi's brother Paul opened the

FRANCE: 1 Freddie Banquet (Villeneuve); 2 Jean-Marc Garcia (UTC); 3 Jean Emmanuel Cassin (Toulouse); 4 Arnaud Dulac (St Gaudens); 5 Claude Sirvent (St Gaudens); 6 Fabien Devecchi (Avignon); 7 Julien Rinaldi (Villeneuve); 8 Rachid Hechiche (Lyon); 9 Vincent Wulf (Villeneuve); 10 Jason Sands (Limoux); 11 Jerome Guisset (Warrington Wolves); 12 Gael Tallec (Halifax Blue Sox); 13 Pascal Jampy (UTC). *Subs (all used):* 14 David Despin (Villeneuve); 15 Laurent Carrasco (Villeneuve); 16 Romain Sort (Villeneuve); 17 Frederic Teixido (Limoux). **Tries:** Banquet (26), Sirvent (36), Dulac (66), Garcia (79), Jampy (80); **Goals:** Banquet 4

TONGA: 1 Paul Koloi (South Mackay); 2 Fifita Moala (Melbourne Storm); 3 Tevita Vaikona (Bradford Bulls); 4 David Fisi'iahi (Eastern Tornadoes); 5 Lipina Kaufusi (Wests Magpies); 6 Phil Howlett (N Queensland Cowboys); 7 Nuko Hifo (Griffith); 8 Martin Masella (C) (Wakefield Trinity Wildcats); 9 Esau Mann (Otahuhu); 10 Talite Liava'a (Auckland Warriors); 11 Willie Mason (Sydney Bulldogs); 12 Brent Kite (Canberra Raiders); 13 Duane Mann (Glenora). *Subs all used:* 14 Paul Fisi'iahi (Eastern Tornadoes); 15 Willie Manu (Wests Magpies); 16 Nelson Lomi (Sydney Roosters); 17 Alfons Masella (St George Illawarra Dragons). **Tries:** D Fisi'iahi (11), P Fisi'iahi (61) **Sin bin:** Lomi (25) - flop **On report:** Lomi (74) - alleged late tackle - no case to answer

Penalties: Fra 11-3; **Half-time:** 12-4; **Referee:** Steve Clark (Australia) **Attendance:** 10,288 **Men of the Match** *France:* Jean-Emmanuel Cassin; *Tonga:* Duane Mann

**French winger Claude Sirvent skips through the challenge of
Tonga's Phil Howlett**

second-half scoring for Tonga after 51 minutes. But this time the French side was made of sterner stuff.

With 14 minutes left, Sirvent's club-mate Arnaud Dulac skipped through a rare defensive hole to make it 16-8.

And - after Sirvent had a try disallowed and Lomi found himself on report for a late tackle - Garcia and Jampy's sensational last-minute double put France in great heart for their Sunday afternoon clash with South Africa.

Tonga coach Murray Hurst, the North Queensland Cowboys assistant, meanwhile, had to prepare his shell-shocked side for a huge showdown against Papua New Guinea in Saint-Esteve the following Monday.

PAPUA NEW GUINEA 16 ....SOUTH AFRICA 0

Played at Stade des Sept Deniers, Toulouse, Thursday 2 November 2000

South Africa took another huge step along the road to becoming a serious international force, when they battled their way to a creditable 16-0 defeat at the hands of Papua New Guinea in Toulouse.

On a rainy night, in front of a much larger than expected crowd, the Kumuls never seriously looked like losing the game.

But they had to wait until the 25th minute to register their first points

PAPUA NEW GUINEA: 1 David Buko (Wagga Wagga); 2 John Wilshere (Brisbane Easts); 3 Eddie Aila (Brisbane Souths); 4 Alfred Songoro (Mackay Souths); 5 Marcus Bai (Melbourne Storm); 6 Stanley Gene (Hull FC); 7 Adrian Lam (C) (Sydney Roosters); 8 Raymond Karl (Enga Mioks); 9 Mark Mom (Port Moresby Vipers); 10 Michael Mondo (Yanco); 11 Duncan Naawi (Redcliffe); 12 Bruce Mamando (N Queensland Cowboys); 13 Tom O'Reilly (Oldham). *Subs (all used):* 14 Elias Paiyo (Kellyville); 15 Alex Krewanty (Sydney Bulls); 16 Andrew Norman (Burdekin Roosters); 17 Mikaili Aizure (Goroka Lahanis). **Tries:** Aila (25), Wilshere (31), Paiyo (52); **Goals:** Wilshere 2

SOUTH AFRICA: 1 Brian Best (Centurion Lions); 2 Archer Dames (Pretoria Bulls); 3 Mark Johnson (Salford City Reds); 4 Leon Barnard (Centurion Lions); 5 Ian Noble (Northwest Leopards); 6 Pierre Van Wyk (Centurion Lions); 7 Jamie Bloem (C) (Halifax Blue Sox); 8 Jaco Booysen (Centurion Lions); 9 Chris Hurter (Centurion Lions); 10 Eugene Powell (Johannesburg Scorpions); 11 Sean Rutgerson (Canberra Raiders); 12 Quinton de Villiers (Pretoria Bulls); 13 Hercules Erasmus (Centurion Lions). *Subs (all used):* 14 Justin Jennings (Pretoria Bulls); 15 Corne Nel (Pretoria Bulls); 16 Hendrik Mulder (Centurion Lions); 17 Francois Cloete (Pretoria Bulls).

Penalties: PNG 9-5; **Half-time:** 12-0;
Referee: Darren Hopewell (New Zealand); **Attendance:** 4,313
Men of the Match
PNG: David Buko; *South Africa:* Jaco Booysen

when Brisbane Souths centre Eddie Aila darted through from 20 metres, with John Wilshere converting.

Half-backs Adrian Lam and Stanley Gene could never quite find the space to utilise their undoubted talents, largely thanks to a phenomenal defensive effort from the Rugby League-raw Rhinos.

Papua New Guinea's Marcus Bai races through the South African defence

So much so that Aila's try and a 31st minute Wilshere effort - together with the winger's second conversion - were the only first-half points PNG could muster.

And had substitute Justin Jennings made the most of a gift chance instead of knocking on with the line at his mercy two minutes into the second half, the outcome could have been very different.

As it was, a combination of over-enthusiasm and inexperience combined to deny the South Africans the try their efforts deserved.

But a second half in which they held PNG to a mere four points - a 52nd minute Elias Paiyo try - gave them plenty of hope for the future.

FRANCE 56 ....SOUTH AFRICA 6

Played at Stade Municipale, Albi, Sunday 5 November 2000

After the shock of their first-match defeat by the Kumuls a week before, France made certain of a quarter-final place with a comprehensive 56-6 success against 12-man South Africa.

France's final home match - watched by another bumper crowd in the treiziste heartland in Albi - was predictable even before the kick-off but South African skipper Jamie Bloem gave France a little assistance by getting sent off on the half-hour, after giving Australian referee Steve Clark an unwanted opinion as he was sin-binned for interference at the play-the-ball.

France's Rachid Hechiche on the burst against South Africa

France were already 14-2 ahead by that time, thanks to Jean-Emmanuel Cassin and Freddie Banquet tries, plus three goals from Banquet.

All South Africa had to show at this stage was a solitary Bloem penalty, awarded for offside.

With the Rhinos captain and chief play-maker gone from the field, Gilles Dumas' men fully capitalised on their numerical advantage.

Five minutes before the break Cassin ran in for his second try, and former Canberra and Warrington forward Jerome Guisset put the game beyond any real doubt when he crashed over under the posts, with Banquet again converting to give France a 26-2 interval lead.

FRANCE: 1 Freddie Banquet (Villeneuve); 2 Jean-Marc Garcia (UTC); 3 Jean-Emmanuel Cassin (Toulouse); 4 Arnaud Dulac (St Gaudens); 5 Claude Sirvent (St Gaudens); 6 Fabien Devecchi (C) (Avignon); 7 Julien Rinaldi (Villeneuve); 8 Rachid Hechiche (Lyon); 9 Vincent Wulf (Villeneuve); 10 Frederic Teixido (Limoux); 11 Jerome Guisset (Warrington Wolves); 12 Gael Tallec (Halifax Blue Sox); 13 Pascal Jampy (UTC). *Subs (all used):* 14 David Despin (Villeneuve); 15 Laurent Carrasco (Villeneuve); 16 Romain Sort (Villeneuve); 17 Jason Sands (Limoux). **Tries:** Cassin (8, 35), Banquet (21), Guisset (40), Jampy (42, 45, 53), Sirvent (65), Tallec (72); **Goals:** Banquet 10
Sin bin: Hechiche (58) - interference

SOUTH AFRICA: 1 Brian Best (Centurion Lions); 2 Ian Noble (Northwest Leopards); 3 Leon Barnard (Centurion Lions); 4 Mark Johnson (Salford City Reds); 5 Archer Dames (Pretoria Bulls); 6 Pierre Van Wyk (Centurion Lions); 7 Jamie Bloem (C) (Halifax Blue Sox); 8 Jaco Booysen (Centurion Lions); 9 Justin Jennings (Pretoria Bulls); 10 Eugene Powell (Johannesburg Scorpions); 11 Quinton de Villiers (Pretoria Bulls); 12 Sean Rutgerson (Canberra Raiders); 13 Hercules Erasmus (Centurion Lions). *Subs (all used):* 14 Chris Hurter (Centurion Lions); 15 Jaco Webb (Blue Bulls); 16 Hendrik Mulder (Centurion Lions); 17 Richard Louw (Kempton).
Try: de Villiers (79); **Goal:** Bloem
Sin bin: Bloem (31) - interference; **Dismissal:** Bloem (31) - dissent

Penalties: Fra 10-3; **Half-time:** 26-2; **Referee:** Steve Clark (Australia)
Attendance: 7.969
Men of the Match
France: Pascal Jampy; *South Africa:* Brian Best

doubt when he crashed over under the posts, with Banquet again converting to give France a 26-2 interval lead.

With the full house crowd in carnival mood and lapping it all up, it was one-way traffic in the second half. South Africa's chief tormentor - Pascal Jampy - scored a hat-trick of tries in the first 13 minutes after the break.

A late Quinton de Villiers try gave the Rhinos some consolation but further French tries from Claude Sirvent and Gael Tallec, with two more Banquet goals, brought the curtain down on France's World Cup home games in style.

PAPUA NEW GUINEA 30..**TONGA 22**

Played at Stade Municipale, St Esteve, Monday 6 November 2000

Hull's Stanley Gene inspired Papa New Guinea into a quarter-final clash with Wales, with a hard-fought win over Tonga.

The unbeaten Kumuls topped group three at the end of the pool stages, with France finishing second.

For Tonga, elimination came as a massive shock after their humbling of South Africa nine days before.

Both sides certainly had everything to play for and swapped early penalties in a thrilling game before another good French crowd.

John Wilshere got PNG on the board in the fifth minute but Fifita Moala drew the Tongans level two minutes later. But Tonga were first across the try line after ten minutes when Moala went in from Phil Howlett's pass, the winger converting his own try.

The Kumuls knew that a win or a draw would be good enough to send them into the last eight, and they stormed back in style when Wigan-bound Adrian Lam and Gene combined superbly to put Michael Mondo in, with Wilshere converting.

PAPUA NEW GUINEA: 1 David Buko (Wagga Wagga); 2 John Wilshere (Brisbane Easts); 3 Eddie Aila (Brisbane Souths); 4 Alfred Songoro (Mackay Souths); 5 Marcus Bai (Melbourne Storm); 6 Stanley Gene (Hull FC); 7 Adrian Lam (C) (Sydney Roosters); 8 Raymond Karl (Enga Mioks); 9 Mark Mom (Port Moresby Vipers); 10 Michael Mondo (Yanco); 11 Duncan Naawi (Redcliffe); 12 Bruce Mamando (N Queensland Cowboys); 13 Tom O'Reilly (Oldham). *Subs (all used):* 14 Elias Paiyo (Kellyville); 15 Alex Krewanty (Sydney Bulls); 16 Andrew Norman (Burdekin Roosters); 17 Mikaili Aizure (Goroka Lahanis).
Tries: Mondo (19), Gene (23,66), Buko (34), Karl (51); **Goals:** Wilshere 5

TONGA: 1 Lipina Kaufusi (Wests Magpies); 2 Fifita Moala (Melbourne Storm); 3 Paul Koloi (South Mackay); 4 Greg Wolfgramm (Canberra Raiders); 5 Tevita Vaikona (Bradford Bulls); 6 Phil Howlett (N Queensland Cowboys); 7 Duane Mann (Glenora); 8 Martin Masella (C) (Wakefield Trinity Wildcats); 9 Esau Mann (Otahuhu); 10 Alfons Masella (St George-Illawarra Dragons); 11 Malupo Kaufusi (Wests Magpies); 12 Willie Mason (Canterbury Bulldogs); 13 Willie Manu (Wests Magpies). *Subs (all used):* 14 David Fisi'iahi (Eastern Tornadoes); 15 Willie Wolfgramm (Queanbeyan); 16 Nelson Lomi (Sydney Roosters); 17 Andrew Lomu (Sydney Roosters).
Tries: Moala (10, 56), Mason (39), Vaikona (59); **Goals:** Moala 3

Penalties: PNG 7-8 ; **Half-time:** 18-12; **Referee:** Steve Ganson (England)
Attendance: 3,666

Men of the Match
PNG: Stanley Gene; *Tonga:* Willie Mason

Tonga's Alfons Masella brought to ground against Papua New Guinea

Papua New Guinea's Bruce Mamando takes on the Tongan defence

Four minutes later, Gene made the most of a spilled ball to pounce and stretch his side's lead to 12-6.

A David Buko try, and another Wilshere conversion, made it 18-6 after Tonga had a try from loose forward Willie Manu disallowed when he knocked on over the line.

But the huge Willie Mason powered his way over under the posts a minute before half-time to give Tonga hope and Moala added the extras to leave PNG sweating on a narrow 18-12 lead.

Wilshere eased the Kumuls' nerves with a penalty two minutes into the second half, and big prop Raymond Karl crashed over to seemingly put PNG well in control.

But, with a noisy crowd behind them - a win for Tonga would have left France at the top of the table - Tonga came storming back with a second try from Moala and a stunning effort from Tevita Vaikona brought his side to within two points at 24-22.

But the game swung firmly in PNG's favour when Gene swooped for his second try of the night as he got on the end of an inch-perfect Lam kick, Wilshere converting.

Spirited Tonga stormed back but they couldn't get the points they needed. PNG skipper Lam put his side's victory into context.

"It is sure to lift the country quite a bit," he said. "Papua New Guinea is the only country in the world where Rugby League is the national sport – 3.8 million people live there and at least 2.8 million will have been listening to this game on the radio. Winning it makes me feel very proud."

GROUP FOUR

IRELAND 30 ....SAMOA 16

Played at Windsor Park, Belfast, Saturday 28 October 2000

IT was a damp and grey World Cup opening in Belfast, as Ireland justified their pre-tournament billing as Group Four winners with a professional job on ring-rusty Samoa.

Sub-gale-force winds and ice-cold rain lashed Ulster all afternoon, deterring all of the floating voters who World Cup organisers were banking on rolling up to the home of the Linfield soccer club.

The wide empty spaces around the ground didn't provide the type of backdrop that the tournament needed for its launch. But the 3,000-plus locals, as well as a handful of Samoan supporters, were absorbed as Ireland's game came together in the last 40 minutes, after a first half of bruising defence from both sides.

There was no panic in the Ireland camp, even after ten minutes of relentless Samoan pressure just before the break had put the game in the balance.

Ireland had a shaky looking 12-10 lead at that point. Barrie McDermott had given them a wonder start when he stepped opposite number Jerry Seu Seu 20 metres out and bumped off Laloa Milford, before offloading to Chris Joynt for the try. Steve Prescott added a fine conversion.

But within five minutes Samoa winger Bryan Leauma somehow got a hand to

IRELAND: 1 Steve Prescott (Wakefield Trinity Wildcats); 2 Brian Carney (Hull FC); 6 Michael Withers (Bradford Bulls); 4 Michael Eagar (Castleford Tigers); 5 Mark Forster (Warrington Wolves); 3 Tommy Martyn (St Helens); 7 Ryan Sheridan (Leeds Rhinos); 8 Terry O'Connor (C) (Wigan Warriors); 9 Danny Williams (Melbourne Storm); 10 Barrie McDermott (Leeds Rhinos); 11 Chris Joynt (St Helens); 12 Kevin Campion (Brisbane Broncos); 13 Luke Ricketson (Sydney Roosters). *Subs (all used):* 14 Liam Bretherton (Leigh Centurions); 15 Johnny Lawless (Huddersfield-Sheffield Giants); 16 David Barnhill (Leeds Rhinos); 17 Paul Southern (Salford City Reds).
Tries: Joynt (3), Ricketsen (24), Eagar (43), Carney (47), Prescott (57); **Goals:** Prescott 5
On report: McDermott (66) – butting (no case to answer)

SAMOA: 1 Loa Milford (Balmain Tigers); 2 Bryan Leauma (Penrith Panthers); 3 Anthony Swann (Canberra Raiders); 4 Joe Galuvao (Auckland Warriors); 5 Francis Meli (Auckland Warriors); 6 Simon Geros (Burleigh Bears); 7 Willie Swann (Hunslet Hawks); 8 Frank Puletua (Penrith Panthers); 9 Monty Betham (Auckland Warriors); 10 Jerry Seu Seu (Auckland Warriors); 11 David Solomona (Sydney Roosters); 12 Fred Petersen (Penrith Panthers); 13 Willie Poching (Wakefield Trinity Wildcats). *Subs:* 14 Tony Tatupu (Wakefield Trinity Wildcats); 15 Farvae Kalolo (Auckland Warriors); 16 Mark Leafa (Sydney Bulldogs); 17 Henry Aau Fa'afili (Auckland Warriors) *not used.*
Tries: Leauma (7), Milford (28), Betham (66); **Goals:** Geros 2

Penalties: 10-10; **Half-time:** 12-10; **Referee:** Tim Mander (Australia)
Attendance: 3,207
Men of the Match
Ireland: Steve Prescott; *Samoa:* David Solomona

Ireland's Michael Withers puts in a big hit on Samoa's David Solomona

Anthony Swann's kick into the right corner. Poching mis-cued the conversion badly, and it wasn't until the 24th minute that Ireland were able to breach the Samoa defence again. A delayed pass from Ryan Sheridan sent Michael Withers through on the angle, and his pass found the excellent Luke Ricketson on the inside for the try.

But fullback Milford pulled back a try just before the half hour on the back of a mounting penalty count, and stand-off Simon Geros's conversion – Poching was excused from the job after missing a kickable penalty – finished the first-half scoring.

The Samoans were very physical, much in the mould of the 1995 team, with many unknown names from the competitions down under. And they had a genuine class player in David Solomona, a giant in the Sydney Roosters pack in 2000.

But the first seven minutes after the turnaround secured Ireland's winning start. On 43 minutes Tommy Martyn gave Michael Eagar a metre to work in down the left, and the Tigers' centre beat three men on a storming run down the wing. Four minutes later Withers put Brian Carney in at the right corner.

Prescott kicked a straight penalty, and then scored a try, when Sheridan's kick against the post protector fooled Milford – who thought he had got a hand to it first - to put Ireland out of sight.

Hooker Monty Betham got a consolation score for Samoa, but they had little hope by then.

SCOTLAND 16 ....AOTEAROA MAORI 17

Played at Firhill Park, Glasgow, Sunday 29 October 2000

Scottish bravery and commitment wasn't quite enough as a late field goal from Gene Ngamu gave the fearsome Maori a winning start in Glasgow.

The Scots had fought their way back from a 16-6 deficit to tie the scores with less than ten minutes remaining before Ngamu's well taken one-pointer gave the Maori the edge.

It provided a thrilling finale to a tremendously well contested 80 minutes in a game which the Maori - with seasoned former Kiwi internationals Tawera Nikau, Ngamu and Sean Hoppe in their side - were expected to win with more ease.

The Scots refused to be intimidated by their physical opponents, and were led superbly from the front by captain Danny Russell and loose forward Adrian Vowles, who both put in magnificent defensive efforts.

But despite the endeavours of the Scots, two tries in five minutes early in the second half gave the Maori a decisive lead and the New Zealand visitors managed to hang on in the dramatic dying stages.

Early big hits from packmen Paul Rauhihi, Tyran Smith and Wairangi Koopu, and centre David Kidwell, set the tone and the Maori took the lead 12 minutes in.

Substitute forward Tahi Reihana was denied a try when the video referee ruled he was short of the line, but two tackles later impressive fullback Clinton Toopi took advantage of a strong Toa Kohe-Love run to cross out wide. Ngamu's conversion sailed wide.

Henry Perenara and Tawera Nikau celebrate the Maori's thrilling win over Scotland

The Scots hit back within six minutes when Hull scrum-half Richard Horne created the space for full-back Lee Penny to dive over. Graham Mackay's conversion gave the home side the lead.

The half ended with Nikau and Scotland substitute Wayne McDonald being sent to the sin bin as tempers boiled over on halfway.

The Maori started the second period a stronger side, and two tries – from Kidwell and Toopi - inside five minutes gave them a crucial lead. Ngamu converted both scores to give the Maori a 16-6 lead.

But the gallant Scots refused to lie down, and fought their way back into the game when McDonald got the ball out of the tackle for

**Scotland's Richard Horne comes in for some close attention from Maori duo
Terry Hermansson (top) and Chris Nahi**

David Maiden to score and Matt Crowther's conversion closed the gap to four points. Three minutes later the Scots were level as a beautifully-timed pass from Vowles sent North Queensland Cowboys centre Geoff Bell over in the left corner. Crowther again stepped up for the conversion, but his attempt was agonisingly short.

The Maori immediately countered as Hare Te Rangi went down the touchline to set up the position for Ngamu's field goal.

SCOTLAND: 1 Lee Penny (Warrington Wolves); 2 Matt Daylight (Cronulla Sharks); 3 Graham Mackay (Leeds Rhinos); 4 Geoff Bell (N Queensland Cowboys); 5 Lee Gilmour (Wigan Warriors) 6 Andrew Purcell (Castleford Tigers); 7 Richard Horne (Hull FC); 8 Daniel Heckenberg (St George-Illawarra Dragons); 9 Danny Russell (C) (Huddersfield-Sheffield Giants); 10 Dale Laughton (Huddersfield-Sheffield Giants); 11 Scott Logan (Sydney City Roosters); 12 Scott Cram (London Broncos); 13 Adrian Vowles (Castleford Tigers). *Subs (all played):* 14 David Maiden (Hull FC); 15 Matt Crowther (Huddersfield-Sheffield Giants); 16 Wayne McDonald (Hull FC); 17 Darren Shaw (Castleford Tigers).
Tries: Penny (18), Maiden (68), Bell (71); **Goals:** Mackay, Crowther
Sin bin: McDonald (40) - fighting

NEW ZEALAND MAORI: 1 Clinton Toopi (Auckland Warriors); 2 Odell Manuel (Auckland Warriors); 3 Toa Kohe-Love (Warrington Wolves); 4 David Kidwell (Parramatta Eels); 5 Sean Hoppe (St Helens); 6 Gene Ngamu (Huddersfield-Sheffield Giants); 7 Hare Te Rangi (Otahuhu Leopards); 8 Paul Rauhihi (Newcastle Knights); 9 Henry Perenara (Auckland Warriors); 10 Terry Hermansson (Auckland Warriors); 11 Wairangi Koopu (Auckland Warriors); 12 Tyran Smith (Wests Tigers); 13 Tawera Nikau (Warrington Wolves). *Subs (all played):* 14 Martin Moana (Halifax Blue Sox); 15 Kyle Leuluai (Wests Tigers); 16 Chris Nahi (Brisbane Easts); 17 Tahi Reihana (Brisbane Souths).
Tries: Toopi (12, 55), Kidwell (50); **Goals:** Ngamu 2; **Field goal:** Ngamu
Sin bin: Nikau (40) - fighting

Penalties: Sco 12-9; **Half-time:** 6-4; **Referee:** Stuart Cummings (England)
Attendance: 2,008
Men of the Match
Scotland: Danny Russell; *Maori:* Tawera Nikau

IRELAND 18 ....SCOTLAND 6

Played at Tolka Park, Dublin, Wednesday 1 November 2000

Solid, if unspectacular, victory in the battle of the Celts meant that Irish eyes were firmly focused on the road ahead after the World Cup roadshow rolled into Dublin.

But there was much endeavour for the lively crowd to admire, with the efforts of Chris Joynt, Luke Ricketson, Adrian Vowles and Scott Logan in particular to the fore. But a surfeit of lost possession ensured that the only real highlights were the three tries, two of which were beauties.

Ireland's Kevin Campion wrapped up by the Scottish defence

Ireland were on the board in the second minute, Ricketson charging down otherwise impressive Scott Rhodes kick, Michael Withers hacking on and Ryan Sheridan winning the race to the touchdown.

Two penalties from Steve Prescott made it 10-0 before Vowles' magnificent pass put Lee Gilmour gliding and stepping into the clear, his well-timed inside ball sending Lee Penny over.

Another Prescott two-pointer made it 12-6 but the game turned in a five-minute spell around the hour mark. First Gilmour failed to cling onto another peach of a scoring pass from Vowles before the Castleford stalwart was sin-binned, a result of cumulative off-sides by the Bravehearts.

In his absence the Irish conjured up the best move of the game to ensure victory. Terry O'Connor started the rumble and magnificent passes out of the tackle as they fell by Prescott and Carney saw Michael Withers power into the corner for a spectacular try. The only other score was a fifth Prescott goal late on.

IRELAND: 1 Steve Prescott (Wakefield Trinity Wildcats); 2 Brian Carney (Hull FC); 6 Michael Withers (Bradford Bulls); 4 Michael Eagar (Castleford Tigers); 5 Ian Herron (Hull FC); 3 Tommy Martyn (St Helens); 7 Ryan Sheridan (Leeds Rhinos); 8 Terry O'Connor (C) (Wigan Warriors); 9 Johnny Lawless (Huddersfield-Sheffield Giants); 10 Barrie McDermott (Leeds Rhinos); 11 Chris Joynt (St Helens); 12 Kevin Campion (Brisbane Broncos); 13 Luke Ricketson (Sydney Roosters). *Subs (all used):* 14 Danny Williams (Melbourne Storm); 15 Jamie Mathiou (Leeds Rhinos); 16 David Barnhill (Leeds Rhinos); 17 Dave Bradbury (Huddersfield-Sheffield Giants)
Tries: Sheridan (2), Withers (68); **Goals:** Prescott 5

SCOTLAND: 1 Danny Arnold (Huddersfield-Sheffield Giants); 2 Matt Daylight (Hull FC); 3 Lee Gilmour (Wigan Warriors); 4 Geoff Bell (N Queensland Cowboys); 5 Matt Crowther (Huddersfield-Sheffield Giants); 6 Richard Horne (Hull FC); 7 Scott Rhodes (Leeds Rhinos); 8 Daniel Heckenberg (St George-Illawarra Dragons); 9 Danny Russell (Huddersfield-Sheffield Giants) (C); 10 Dale Laughton (Huddersfield-Sheffield Giants); 11 Scott Logan (Sydney City Roosters); 12 Scott Cram (London Broncos); 13 Adrian Vowles (Castleford Tigers). *Subs (all played):* 14 David Maiden (Hull FC); 15 Nathan Graham (Dewsbury Rams); 16 Wayne McDonald (Hull FC); 17 Darren Shaw (Castleford Tigers)
Try: Arnold (37); **Goal:** Crowther
Sin bin: Vowles (59) - persistent offside

Penalties: Ire 10-7; **Half-time:** 10-6; **Referee:** Russell Smith (England)
Attendance: 1,782
Men of the Match
Ireland: Luke Ricketson; *Scotland:* Adrian Vowles

SAMOA 21 ....MAORI 16

Played at Derwent Park, Wednesday 1 November

Samoa stunned the Maori on a magical night on the River Derwent as the South Seas came to Workington.

Samoa and Maori played out a wonderful drama before an enthralled Cumbrian crowd as the rain gods relented to provide a fine, calm evening.

The crowd was already enthused by the pre-match hakas, with the Maori performing their pre-match ritual twice. The Samoans, though, outdid them after a tremendous win by repeating their's twice for the crowd that was reluctant to go home.

The Maori seemed to hold all the aces with their big pack and the win over Scotland already under their belts. But the out-weighed Samoans stood up to the physical challenge and proved to be quicker in thought and deed.

Maori coach Cameron Bell's squad rotation back-fired as the rested Gene Ngamu wasn't on hand to decide the tie, replacement stand-off Luke Goodwin fluffing two field goal attempts when the game was poised at 16-16 late on.

On the other hand, Darrell Williams was delighted with the changes he had wrung, especially bringing in Auckland Warrior Henry Aau Fa'afili at stand-off, who was outstanding, with power, pace and skill, and a devastating side-step.

SAMOA: 1 Loa Milford (Balmain Tigers); 2 Francis Meli (Auckland Warriors); 3 Anthony Swann (Canberra Raiders); 4 Joe Galuvao (Auckland Warriors); 5 Bryan Leauma (Penrith Panthers); 6 Henry Aau Fa'afili (Auckland Warriors); 7 Willie Swann (Hunslet Hawks); 8 Frank Puletua (Penrith Panthers); 9 Monty Betham (Auckland Warriors); 10 Jerry Seu Seu (Auckland Warriors); 11 David Solomona (Sydney Roosters); 12 Mark Leafa (Sydney Bulldogs); 13 Willie Poching (C) (Wakefield Trinity Wildcats). *Subs (all used):* 14 Tony Tatupu (Wakefield Trinity Wildcats); 15 Philip Leuluai (Auckland Warriors); 16 Simon Geros (Burleigh Bears); 17 Max Fala (Northcote Tigers).
Tries: Fa'afili (42, 54), W Swann (57), Milford (79); **Goals:** Poching 2; **Field goal:** W Swann

NEW ZEALAND MAORI: 1 Clinton Toopi (Auckland Warriors); 2 Jarred Mills (Newtown); 3 Paul Whaituira (Auckland Warriors); 4 Boycie Nelson (Glenora Bears); 5 Steve Matthews (Glenora Bears); 6 Luke Goodwin (Newtown); 7 Jeremy Smith (Sydney Roosters); 8 Paul Rauhihi (Newcastle Knights); 9 James Cook (Northcote Tigers); 10 Tahi Reihana (Brisbane Souths); 11 Kyle Leuluai (Wests Tigers); 12 Tyran Smith (Wests Tigers); 13 Tawera Nikau (Warrington Wolves). *Subs (all played):* 14 Toa Kohe-Love (Warrington Wolves); 15 Martin Moana (Halifax Blue Sox); 16 David Kidwell (Parramatta Eels); 17 Terry Hermansson (Auckland Warriors).
Tries: Matthews (2), Nelson (49), Rauhihi (70); **Goals:** Goodwin 2

Penalties: Samoa 9-7; **Half-time:** Maori 4-0;
Referee: Bill Harrigan (Australia); **Attendance:** 4,107
Men of the Match
Samoa: Henry Aau Fa'afili; *Maori:* Paul Rauhihi

Maori had the perfect start too when Goodwin put in a huge bomb which was patted back and winger Steve Matthews pounced for a four-pointer.

Then it was end-to-end with fearsome hits, great handling, and amazing last-ditch tackling from both sides. It was amazing that the score was still 4-0 at half-time.

Samoa came out and stormed into the lead with the classy Fa'afili stepping and swerving for the first of his brace of tries.

The Maori stepped up the pace and Jeremy Smith's rehearsed grubber allowed Boycie Nelson to win the race to regain the lead. Goodwin, whose field kicking game was excellent throughout, landed a good conversion too.

Samoa's David Solomona offloads as Maori fullback Clinton Toopi closes in

Now Samoa took control with Fa'afili's second, then Willie Swann stepped and ducked in from close range.

Back came the Maori with a long spell of pressure. Paul Rauhihi at prop was striving valiantly and he ran onto Martin Moana's short pass to charge over. Goodwin's conversion tied up the scores.

The Maori looked like winners, but Samoa hadn't read the script, and Willie Swann landed a good field goal himself to steal the game. Loa Milford's last-second try was just the full-stop at the end of a superb night.

The group couldn't have left the Celtic group more finely balanced. Going into the last round of games, any one of the four sides could still make it to the quarter-finals.

IRELAND 30 ....AOTEAROA MAORI 16

Played at Tolka Park, Dublin, Saturday 4 November 2000

A magnificent performance from Ireland's forwards was at the centre of a compelling win against the eliminated Maori, confirming their position at the top of Group Four.

Ireland out-muscled their physical opponents in the battle up front, with props Terry O'Connor and Barrie McDermott providing them with tremendous go-forward and back-rowers David Barnhill and Kevin Campion tireless workers throughout.

Steve Prescott kicked

IRELAND: 1 Steve Prescott (Wakefield Trinity Wildcats); 2 Brian Carney (Hull FC); 3 Michael Withers (Bradford Bulls); 4 Luke Ricketson (Sydney City Roosters); 5 Mark Forster (Warrington Wolves); 6 Gavin Clinch (Huddersfield-Sheffield Giants); 7 Ryan Sheridan (Leeds Rhinos); 8 Terry O'Connor (C) (Wigan Warriors); 9 Danny Williams (Melbourne Storm); 10 Barrie McDermott (Leeds Rhinos); 11 Chris Joynt (St Helens); 12 David Barnhill (Leeds Rhinos); 13 Kevin Campion (Brisbane Broncos). *Subs (all used):* 14 Liam Bretherton (Leigh Centurions); 15 Johnny Lawless (Huddersfield-Sheffield Giants); 16 Liam Tallon (Brisbane Norths); 17 Paul Southern (Salford City Reds).
Tries: Forster (34), Carney (40), Barnhill (47), Withers (61), Sheridan (80); **Goals:** Prescott 5

NEW ZEALAND MAORI: 1 Clinton Toopi (Auckland Warriors); 2 Odell Manuel (Auckland Warriors); 3 Toa Kohe-Love (Warrington Wolves); 4 David Kidwell (Parramatta Eels); 5 Sean Hoppe (St Helens); 6 Gene Ngamu (Huddersfield-Sheffield Giants); 7 Hare Te Rangi (Otahuhu Leopards); 8 Paul Rauhihi (Newcastle Knights); 9 Henry Perenara (Auckland Warriors); 10 Terry Hermansson (Auckland Warriors); 11 Wairangi Koopu (Auckland Warriors); 12 Tyran Smith (Wests Tigers); 13 Tawera Nikau (Warrington Wolves). *Subs (all used):* 14 Martin Moana (Halifax Blue Sox); 15 Boycie Nelson (Glenora Bears); 16 Chris Nahi (Brisbane Easts); 17 Tahi Reihana (Brisbane Souths).
Tries: Nelson (52), Te Rangi (69), Koopu (78); **Goals:** Perenara, Ngamu

Penalties: Ire 9-4; **Half-time:** 12-0 ; **Referee:** Bill Harrigan (Australia)
Attendance: 3,164
Men of the Match
Ireland: Terry O'Connor; *Maori:* Henry Perenara

the Irish into a 2-0 lead on 19 minutes, after Ryan Sheridan was prevented from playing the ball on the last tackle.

The crowd had to wait until the 34th minute for the game's first try, but when it arrived, it provided one of the scores of the tournament.

Odell Manuel put in a speculative kick 20 metres inside the Ireland half, only to

Ireland skipper Terry O'Connor drives past Maori hooker Henry Perenara

see it charged down by opposite winger Mark Forster. The veteran flyer then set off down the left touchline, escaping the clutches of Warrington teammate Toa Kohe-Love and winning a footrace with the covering Hare Te Rangi on a thrilling run to the line.

Forster almost added a second five minutes later when he gathered a clever Clinch chip only for Manuel to atone for his earlier mistake by pulling off a superb tackle to turn the Ireland man on his back.

But from the ensuing set of six the ball was moved quickly to the right and Michael Withers' inside ball saw Brian Carney display his bravery and strength to take two defenders over the line with him.

Prescott add the conversion for a 12-0 half-time lead, and added a penalty less than two minutes into the second period after tempers boiled over between McDermott and Paul Rauhihi.

Five minutes later, and the Irish pulled further in front.

Gene Ngamu failed to hold a Tawera Nikau pass and Barnhill collected and raced 30 metres to the line for a try that was given on the nod of the video referee.

The Maori opened their account when substitute Boycie Nelson squeezed over in the left hand corner but Nelson was at fault for Ireland's fourth try on the hour, missing a tackle on Withers after Clinch had brilliantly stolen the ball from Manuel.

The New Zealanders did raise hopes of a late comeback when a brilliant ball from Nikau sent Te Rangi through a gap and around the wrong-footed Prescott.

But those hopes all but disappeared when Nikau was sent to the sin bin for a late, high shot on Clinch.

They added a consolation when a brilliant pass from the impressive Henry Perenara sent Wairangi Koopu over out wide, but the Irish had the final word, Sheridan stepping through and evading the flying challenge of fullback Clinton Toopi.

Ireland start the celebrations after they had defeated the Maori to reach the quarter finals

SCOTLAND 12 ....SAMOA 20

Played at Tynecastle, Edinburgh, Sunday 5 November 2000

SCOTLAND's World Cup hopes were finally extinguished as Samoa earned the dubious privilege of a quarter-final meeting with Australia.

Scotland, despite having lost both their previous games, needed to win by two or more points to make the quarter-finals but Samoa won a deserved victory inspired by their brilliant full-back Loa Milford and two-try winger Bryan Leauma.

Leauma's opportunist try midway through the second half enabled the enterprising Samoans to ward off a stirring Scottish comeback early in the second half.

The Scots got the perfect start when Matt Crowther landed a 30-metre penalty for a third minute lead.

But when Matt Daylight failed to gather Shane Laloata's high swirling cross-field kick, Tony Tatupu and Anthony Swann combined to send Leauma over for the opening try.

The second try was not long delayed as Frank Puletua offloaded and Henry Aau Fa'afili's inside pass sent David Solomona on the charge, the Roosters forward scattering the close range cover for a try that Laloata converted.

A third Samoan try, which was a splendid individual effort by Milford, extended the lead to 14-2. Milford pounced on a loose ball after Daylight, chasing Adrian Vowles' chip to the left, was collared by Leauma. Milford hared off down the right touch-line and left the Scots defence trailing in his wake as he notched a memorable 70-metre effort that remained unconverted.

SCOTLAND: 1 Danny Arnold (Huddersfield-Sheffield Giants); 5 Matt Crowther (Huddersfield-Sheffield Giants); 3 Lee Gilmour (Wigan Warriors); 4 Geoff Bell (North Queensland Cowboys); 2 Matt Daylight (Hull FC); 6 Andrew Purcell (Castleford Tigers); 7 Richard Horne (Hull FC); 8 Daniel Heckenberg (St George-Illawarra Dragons); 9 Danny Russell (C) (Huddersfield-Sheffield Giants); 10 Dale Laughton (Huddersfield-Sheffield Giants); 11 Scott Logan (Sydney Roosters); 12 Scott Cram (London Broncos); 13 Adrian Vowles (Castleford Tigers). *Subs (all played):* 14 Scott Rhodes (Leeds Rhinos); 15 David Maiden (Hull FC); 16 Wayne McDonald (Hull FC); 17 Darren Shaw (Castleford Tigers).
Tries: Vowles (44), Rhodes (47); **Goals:** Crowther 2

SAMOA: 1 Loa Milford (Wests Tigers); 5 Bryan Leauma (Penrith Panthers); 3 Anthony Swann (Canberra Raiders); 4 Shane Laloata (Nelson Bay); 2 Peter Lima (Toulouse); 6 Henry Aau Fa'afili (Auckland Warriors); 7 Albert Talapeau (Sydney Roosters); 8 Frank Puletua (Penrith Panthers); 9 Monty Betham (Auckland Warriors); 10 Jeremy Seu Seu (Auckland Warriors); 11 David Solomona (Sydney Roosters); 12 Tony Tatupu (Wakefield Trinity Wildcats); 13 Willie Poching (C) (Wakefield Trinity Wildcats). *Subs (all used):* 14 Willie Swann (Hunslet Hawks); 15 Philip Leuluai (Auckland Warriors); 16 Mark Leafa (Canterbury Bulldogs); 17 Max Fala (Northcote Tigers).
Tries: Leauma (17, 58), Solomona (21), Milford (31); **Goals:** Laloata 2

Penalties: Sco 12-10; **Half-time:** 2-14;
Referee: David Pakieto (New Zealand); **Attendance:** 1,579
Men of the Match
Scotland: Adrian Vowles; *Samoa:* Loa Milford

The start of the second half, though, signalled an astonishing turnaround as the Scots tore into the Samoan defence and dominated possession on the back of four successive penalty awards.

Russell grubber-kicked through twice only to be denied by Milford at the expense of a drop-out but, as the pressure continued, Vowles burrowed over by the left corner flag, after a McDonald offload.

The Scots' revival gathered momentum as Scott Rhodes jinked through to score their second try after Darren Shaw was held up just short and Crowther's

**Samoa's Bryan Leauma hit by Scotland duo
Dale Laughton and Daniel Heckenberg**

conversion reduced the arrears to just two points.

But Laloata gave his side some breathing space with a 55th minute penalty, an angled attempt from 22 metres, after Scott Cram was guilty of an offence at the ruck.

Rhodes, playing with confidence, almost wriggled through again before an error by Arnold left his side with a mountain to climb.

Arnold tried to stop a raking Aau Fa'afili 40-20 from going into touch but, before he could regather, Leauma was on the loose ball in a flash. The winger hacked ahead from 20 metres out and won the race for the touchdown.

Though Laloata was unable to convert, the Samoans now held a 20-12 lead going into the final quarter and it took a brilliant tackle by Vowles on Talapeau to keep his side in the contest.

The Scots last chance disappeared when Horne was held up in a massed tackle two minutes from the end.

THE PLAY-OFFS

ENGLAND 26 ....IRELAND 16

Played at Headingley, Leeds, Saturday 11 November 2000

The first meeting between the two home nations was all that had been predicted, with Ireland forcing England to battle all the way for their place in the semi-finals.

England needed to re-group when Ireland led 10-4 midway through the first half. And having fought back, they spread the ball wide to run in three excellent tries.

England's younger players continued to grow in stature and Stuart Fielden certainly enhanced his reputation with a

ENGLAND: 1 Paul Wellens (St Helens); 2 Chev Walker (Leeds Rhinos); 3 Kris Radlinski (Wigan Warriors); 4 Keith Senior (Leeds Rhinos); 5 Darren Rogers (Castleford Tigers); 6 Sean Long (St Helens); 7 Paul Deacon (Bradford Bulls); 8 Stuart Fielden (Bradford Bulls); 9 Paul Rowley (Halifax Blue Sox); 10 Paul Anderson (Bradford Bulls); 11 Adrian Morley (Leeds Rhinos); 12 Mike Forshaw (Bradford Bulls); 13 Andrew Farrell (C) (Wigan Warriors). *Subs (all used):* 14 Tony Smith (Wigan Warriors); 15 Scott Naylor (Bradford Bulls); 16 Jamie Peacock (Bradford Bulls); 17 Harvey Howard (Brisbane Broncos).
Tries: Senior (4), Peacock (39), Smith (59), Walker (69); **Goals:** Farrell 5

IRELAND: 1 Steve Prescott (Wakefield Trinity Wildcats); 2 Brian Carney (Hull FC); 6 Michael Withers (Bradford Bulls); 4 Michael Eagar (Castleford Tigers); 5 Mark Forster (Warrington Wolves); 3 Tommy Martyn (St Helens); 7 Ryan Sheridan (Leeds Rhinos); 8 Terry O'Connor (C) (Wigan Warriors); 9 Danny Williams (Melbourne Storm); 10 Barrie McDermott (Leeds Rhinos); 11 Chris Joynt (St. Helens); 12 Kevin Campion (Brisbane Broncos); 13 Luke Ricketson (Sydney Roosters). *Subs (all used):* 14 Gavin Clinch (Huddersfield-Sheffield Giants); 15 David Barnhill (Leeds Rhinos); 16 Jamie Mathiou (Leeds Rhinos); 17 Paul Southern (Salford City Reds).
Tries: Withers (8,78), Martyn (12); **Goals:** Prescott 2
Sin bin: Steve Prescott (52) – holding down
On report: Barrie McDermott (45) – high tackle

Penalties: Eng 8-6; **Half-time:** 12-10; **Referee:** Tim Mander (Australia)
Attendance: 15,405
Men of the Match
England: Stuart Fielden; *Ireland:* Michael Withers

towering performance. The 21 year old Bradford prop took the man of the match award after coming out on top in a torrid front row battle against hardened warriors Barrie McDermott and Terry O'Connor.

England's Andy Farrell collides with Ireland's David Barnhill

Fielden battered the Irish front line, and also stood out in defence, overhauling Kevin Campion to end the second-rower's 60-metre break just short of the England line. It was a crucial tackle as a try and goal would have pulled Ireland back to only 20-16 down with 15 minutes left.

England took full advantage of the try-saver to scramble possession from Ireland's next play and power back with a match-clinching try from Chev Walker.

Andy Farrell added his fifth goal to complete his major contribution to the victory. The England captain was involved in Walker's touchdown and also in the try of the match in the 59th minute when Ireland were down to 12 men after Steve Prescott had been sent to the sin bin for holding down.

AUSTRALIA 66 ....SAMOA 10

Played at Vicarage Road, Watford, Saturday 11 November 2000

Australia's 12-try romp over the brave but eventually outclassed Samoans brought the world champions' points-tally to 264 in four games.

Second row forward Bryan Fletcher led the way with his first senior hat-trick as Andrew Johns, the official man of the match, and Brett Kimmorley bossed the midfield, allowing Scott Hill and skipper Brad Fittler to make hay in the teeming rain.

At 40-10, with ten minutes to go, Samoa coach Darrell Williams could have been well pleased with his side's efforts. But Australia ran in 26 points, including five tries, in the closing ten minutes as the mighty effort of the first half took its toll on the Samoan defence.

Australia's Brad Fittler picks his way through the Samoan defence

The Australians scored only one try in the first quarter as Darren Lockyer and Robbie Kearns laid on Ryan Girdler's sixth try of the tournament in the fifth minute.

After tries from Fittler and Fletcher, the Samoans showed they were made of stern stuff as David Solomona brought the house down as he dummied and cut through to score.

The Samoans showed their fighting spirit with a length-of-the field second-half effort by Bryan Leauma, his fourth try of the World Cup.

But they had nothing left in the tank in the closing stages and Fletcher brought up the half-century with two tries inside three minutes; and MacDougall, Hill and Johns each scored their second tries, with Mat Rogers taking his goal-tally to nine from 12 attempts.

AUSTRALIA: 1 Darren Lockyer (Brisbane Broncos); 5 Wendell Sailor (Brisbane Broncos); 4 Matthew Gidley (Newcastle Knights); 3 Ryan Girdler (Penrith Panthers); 2 Mat Rogers (Cronulla Sharks); 6 Brad Fittler (C) (Sydney City Roosters); 7 Brett Kimmorley (Melbourne Storm); 8 Shane Webcke (Brisbane Broncos); 9 Andrew Johns (Newcastle Knights); 10 Robbie Kearns (Melbourne Storm); 11 Gorden Tallis (Brisbane Broncos); 12 Bryan Fletcher (Sydney Roosters); 13 Scott Hill (Melbourne Storm). *Subs (all used):* 14 Adam MacDougall (Newcastle Knights); 15 Jason Croker (Canberra Raiders); 16 Darren Britt (Canterbury Bulldogs); 17 Jason Stevens (Cronulla Sharks).
Tries: Girdler (5), Fittler (24), Fletcher (27, 70, 73), Sailor (40), Johns (42, 80), Hill (50, 78), MacDougall (57, 75); **Goals:** Rogers 9

SAMOA: 1 Laloa Milford (Wests Tigers); 2 Bryan Leauma (Penrith Panthers); 3 Anthony Swann (Canberra Raiders); 4 Shane Laloata (Nelson Bay); 5 Peter Lima (Toulouse); 6 Henry Aau Fa'afili (Auckland Warriors); 7 Willie Swann (Hunslet Hawks); 8 Frank Puletua (Penrith Panthers); 9 Monty Betham (Auckland Warriors); 10 Jerry Seu Seu (Auckland Warriors); 11 David Solomona (Sydney Roosters); 12 Philip Leuluai (Auckland Warriors); 13 Willie Poching (C) (Wakefield Trinity Wildcats). *Subs (all used):* 14 Tony Tatupu (Wakefield Trinity Wildcats); 15 Mark Leafa (Canterbury Bulldogs); 16 Max Fala (Northcote Tigers); 17 Francis Meli (Auckland Warriors).
Tries: Solomona (33), Leauma (63); **Goal:** Laloata

Penalties: Aus 6-8; **Half-time:** 24-4; **Referee:** Stuart Cummings (England)
Attendance: 5,404
Men of the Match
Australia: Andrew Johns; **Samoa:** David Solomona

WALES 22 ....PAPUA NEW GUINEA 8

Played at Auto Quest Stadium, Widnes, Sunday 11 November 2000

Wales progressed with unexpected ease against a Papua New Guinea side that played with plenty of passion, courage and no little flair, but paid the price for a lack of concentration midway through the first half.

The Kumuls returned home to bask in a heroes' welcome despite never really hitting their straps against a determined Welsh side.

After Iestyn Harris and John Wilshere traded penalty goals, the Kumuls stuck to their defensive structure, and all seemed to be going to plan until a five-minute spell in the middle of the half saw Wales score two vital tries.

First Lam, attempting to offload in a tackle, sent the ball straight into the hands of Jason Critchley who romped away from 40 metres for the game's opening try.

Then, after Keiron Cunningham had gone close, Lee Briers dummied through near the left corner. With the interval approaching, Wes Davies slid over, and Harris added the touchline conversion for a 20-2 lead.

After the break the Kumuls defended manfully, allowing Wales a solitary two points from a penalty. And they scored a deserved try when Duncan Naawi popped up a pass in an Atcheson-Sullivan double tackle for Wilshere to cross unopposed.

It was a mighty defensive effort from the Welsh with Paul Highton leading the tackling stint with 41 tackles - the highest tackle count in the tournament so far, topping the 40 by Samoan hooker Monty Betham in the opening match against Ireland.

WALES: 1 Paul Atcheson (St Helens); 2 Paul Sterling (Leeds Rhinos); 4 Jason Critchley (unattached); 3 Kris Tassell (Salford City Reds); 5 Anthony Sullivan (St Helens); 6 Iestyn Harris (C) (Leeds Rhinos); 7 Lee Briers (Warrington Wolves); 8 Anthony Farrell (Leeds Rhinos); 9 Keiron Cunningham (St Helens); 10 Justin Morgan (Canberra Raiders); 11 Mick Jenkins (Hull FC); 12 Paul Highton (Salford City Reds); 13 Dean Busby (Warrington Wolves). *Subs (all used):* 14 Wes Davies (Wigan Warriors); 15 Chris Morley (Sheffield Eagles); 16 John Devereux (unattached); 17 Paul Moriarty (unattached).
Tries: Critchley (21), Briers (25), Davies (38); **Goals:** Harris 5

PAPUA NEW GUINEA: 1 David Buko (Wagga Wagga); 2 John Wilshere (Brisbane Easts); 3 Eddie Aila (Brisbane Souths); 4 Alfred Songoro (Mackay Souths); 5 Marcus Bai (Melbourne Storm); 6 Stanley Gene (Hull FC); 7 Adrian Lam (C) (Wigan Warriors); 8 Raymond Karl (Enga Mioks); 9 Mark Mom (Port Moresby Vipers); 10 Michael Mondo (Yanco); 11 Duncan Naawi (Redcliffe); 12 Bruce Mamando (N Queensland Cowboys); 13 Tom O'Reilly (Oldham). *Subs (all used):* 14 Elias Paiyo (Kellyville); 15 Alex Krewanty (Sydney Bulls); 16 Andrew Norman (Burdekin Roosters); 17 Mikaili Aizure (Goroka Lahanis).
Try: Wilshere (70); **Goal:** Wilshere 2
On report: Mondo (78) - dangerous tackle

Penalties: Wales 5-9; **Half-time:** 20-2;
Referee: David Pakieto (New Zealand); **Attendance:** 5,211
Men of the Match
Wales: Lee Briers; *PNG:* John Wilshere

Wales' Anthony Farrell meets Papua New Guinea's Tom O'Reilly head on

FRANCE 6 ....NEW ZEALAND 54

Played at The Jungle, Castleford, Sunday 12 November 2000

New Zealand's Henry Paul brought down by France's Gael Tallec

The Kiwis made smooth progress through to the semi-finals with a ten-try demolition of the French at Castleford.

They were too big, fast and powerful for a gallant France side with Robbie Paul - standing in for the rested Stacey Jones - leading the way with three tries and brother Henry adding seven goals.

History was against a French side that had improved steadily as the tournament had progressed as their last win over the Kiwis was 20 years ago, by a 6-5 margin in Perpignan.

And the French made a disastrous start as Jerome Guisset was penalised for ball-stealing and Henry Paul kicked the Kiwis into a second minute lead. Then Freddie Banquet kicked-off directly into touch and Richard Swain and Robbie Paul combined to send Matt Rua charging over in the right corner for an unconverted try.

And by the break it was 30-0, props Quentin Pongia and Craig Smith, Robbie Paul and Stephen Kearney all scoring tries.

Robbie Paul's second try, three minutes after the re-start, signalled it would be more of the same for France in the second half, Brian Jellick and Willie Talau adding further tries before the French finally gave their supporters something to cheer. Kiwi winger Nigel Vagana twice mishandled in attempting to clear Devecchi's grubber kick and Claude Sirvent pounced for the touchdown, Freddie Banquet converting to make it 44-6.

It proved to be merely a brief respite as another Blackmore touchdown and Robbie Paul's hat-trick try ended the scoring.

FRANCE: 1 Freddie Banquet (Villeneuve); 5 Claude Sirvent (St-Gaudens); 4 Arnaud Dulac (St-Gaudens); 3 Jean-Emmanuel Cassin (Toulouse); 2 Jean-Marc Garcia (UTC); 6 Fabien Devecchi (C) (Avignon); 7 Julien Rinaldi (Villeneuve); 8 Rachid Hechiche (Lyon); 9 Vincent Wulf (Villeneuve); 10 Jason Sands (Limoux); 11 Jerome Guisset (Warrington Wolves); 12 Gael Tallec (Halifax Blue Sox); 13 Pascal Jampy (UTC). *Subs (all used):* 14 David Despin (Villeneuve); 15 Laurent Carrasco (Villeneuve); 16 Romain Sort (Villeneuve); 17 Frederic Teixido (Limoux)
Try: Sirvent (59); **Goal:** Banquet

NEW ZEALAND: 1 Richie Barnett (C) (Sydney Roosters); 2 Brian Jellick (North Queensland Cowboys); 3 Richie Blackmore (Leeds Rhinos); 4 Willie Talau (Canterbury Bulldogs); 5 Nigel Vagana (Auckland Warriors); 6 Henry Paul (Bradford Bulls); 7 Robbie Paul (Bradford Bulls); 8 Craig Smith (St George-Illawarra Dragons); 9 Richard Swain (Melbourne Storm); 10 Quentin Pongia (Sydney City Roosters); 11 Matt Rua (Melbourne Storm); 12 Stephen Kearney (Melbourne Storm); 13 Logan Swann (Auckland Warriors). *Subs (all used):* 14 Nathan Cayless (Parramatta Eels); 15 Joe Vagana (Auckland Warriors); 16 Ruben Wiki (Canberra Raiders); 17 Tonie Carroll (Brisbane Broncos).
Tries: Rua (3), Pongia (18), Smith (20), R Paul (31, 43, 65), Kearney (39), Jellick (48), Talau (50), Blackmore (62); **Goals:** H Paul 7

Penalties: 6-6; **Half-time:** 30-0; **Referee:** Bill Harrigan (Australia)
Attendance: 5,158
Men of the Match
France: Vincent Wulf; *New Zealand:* Robbie Paul

ENGLAND 6 ....NEW ZEALAND 49

Played at Reebok Stadium, Bolton, Saturday 18 November 2000

Red-hot New Zealand shattered England's dream of a second successive World Cup final with a near-perfect display.

Every Kiwi looked top class, none more so than Bradford Bulls' stand-off Henry Paul, who gave one of the outstanding performances of the tournament.

From the second minute, when he sent in Stephen Kearney for the first try to when he put Logan Swann through for the last, Paul was in total command. He was involved in five tries altogether and kicked nine goals including a field goal, with his first two-pointer giving him a century of points for New Zealand in Test and World Cup matches.

There was an eight-minute spell early in the second half when England just couldn't handle Henry. It began with him snapping up a lost England ball to spark off a rapid counter-attack which finished with Willie Talau scoring out wide.

The best of many marvellous moments followed when Paul sent in Nigel Vagana for a superb try.

Three minutes later, Paul linked with his three-quarters for Talau to send Lesley Vainikolo pounding clear for his second try.

Kearney had made it look so easy when, with England's centres bamboozled by the decoy, he burst through for his second minute try,

ENGLAND: 1 Kris Radlinski (Wigan Warriors); 2 Chev Walker (Leeds Rhinos); 3 Scott Naylor (Bradford Bulls); 4 Keith Senior (Leeds Rhinos); 5 Paul Wellens (St Helens); 7 Sean Long (St Helens); 6 Paul Deacon (Bradford Bulls); 8 Stuart Fielden (Bradford Bulls); 9 Tony Smith (Wigan Warriors); 10 Harvey Howard (Brisbane Broncos); 11 Paul Sculthorpe (St Helens); 12 Mike Forshaw (Bradford Bulls); 13 Andrew Farrell (C) (Wigan Warriors). *Subs (all used):* 14 Jamie Peacock (Bradford Bulls); 15 Andy Hay (Leeds Rhinos); 16 Darren Fleary (Leeds Rhinos); 17 Paul Anderson (Bradford Bulls).
Try: Smith (44); **Goal:** Farrell
On report: Darren Fleary (39) – late, high tackle

NEW ZEALAND: 1 Richie Barnett (C) (Sydney City Roosters); 2 Nigel Vagana (Auckland Warriors); 3 Tonie Carroll (Brisbane Broncos); 4 Willie Talau (Canterbury Bulldogs); 5 Lesley Vainikolo (Canberra Raiders); 6 Henry Paul (Bradford Bulls); 7 Stacey Jones (Auckland Warriors); 8 Craig Smith (St George-Illawarra); 9 Richard Swain (Melbourne Storm); 10 Quentin Pongia (Sydney City Roosters); 11 Matt Rua (Melbourne Storm); 12 Stephen Kearney (Melbourne Storm); 13 Ruben Wiki (Canberra Raiders). *Subs (all used):* 14 Robbie Paul (Bradford Bulls); 15 Joe Vagana (Auckland Warriors); 16 Nathan Cayless (Parramatta Eels); 17 Logan Swann (Auckland Warriors).
Tries: Vainikolo (33,56), Talau (48,62), Kearney (2), Wiki (36), N. Vagana (53), Swann (75); **Goals:** H Paul 8; **Field goal:** H Paul

Penalties: Eng 5-9; **Half-time:** 0-21; **Referee:** Tim Mander (Australia)
Attendance: 16,032
Men of the Match
England: Tony Smith; *New Zealand:* Henry Paul

stepping inside Kris Radlinski to start the rout. Paul must have been expecting a close game as, after adding the extras, he popped over a field goal.

England held out until the 33rd minute when a shattering tackle from Tonie Carroll caused England skipper Andrew Farrell to spill the ball on the Kiwi '20' and Nigel Vagana scooped it up to sprint away.

Jamie Peacock brought the winger down just short of the line with the chase of the World Cup, only for Vainikolo to power over from the play-the-ball.

The game was up. Three minutes later Ruben Wiki produced a classic piece of loose forward play, picking up the ball from a scrum and beating two defenders round the blind side in his burst for the line. Paul added the goals to both tries plus

New Zealand's Stacey Jones collared by England captain Andy Farrell

a penalty to make it 21-0 to the Kiwis at half-time.

England raised faint hopes of a rally when they scored their only try early in the second half with Tony Smith touching down Sean Long's neat kick and Farrell adding the goal.

But New Zealand's response was to deliver another shattering blow as a typical hefty tackle caused Paul Sculthorpe to cough up the ball and a few swift passes brought Talau his first try.

It became a procession after that as Nigel Vagana, Vainikolo, Talau and Swann swept in for tries to rack up a record defeat for England, beating the 42-13 loss against France back in 1951.

61

AUSTRALIA 46 ....WALES 22

Played at McAlpine Stadium, Huddersfield, Sunday 19 November 2000

Australia made their predicted progress through to the World Cup Final but not before Clive Griffiths' gallant Welsh side had lifted the spirits of a nation.

The Welsh produced an outstanding display of enterprise and commitment to the cause, holding a 22-14 lead early in the second half before the Kangaroos dominated the latter stages of a truly memorable encounter.

Lee Briers, Keiron Cunningham, Paul Highton and skipper Iestyn Harris all played superbly in a wonderful team effort as the mighty Kangaroos were rocked by the sheer pride of a Wales side written off as no-hopers before the tournament.

But second-half tries by Bryan Fletcher, Darren Lockyer (two), Brad Fittler, Craig Gower and Ben Kennedy - the culmination of one of the most glorious passages of football ever seen in a World Cup - ended the impossible dream.

There was no hint of the drama to come when Brett Kimmorley pierced the close-range Welsh defence from first receiver for a fifth minute try and Wendell Sailor added his eighth try of the tournament six minutes later.

But Cunningham and Harris sparked an amazing Welsh revival with some determined runs down centre-field before scrum-half Ian Watson scored a 14th minute try out of the top drawer.

AUSTRALIA: 1 Darren Lockyer (Brisbane Broncos); 5 Wendell Sailor (Brisbane Broncos); 4 Matthew Gidley (Newcastle Knights); 3 Ryan Girdler (Penrith Panthers); 2 Adam MacDougall (Newcastle Knights); 6 Brad Fittler (C) (Sydney City Roosters); 7 Brett Kimmorley (Melbourne Storm); 8 Shane Webcke (Brisbane Broncos); 9 Craig Gower (Penrith Panthers); 10 Michael Vella (Parramatta Eels); 11 Gorden Tallis (Brisbane Broncos); 12 Bryan Fletcher (Sydney City Roosters); 13 Scott Hill (Melbourne Storm). *Subs (all used):* 14 Trent Barrett (St George-Illawarra Dragons); 15 Robbie Kearns (Melbourne Storm); 16 Ben Kennedy (Newcastle Knights); 17 Nathan Hindmarsh (Parramatta Eels).
Tries: Kimmorley (5), Sailor (11), Fittler (28, 61), Fletcher (54), Lockyer (57, 64), Gower (70), Kennedy (80); **Goals:** Girdler, Lockyer 4;
On report: Webcke (77) - striking

WALES: 1 Iestyn Harris (C) (Leeds Rhinos); 2 Chris Smith (St Helens); 4 Jason Critchley (unattached); 3 Kris Tassell (Salford City Reds); 5 Anthony Sullivan (St Helens); 6 Lee Briers (Warrington Wolves); 7 Ian Watson (Widnes Vikings); 8 Anthony Farrell (Leeds Rhinos); 9 Keiron Cunningham (St Helens); 10 Paul Moriarty (unattached); 11 Justin Morgan (Canberra Raiders); 12 Paul Highton (Salford City Reds) 13 Chris Morley (Sheffield Eagles). *Subs (all used):* 14 Wes Davies (Wigan Warriors); 15 Paul Atcheson (St Helens); 16 John Devereux (unattached); 17 David Luckwell (Batley Bulldogs).
Tries: Watson (14), Tassell (18), Briers (23); **Goals:** Harris 4;
Field goals: Briers 2

Penalty count: Aus 9-3; **Half-time:** 14-20;
Referee: Russell Smith (England); **Attendance:** 8,114
Men of the Match
Australia: Brett Kimmorley; *Wales:* Lee Briers

After Gorden Tallis had lost possession for the Kangaroos, Wales took advantage and Briers' cut-out pass to the left was brilliantly gathered on the bounce by centre Kris Tassell who scored his fourth try of the tournament wide out on the left.

When Harris hoisted a towering kick from 40 metres out, Briers chased and timed his leap to perfection to beat Lockyer to the ball and go over unopposed, sealing his moment of triumph with a glorious swallow dive. Harris goaled and Wales had scored three tries in an amazing ten-minute spell.

Briers added to the Australians' discomfort with two perfectly struck field goals

**Australia's Wendell Sailor crashes through the challenge of Wales'
Justin Morgan to score**

to give his side a 20-8 lead after 27 minutes.

The shell-shocked Kangaroos needed inspiration quickly and, typically, it came from skipper Fittler who took Kimmorley's pass to score a reviving try from close range that Girdler converted.

With Wales now forced to defend desperately, Anthony Sullivan went agonisingly close to a sensational interception - shades of dad Clive in the '72 final - after Kimmorley flung a long ball to the right. If the ball had stuck.....

Wales kept up the intensity of their display as the second half opened, Briers failing with a field goal attempt before Harris added a penalty five minutes after the re-start after Kearns was penalised at the ruck.

But with Australia mounting wave after wave of attacks, the pressure was bound to tell as the Welsh visibly tired under an unstoppable assault.

GROUP ONE

ENGLAND 2 ....**AUSTRALIA 22**
England: G - Farrell
Australia: T - Sailor 2, Gidley, MacDougall; G - Rogers 3

FIJI 38 ....**RUSSIA 12**
Fiji: T - Vunivalu 3, Tuqiri 2, Kuruduadua, Sovatabua; G - Tuqiri 5
Russia: T - Iliassov, Rullis; G - Jiltsov, Mitrofanov

AUSTRALIA 66 ....**FIJI 8**
Australia: T - Rogers 4, Kennedy 2, Girdler 2, Barrett, Hindmarsh, MacDougall, Gidley; G - Rogers 9
Fiji: T - Cakacaka, Tuqiri

ENGLAND 76 ....**RUSSIA 4**
England: T - Sinfield 3, Rowley 2, Peacock 2, Long 2, Hay, Walker, Pryce, Stephenson, Deacon; G - Farrell 5, Long 5
Russia: G - Mitrofanov 2

AUSTRALIA 110 ....**RUSSIA 4**
Australia: T - Sailor 4, Girdler 3, Barrett 2, Croker 2, Hindmarsh 2, MacDougall, Fletcher, Webcke, Tallis, Johns, Gidley; G - Girdler 17
Russia: T - Donovan

ENGLAND 66 ....**FIJI 10**
England: T - Peacock 3, Wellens 3, Rogers 2, Hay, Smith, Farrell, Naylor, Radlinski; G - Farrell 9
Fiji: T - Navale, Tuqiri; G - Vunivalu

Group One - Final Standings

	P	W	D	L	F	A	D	Pts
Australia	3	3	0	0	198	14	184	6
England	3	2	0	1	144	36	108	4
Fiji	3	1	0	2	56	144	-88	2
Russia	3	0	0	3	20	224	-204	0

GROUP TWO

LEBANON 0 ....**NEW ZEALAND 64**
New Zealand: T - Barnett 2, Carroll 2, Talau 2, Vainikolo 2, Jones 2, Jellick, Swann; G - Jones 6, H Paul 2

WALES 38 ....**COOK ISLANDS 6**
Wales: T - Tassell 3, Briers, Jenkins, Cunningham; G - Harris 7
Cook Islands: T - Temata; G - Piakura

COOK ISLANDS 10 ....**NEW ZEALAND 84**
Cook Islands: T - Noovao, Iro; G - Piakura
New Zealand: T - Barnett 2, Vaealiki 2, Lavea 2, R Paul 2, N Vagana, Vainikolo, Cayless, Lauiti'iti, Puletua, Wiki, Pongia; G - Lavea 12

WALES 24 ....**LEBANON 22**
Wales: T - Harris 2, Sterling, Cunningham, Davies; G - Harris 2
Lebanon: T - Saleh 2, Coorey, S El Masri; G - H El Masri 3

COOK ISLANDS 22 ....**LEBANON 22**
Cook Islands: T - Berryman 2, Joe, Toa; G - Berryman 2, Piakura
Lebanon: T - H El Masri 2, Touma, H Saleh; G - H El Masri 3

WALES 18 ....**NEW ZEALAND 58**
Wales: T - Briers, Atcheson, Farrell; G - Harris 3
New Zealand: T - Vainikolo 3, Barnett 2, Talau, H Paul, Wiki, Carroll, Lauiti'iti, N Vagana; G - H Paul 5, Lavea 2

Group Two - Final Standings

	P	W	D	L	F	A	D	Pts
New Zealand	3	3	0	0	206	28	178	6
Wales	3	2	0	1	80	86	-6	4
Lebanon	3	0	1	2	44	110	-66	1
Cook Islands	3	0	1	2	38	144	-106	1

GROUP THREE

FRANCE 20 ....**PAPUA NEW GUINEA 23**
France: T - Hechiche 2, Benausse, Dekkiche; G - Banquet 2
Papua New Guinea: T - Bai, Krewanty, Buko, Lam; G - Wilshere 2, Buko; FG - Lam

SOUTH AFRICA 18 ....**TONGA 16**
South Africa: T - Breytenbach, Barnard, Best; G - Bloem 2, O'Shea
Tonga: T - Vaikona 3, D Mann 2, W Wolfgramm, Liava'a, Masella, Moala, E Mann, Lomi, Kaufusi, Mason; G - Moala 6, D Mann

FRANCE 28 ....**TONGA 8**
France: T - Banquet, Sirvent, Dulac, Garcia, Jampy; G - Banquet 4
Tonga: T - D Fisi'iahi, P Fisi'iahi

PAPUA NEW GUINEA 16 ....**SOUTH AFRICA 0**
Papua New Guinea: T - Aila, Wilshere, Paiyo; G - Wilshere 2

FRANCE 56 ....**SOUTH AFRICA 6**
France: T - Jampy 3, Cassin 2, Banquet, Guisset, Sirvent, Tallec; G - Banquet 10
South Africa: T - de Villiers; G - Bloem

PAPUA NEW GUINEA 30 ....**TONGA 22**
Papua New Guinea: T - Gene 2, Mondo, Buko, Karl; G - Wilshere 5
Tonga: T - Moala 2, Vaikona, Mason; G - Moala 3

Group Three - Final Standings

	P	W	D	L	F	A	D	Pts
Papua New Guinea	3	3	0	0	69	42	27	6
France	3	2	0	1	104	37	67	4
Tonga	3	1	0	2	96	76	20	2
South Africa	3	0	0	3	24	138	-114	0

GROUP FOUR

IRELAND 30 ....**SAMOA 16**
Ireland: T - Joynt, Ricketson, Eagar, Carney, Prescott; G - Prescott 5
Samoa: T - Leauma, Milford, Betham; G - Geros 2

SCOTLAND 16 ....**AOTEAROA MAORI 17**
Scotland: T - Penny, Maiden, Bell; G - Mackay, Crowther
Aotearoa Maori: T - Toopi 2, Kidwell; G - Ngamu 2; FG - Ngamu

IRELAND 18 ....**SCOTLAND 6**
Ireland: T - Sheridan, Withers; G - Prescott 5
Scotland: T - Arnold; G - Crowther

AOTEAROA MAORI 16 ....**SAMOA 21**
Maori: T - Matthews, Nelson, Rauhihi; G - Goodwin 2
Samoa: T - Fa'afili 2, W Swann, Milford; G - Poching 2; FG - W Swann

IRELAND 30 ....**AOTEAROA MAORI 16**
Ireland: T - Forster, Carney, Barnhill, Withers, Sheridan; G - Prescott 5
Maori: T - Nelson, Te Rangi, Koopu; G - Perenara, Ngamu

SCOTLAND 12 ....**SAMOA 20**
Scotland: T - Vowles, Rhodes; G - Crowther 2
Samoa: T - Leauma 2, Solomona, Milford; G - Laloata 2

Group Four - Final Standings

	P	W	D	L	F	A	D	Pts
Ireland	3	3	0	0	78	38	40	6
Samoa	3	2	0	1	57	58	-1	4
Maori	3	1	0	2	49	67	-18	2
Scotland	3	0	0	3	34	55	-21	0

QUARTER FINALS

AUSTRALIA 66 ....**SAMOA 10**
Australia: T - Fletcher 3, Johns 2, Hill 2, MacDougall 2, Girdler, Fittler, Sailor; G - Rogers 9
Samoa: T - Solomona, Leauma; G - Laloata

ENGLAND 26 ....**IRELAND 16**
England: T - Senior, Peacock, Smith, Walker; G - Farrell 5
Ireland: T - Withers 2, Martyn; G - Prescott 2

NEW ZEALAND 54 ....**FRANCE 6**
New Zealand: T - R Paul 3, Rua, Pongia, Smith, Kearney, Jellick, Talau, Blackmore; G - H Paul 7
France: T - Sirvent; G - Banquet

WALES 22 ....**PAPUA NEW GUINEA 8**
Wales: T - Critchley, Briers, Davies; G - Harris 5
Papua New Guinea: T - Wilshere; G - Wilshere 2

SEMI FINALS

AUSTRALIA 46 ....**WALES 22**
Australia: T - Fittler 2, Lockyer 2, Kimmorley, Sailor, Fletcher, Gower, Kennedy; G - Lockyer 4; Girdler
Wales: T - Watson, Tassell, Briers; G - Harris 4; FG - Briers 2

ENGLAND 6 ....**NEW ZEALAND 49**
England: T - Smith; G - Farrell
New Zealand: T - Vainikolo 2, Talau 2, Kearney, Wiki, N Vagana, Swann; G - H Paul 8; FG - H Paul

WORLD CUP FINAL 2000

AUSTRALIA 40 ....**NEW ZEALAND 12**
Australia: T - Sailor 2, Gidley, N Hindmarsh, Lockyer, Fittler, Barrett; G - Rogers 6
New Zealand: T - Vainikolo, Carroll; G - H Paul 2

TOP TRYSCORER: Wendell Sailor (Australia) 10
TOP GOALKICKER: Mat Rogers (Australia) 27
TOP POINTSCORER: Mat Rogers (Australia) 70 *(4 tries, 27 goals)*

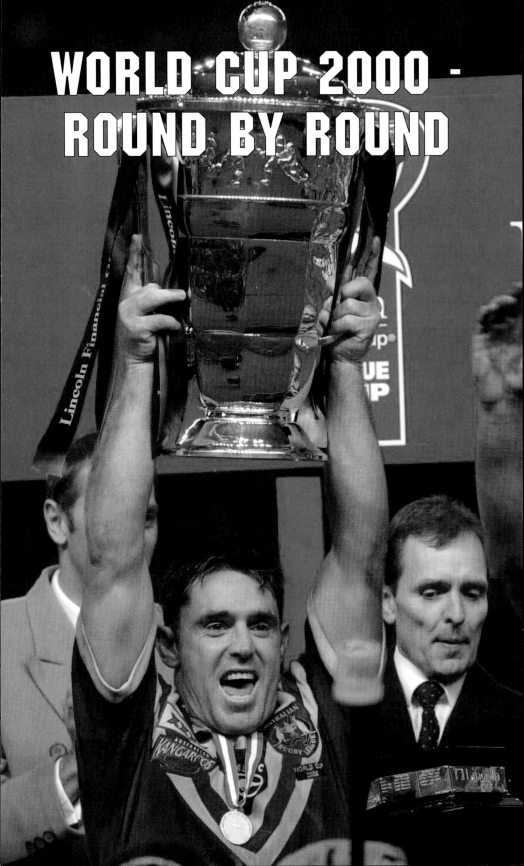

WORLD CUP 2000 - ROUND BY ROUND

GROUP ONE

MAIN PICTURE: Adrian Morley receives some close attention from Scott Hill at Twickenham as England go down to Australia in the opening game.
ABOVE: Australia's Nathan Hindmarsh on the burst against Fiji.
RIGHT: Fiji's Etuate Vakatawa held by Russia's Ian Rubin.

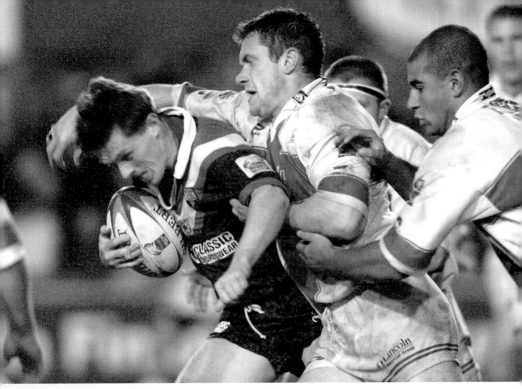

TOP: Andre Olar finds no way past Jamie Peacock and Chev Walker as England defeat Russia at Knowsley Road.
ABOVE: Sean Long on the attack for England as they see off Fiji.
RIGHT: Australia's Shane Webcke is held by the Russian defence.

ABOVE: New Zealand's Ali Lauiti'iti fends off the advancing Cook Islands defence.
BELOW: Cook Islands' Tyrone Pau dives over for a try at the Millennium Stadium against Lebanon.
BOTTOM: New Zealand's Willie Talau loses the ball in win against the Lebanon.

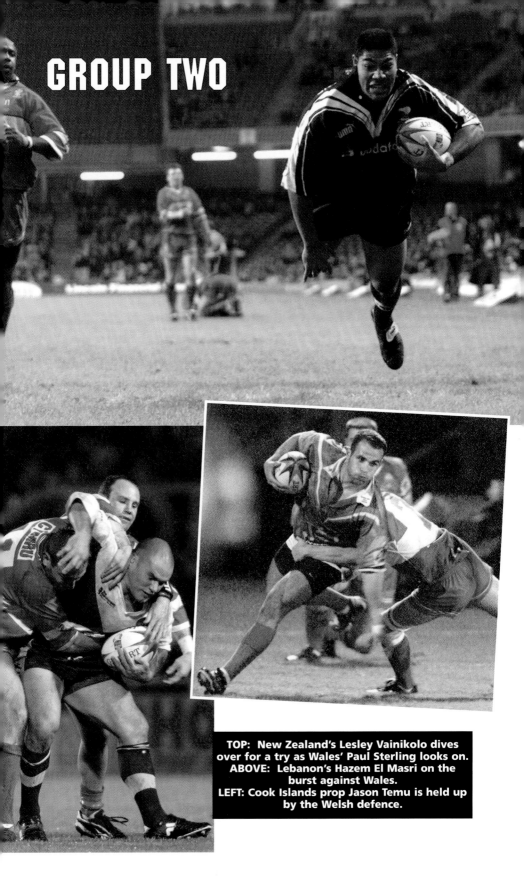

GROUP TWO

TOP: New Zealand's Lesley Vainikolo dives over for a try as Wales' Paul Sterling looks on.
ABOVE: Lebanon's Hazem El Masri on the burst against Wales.
LEFT: Cook Islands prop Jason Temu is held up by the Welsh defence.

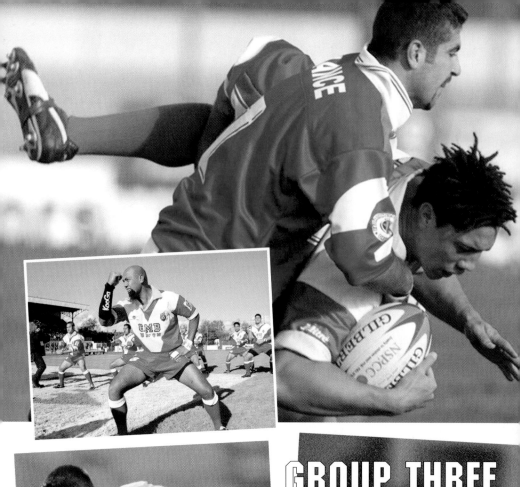

GROUP THREE

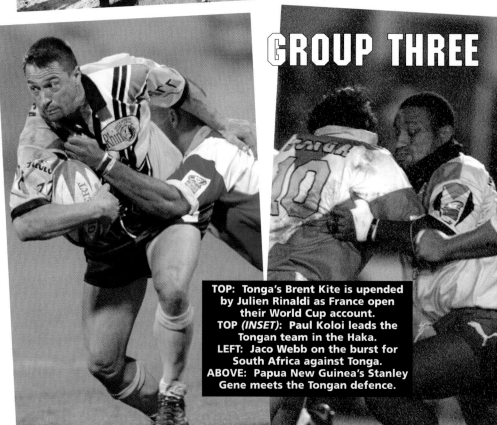

TOP: Tonga's Brent Kite is upended by Julien Rinaldi as France open their World Cup account.
TOP *(INSET)*: Paul Koloi leads the Tongan team in the Haka.
LEFT: Jaco Webb on the burst for South Africa against Tonga.
ABOVE: Papua New Guinea's Stanley Gene meets the Tongan defence.

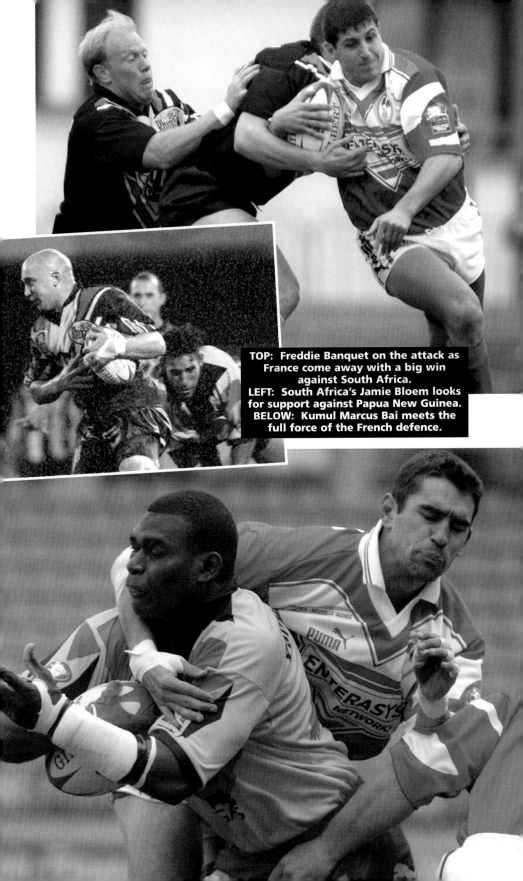

TOP: Freddie Banquet on the attack as France come away with a big win against South Africa.
LEFT: South Africa's Jamie Bloem looks for support against Papua New Guinea.
BELOW: Kumul Marcus Bai meets the full force of the French defence.

GROUP FOUR

ABOVE: David Kidwell dives over for a try as the Maori defeat Scotland by a single point.
LEFT: Terry O'Connor feels the force of the Maori defence.
BELOW: Scotland's Andrew Purcell is all wrapped up by the Samoans.

ABOVE: Jerry Seu Seu is collared as Samoa shock the Maori at Workington.
RIGHT: Ireland's Michael Eagar on the burst against Scotland.
BELOW: Luke Ricketson dives over for a try as Ireland prove too strong for Samoa.

TOP: England's Paul Deacon looks for a gap in the Irish defence.
LEFT: Kris Radlinski jumps for a high ball.
ABOVE: Chev Walker is hauled down by Ireland's Terry O'Connor.

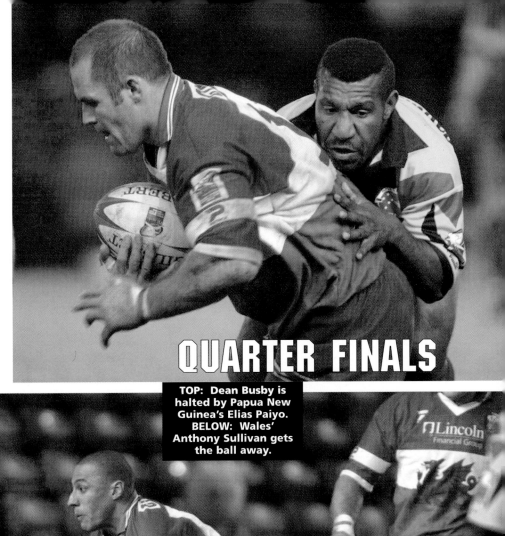

QUARTER FINALS

TOP: Dean Busby is halted by Papua New Guinea's Elias Paiyo. BELOW: Wales' Anthony Sullivan gets the ball away.

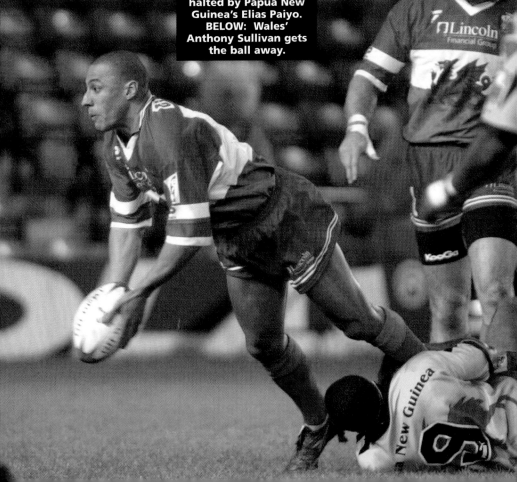

QUARTER FINALS

**TOP: Samoa's Jerry Seu Seu is dumped by Scott Hill and Bryan Fletcher as Australia ease through to the semi-finals.
BELOW: Brian Jellick takes the ball up for New Zealand as they beat France 54-6.
BELOW LEFT: Matt Rua on the charge for New Zealand.**

SEMI FINAL

TOP: England's Paul Sculthorpe is dumped by the New Zealand defence.
INSET: Ruben Wiki is congratulated on his try by Richie Barnett.
ABOVE: Nathan Cayless is halted by Andy Farrell and Paul Anderson.

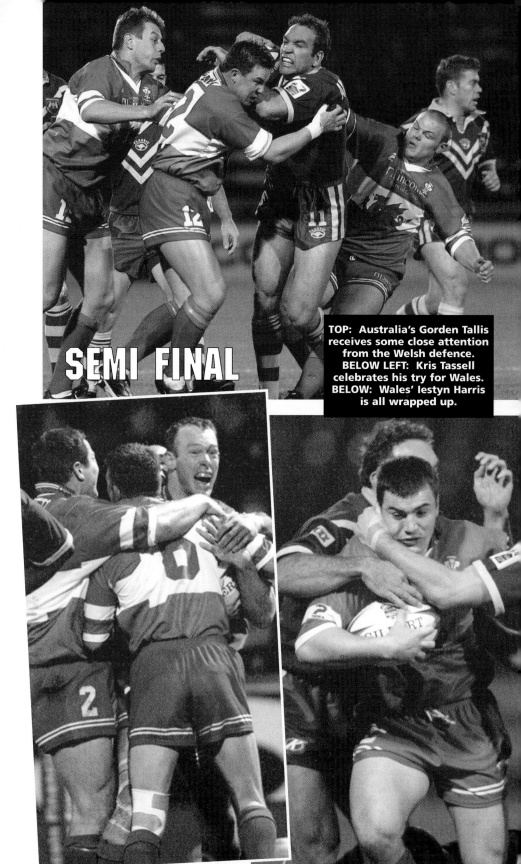

SEMI FINAL

TOP: Australia's Gorden Tallis receives some close attention from the Welsh defence.
BELOW LEFT: Kris Tassell celebrates his try for Wales.
BELOW: Wales' Iestyn Harris is all wrapped up.

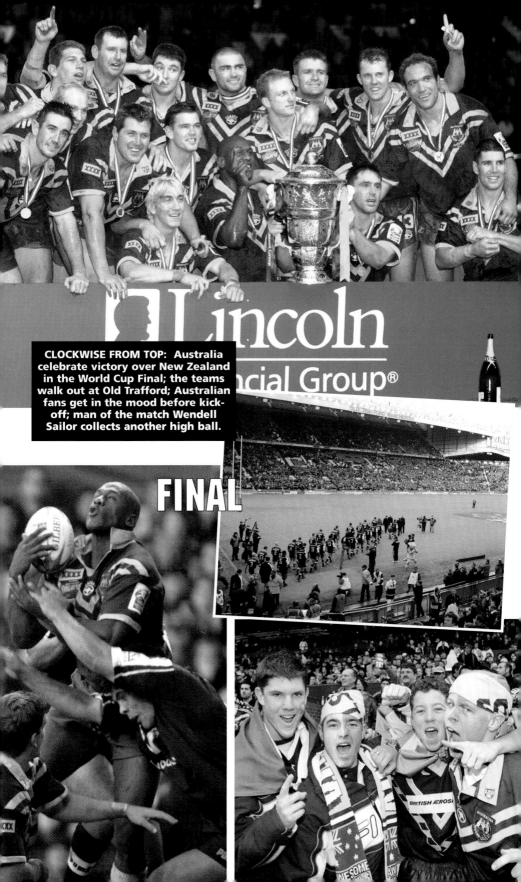

CLOCKWISE FROM TOP: Australia celebrate victory over New Zealand in the World Cup Final; the teams walk out at Old Trafford; Australian fans get in the mood before kick-off; man of the match Wendell Sailor collects another high ball.

FINAL

TOP: BARLA Great Britain & Ireland celebrate winning the Emerging Nations final against Italy.
BELOW: USA's Robert Balachandran on the attack as they defeat Morocco in the play-offs.
RIGHT: Japan's Daisuke Kobayashi on the burst against Canada.
BOTTOM RIGHT: Daniel Albertini is held up by the BARLA defence as Italy lose the final.

EMERGING NATIONS

2

A HISTORY OF THE RUGBY LEAGUE WORLD CUP

1954

As sporting legends go, they don't come much better than the story of Great Britain's triumph in the very first Rugby League World Cup 46 years ago.

Inspired by their captain Dave Valentine, the British boys defied all the pre-tournament predictions. Described by critics back home as 'no hopers', they crossed the Channel and returned as conquering heroes.

The triumph of Scotsman Valentine and his men put the icing on the cake of what, with hindsight, has come to be recognised as a wonderfully successful inaugural World Cup tournament. It remains yet another example of Rugby League leading the way for other sports to follow.

Most of the credit for getting the World Cup off the ground must go to the French.

Almost as soon as France began playing League 20 years earlier they had urged their British neighbours to recognise the value of an international World Championship.

Nothing happened then, but by early 1952, on the back of their sensationally successful first tour of Australia the summer before, the dynamic young president of the French League, Paul Barriere, was more eager than ever to grasp the opportunities offered by a World Cup.

Air travel to and from the southern hemisphere was becoming a reality for Rugby League teams, and with only four Test playing nations - France, Great Britain, Australia and New Zealand - the logistics of bringing them all together for a World Cup appeared to be fairly straightforward. And Barriere's idea was backed by RFL secretary, Bill Fallowfield.

But the Australians were opposed to having a World Cup. It was only after the French offered to stage the first tournament in the autumn of 1954, with a financial guarantee of £25,000 to cover the travel costs of the visiting teams, that the Aussies were persuaded to go ahead.

Barriere arranged for the Federation Francaise de Jeu a Treize (remember, our game was still denied use of the word 'rugby' by the French authorities in those days) to donate the original World Cup - a magnificent trophy, standing two and a half feet high and weighing over half a hundredweight. This trophy has now been restored and will again be presented to the winners of the year 2000 competition.

And so the World Cup story was born. And a lot of our best known Rugby League players were left to rue the fact that they turned down the opportunity to go

Great Britain captain Dave Valentine holds aloft the World Cup after the Lions had triumphed in the first tournament

down in history as a member of the first British team, in any sport, to be crowned World Cup winners.

It's part of our game's folklore now that, coming so soon after a long and particularly gruelling tour to Australia and New Zealand in the summer of 1954, most of Great Britain's recognised international players declared themselves unavailable to travel to France for the first World Cup. Only three of the returned tourists - Dave Valentine, Phil Jackson and Gerry Helme - took part in what turned out to be an amazing triumph.

The Australians, having just won back the Ashes from Great Britain, went to France as favourites for the World Cup. But both the Aussies and the New Zealanders would be handicapped by a lack of match fitness, their domestic seasons having finished some two months before the tournament started, and neither having played any warm-up games.

The Kiwis had the honour of playing in the very first World Cup game against the host nation as the competition kicked off on Saturday, October 30th, 1954 in Paris. A crowd of 13,240 paying spectators were at the Parc des Princes to see the World Cup open in an atmosphere of uncertainty. The relative form of the teams were unknown, and the success of the tournament as a whole could have been made or marred by that first game.

There was no need to worry. Right from the kick-off, a high standard of play was set, which was maintained throughout the series, rising to a dramatic crescendo in the final (unscheduled) deciding match - also at the Parc des Princes.

France, captained by their famous full-back Puig Aubert, got off to the winning start they and the tournament needed, beating the gallant Kiwis 22-13. That left the spotlight to fall on Great Britain's opening match against Australia the following day in Lyon.

Britain's 28-13 victory was greeted with great enthusiasm, the new look young team, superbly led by captain Valentine, upsetting all the odds with a courageous display to be ranked alongside many of their finest moments in the history of Test football.

"Salute the new Britain," commented one national newspaper report.

"Forty years later the spirit of Rorke's Drift can still confound the Aussies."

It was a game that marked the Great Britain debut of 20 year old Mick Sullivan, then of Huddersfield, who went on to become the most capped British player in the history of the game.

And it was also a game that confirmed, surprising as this may be for present day followers of the game some 46 years later, the balance of power in the world of Rugby League at that time firmly rested in Europe, and not the southern hemisphere.

A week after their morale-boosting triumph against Australia, Great Britain travelled south to meet the French in Toulouse.

In front of a sensational crowd of 37,471 - the biggest attendance ever recorded for a Rugby League match in France - the two European nations produced a thrilling

THE FIRST WORLD CUP FINAL

GREAT BRITAIN beat FRANCE 16-12.
November 13, 1954
at Parc des Princes, Paris.

GREAT BRITAIN: Ledgard, Rose, Jackson, Naughton, Sullivan, Brown, Helme, Thorley, Smith, Coverdale, Watts, Robinson, Valentine.
Tries: Brown 2, Rose, Helme.
Goals: Ledgard 2

FRANCE: Puig Aubert, Contrastin, Merquey, Tesseire, Cantoni, Jiminez, Crespo, Rinaldi, Audobert, Krawzyk, Save, Pambrun, Verdier.
Tries: Cantoni, Contrastin.
Goals: Puig Aubert 3

Referee: Charlie Appleton (Warrington, England)
Attendance: 30,368

1954 WORLD CUP RESULTS

FRANCE beat NEW ZEALAND 22-13
At Parc de Princes, Paris. Crowd: 13,240

GREAT BRITAIN beat AUSTRALIA 28-13
At Lyon. Crowd: 10,250

AUSTRALIA beat NEW ZEALAND 34-15
At Marseille. Crowd: 20,000

FRANCE drew with GREAT BRITAIN 13-13
At Toulouse. Crowd: 37,471

FRANCE beat AUSTRALIA 15-5
At Nantes. Crowd: 13,000

GREAT BRITAIN beat NEW ZEALAND 26-6
At Bordeaux. Crowd: 14,000

FINAL TABLE

	P	W	D	L	F	A	Pts
Great Britain	3	2	1	0	67	32	5
France	3	2	1	0	50	31	5
Australia	3	1	0	2	52	58	2
New Zealand	3	0	0	3	34	82	0

Great Britain's John Thorley halted by the Australian defence

match that ended in a 13-all draw.

That proved to be a crucial stroke of good fortune for the inaugural World Cup tournament because, as events unfolded, the draw meant France and Great Britain finished the scheduled fixtures level on points, and a play-off became necessary to decide the title.

Remarkably, the Rugby League authorities didn't take the hint and recognise the dramatic impact of having a final as the climax of each World Cup. The game had to wait another 14 years, until the 1968 tournament, before an 'official' World Cup final would be played.

Whilst Great Britain and France were enthralled in that epic draw in Toulouse, Australia and New Zealand met in Marseille, before another 20,000 spectators, and it was the Aussies, inspired by their captain Clive Churchill, who came out on top 34-15.

That left the two European nations both needing to win their remaining match to finish level. And both did, on Thursday, November 11, with Great Britain comfortably overcoming New Zealand in Bordeaux 26-6, and France killing off Australia's hopes of salvaging something from the tournament by winning 15-5 in front of over 13,000 people in the city of Nantes.

And so the stage was set for the first ever Rugby League World Cup final, remarkably arranged at just two day's notice. A crowd of over 30,000 filled the Parc des Princes in Paris almost to capacity to see France, skippered by Puig Aubert, and Great Britain, led by Dave Valentine, produce a match full of passion, colour and excitement.

The end result was a 16-12 win for the British, and their heroes Valentine and Gerry Helme were carried shoulder-high at the end by delighted team-mates to the cheers of the small band of British press-men and supporters who were privileged enough to be in Paris on that famous day - Saturday, November 13, 1954.

The team, with so little international experience, had been given no chance before the tournament, but Valentine and his men achieved one of Britain's finest hours. Players like goal-kicking full-back Jimmy Ledgard, centre Phil Jackson, flying Scotsman on the wing David Rose, clever stand-off Gordon Brown, and a yeoman pack who rallied to the call of their captain, became British sporting heroes that day.

The enormity of what the Great Britain team achieved can never be overstated. But for the game as a whole, the spoils were even greater. As well as seeing over 30,000 people in Paris, and other stadiums packed in the major cities of the country as Rugby League fever swept the French nation (and we can only speculate just what the game could have done in France had Puig Aubert's team been crowned the first French World Cup winners in any sport), the final was televised live in the United Kingdom.

FOGGY LA

ON their way home after the inaugural World Cup in France, Australia and New Zealand played two exhibition games in California.

The ballyhoo before the games at Long Beach Memorial Stadium and the Los Angeles Coliseum was typically American. Australian captain, Clive Churchill, was given the Key to the City and escorted to the arena by police with their car sirens blaring.

Australia won both matches - 30-13 (before 1,000 spectators) and 28-18 (4,554 attendance).

The second encounter was called off early after a pea-soup fog descended on the ground and the players couldn't find the ball after it had been kicked into touch.

About 10 minutes after the players had left the field, it was realised that Australian winger Des Flannery was nowhere to be seen. He was found still in the fog, calling out for his mates. Or so the story goes!

The impact of that was enormous, as one of the very first sporting events to be beamed back live from the continent, and most certainly the very first occasion, in any sport, that a British team had been seen in action on foreign soil in a World Cup final. Millions of television viewers throughout the country saw a marvellous exhibition of Rugby League, and a wonderful British victory.

FOOTNOTE: *Such was British Rugby League's lack of enthusiasm and belief that their team could win the first World Cup, the game's authorities declined to cover the cost of sending a coach with the team to France.*

Before they left, ex-Wigan and Great Britain hooker Joe Egan had taken the team for a couple of training sessions. Ever the diplomat, Joe, in expressing his delight at the success of Dave Valentine's team, said he had got reward enough from knowing how well the team had played.

1957

Australia had been somewhat reluctant participants in the first Rugby League World Cup in 1954.

But such was the success of the inaugural tournament that the Aussies' attitude had changed dramatically. So much so that they could hardly wait to stage the second World Cup themselves, and they got their wish just three years later.

The 1957 tournament coincided with Australian Rugby League's golden jubilee, and what a 50th birthday present the Green and Golds delivered, under the captaincy of Newtown centre Dick Poole.

And the contrasts didn't stop with the Aussies. Great Britain's mood as they approached the second World Cup could hardly have been more different to that which saw their inexperienced team cross the Channel in 1954 described as 'no hopers'.

In 1957 Great Britain weren't just the holders of the World Cup, they had also won the Ashes back from Australia in convincing fashion late in 1956. And with a team laden with established stars from the country's top clubs, in marked contrast to the makeshift heroes of 1954, the British were hot favourites second time around.

Eddie Waring, the doyen of British writers and commentators, said at the time that, so strong was the team captained by Alan Prescott, the 1957 World Cup competition looked like being a walkover.

"I incurred the wrath of some Australian fans by writing that it was hardly worth paying the cost of taking the big trophy to Sydney, with the side the British had against the sort of team Australia could field," remembered Eddie.

But the tournament collapsed badly for Britain, with a couple of injuries to key men having a big effect. The problems started when an extra warm-up game was played in Perth on the way to Sydney, in which stand-off Ray Price was injured. As a result, the Warrington man couldn't play in any of the World Cup games and Lewis Jones had to come into the pivotal role.

Great Britain started well enough, beating France 23-5 at the Sydney Cricket Ground. With their awesome threequarter line of Billy Boston, Phil Jackson, Alan Davies and Mick Sullivan in powerful form, the World Cup favourites tag seemed to fit well on the British.

France were in a transitional stage, nowhere near as good as their successful first touring teams of 1951 and '55, or their 1954 World Cup team, but still with two of their all-time greats in the backline in Jackie Merquey and Gilbert Benausse.

Over 50,000 spectators packed the SCG to see Britain play France, and on the same afternoon, June 15, 1957, almost 30,000 were in Brisbane to see the host nation win comfortably over New Zealand. The Kiwis were very much the underdogs among the four Rugby League Test playing nations during the mid-fifties, and once Great Britain had beaten the French it became obvious that Britain's showdown with Australia would be the match to decide the destiny of the World Cup.

There was no final play-off scheduled in the 1957 World Cup, the winners were to be the country which finished top of the league table after the round robin.

Australia had their own injury problems going into the vital game with Great Britain, just two days after both sides had beaten New Zealand and France respectively. Their star scrum-half Keith Holman, goal-kicking full-back Keith Barnes, and first choice stand-off Greg Hawick, were all injured against the Kiwis and couldn't turn out against the British.

The enforced changes proved to be the making of Australia's World Cup triumph, as winger Brian Carlson switched to full-back and tough-tackling loose-forward Brian 'Poppa' Clay moved to stand-off.

Great Britain were hit by a bodyblow within the first quarter of the game, when centre Alan Davies was injured in a heavy tackle and was forced to leave the field. Remember, there were no substitutes in those days, so Britain had to play with 12 men and without one of their most potent attacking forces.

Australia went on to outplay Great Britain that day, in front of almost 58,000 people in Sydney. Playing against the powerful Brian Clay proved to be a nightmare for Lewis Jones. The former 'golden boy' of Welsh rugby union did not have a happy day, and was severely criticised in the managers' report on their return to Britain. Jones actually scored all Great Britain's points that day, with three goals, but after being blamed in some quarters for his team's flop, the Welshman was never picked for Great Britain again.

1957 WORLD CUP RESULTS

GREAT BRITAIN beat FRANCE 23-5
At Sydney. Crowd: 50,007

AUSTRALIA beat NEW ZEALAND 25-5
At Brisbane. Crowd: 29,636

AUSTRALIA beat GREAT BRITAIN 31-6
At Sydney. Crowd: 57,955

FRANCE beat NEW ZEALAND 14-10
At Brisbane. Crowd: 28,000

AUSTRALIA beat FRANCE 26-9
At Sydney. Crowd: 35,158

NEW ZEALAND beat GREAT BRITAIN 29-21
At Sydney. Crowd: 14,263

FINAL TABLE

	P	W	D	L	F	A	Pts
Australia	3	3	0	0	82	20	6
Great Britain	3	1	0	2	50	65	2
New Zealand	3	1	0	2	44	60	2
France	3	1	0	2	28	59	2

A crushing 31-6 victory over the British - the biggest margin of all in the 1957 World Cup - left Australia needing to beat France in their third and final game to clinch the trophy. In windy and muddy conditions at the Sydney Cricket Ground, a 35,000 crowd saw the Australians find the French tougher opponents than Great Britain had been, but not enough to prevent Dick Poole's men grinding out a 26-9 win, thanks in no small part to an outstanding contribution by full-back Carlson, the scorer of one try and seven goals.

With three wins out of three, Australia had won the World Cup, leaving Great Britain and New Zealand to battle over the wooden-spoon in what was a huge anti-climax for Alan Prescott's British team. The lowest crowd of the tournament - just over 14,000 - turned out on a Tuesday afternoon at the Sydney Cricket Ground, and they saw things go from bad to worse for the British as they lost 29-21 to the Kiwis.

It was New Zealand's first ever win in World Cup football. Remember, they had lost all three games in the 1954 tournament.

To celebrate Australia's triumph, an additional game was played between them, as the new holders of the World Cup, and a 'Rest of the World' side selected from the other three nations. The Aussies won 20-11 against a 'Rest' team captained by Frenchman Jackie Merquey, and featuring four British players: Lewis Jones, Eric Ashton, Geoff Gunney and John Whiteley.

So, while Great Britain came home disappointed and disillusioned - rarely had they been such hot favourites - ready to regroup in time for the 1958 Lions tour, the Australians were left to celebrate. In their 50th year it was the first time they could bask in the glory of being true World Champions having, at last, managed to beat the challenge of both Great Britain and France.

And, with such excellent crowds, the host nation, along with all three visiting countries, were able to report a healthy profit from the 1957 World Cup.

The enthusiasm and financial returns generated in Australia, appeared to have cemented the future of the Rugby League World Cup as a vital and positive vehicle for the game.

Later in his career Wigan centre Eric Ashton would captain what is generally regarded as the finest Great Britain team ever to tour Australia, when he would lead the famous 1962 Ashes-winning Great Britain tourists.

> **PERSONA NON GRATA**
>
> *AUSTRALIA'S 1957 World Cup hero Brian Carlson is unique in so far as he did not have a club when he played in the tournament. Carlson was chosen as a winger in the Australian squad, but switched to full-back after the regular custodian, Keith Barnes, was injured in the first game. Carlson's play in the remaining matches was a decisive factor in Australia's first Cup success.*
>
> *Despite all this, as far as the club with which he had been playing was concerned, he was persona non grata. Carlson was captain-coach of the Blackall side in the Queensland country when he was selected for the Cup. The Blackall officials asked him to pull out of the squad and concentrate on club football. When he refused, the club dismissed him.*
>
> *Unconcerned, Carlson went ahead to become the top-scorer in the World Cup with two tries and 15 goals. And North Sydney was only too pleased to snap up his services once the tournament was over.*

But five years earlier, Ashton was a young player making his way in the game, and he admits that his selection for the 1957 World Cup was a tremendous surprise what opened up a new world.

"I was just 21, and had been in the game for two years, after signing for Wigan when I came out of the Army after my national service," says Ashton.

"I was very surprised to be selected. Some selectors had been at Oldham three matches before the end of the season, although I hadn't realised that until Ernie Ashcroft told me I had played well enough to have a realistic chance of getting in the side."

And what an adventure the World Cup trip turned out to be!

"The plane took three days to get there. We had to come down and re-fuel frequently in those days, because the maximum flying time was just four or five hours.

"But when we arrived in Sydney it was amazing. I'd never experienced a city like it that was Rugby League mad. The game was so popular, and everybody wanted to see the tourists. We started with a function in Sydney Town Hall, and we were feted everywhere we went. I thought all my birthdays had come at once. They couldn't do enough for us."

The friendship ended once the games began, however, although Ashton would only play against New Zealand in the tournament proper, before his selection for the Rest of the World side that took on the Aussies after the tournament had been completed.

"We were run off the park against Australia," admits Ashton.

"Brian Carlson was the man of the moment. He was voted the player of the series, and he was a big, strong, bustling player."

UNIQUE BROTHERS

AUCKLAND'S Vic and Sel Belsham are two of the select few brothers to have played for New Zealand. But that's not why they are best remembered in the annals of Rugby League history.

Vic's international career was short-lived, touring Australia with the 1948 Kiwis, missing out on selection in the two Tests but playing in four of the six minor games. He achieved much more in later years by becoming one of only three New Zealand international players to referee Tests and the only one to control a World Cup game. He and Australia's Darcy Lawler were in charge during the 1957 World Cup.

Scrum-half Sel Belsham made his Test debut at the age of 24 on the 1955-56 tour of Great Britain and France, toured Australia in 1956 and returned a year later for the World Cup, his last international appearance.

Twice during the World Cup, Vic Belsham refereed matches in which his brother played - New Zealand v Australia and the Rest-of-the-World v Australia.

This feat is unique in international Rugby League.

Carlson might not have played in the World Cup, however. His Queensland club Blackall had tried to prevent him playing in the tournament, but he walked out on the club to become the tournament's star player, afterwards joining North Sydney.

After the World Cup the British and French visited South Africa, where they played three games against each other in Johannesburg, Durban and East London.

"For a young man to visit Australia and South Africa in those days was just a magnificent experience, and is one I will never forget," reflects Eric.

1960

After seeing France and Australia stage the first two very successful tournaments in 1954 and 1957, the British got their turn to host the World Cup in 1960.

And it would be Great Britain who would win back the famous trophy first held aloft by Dave Valentine on that memorable day in Paris six years before.

However, victory in the 1960 World Cup, whilst it might have tasted just as sweet for the players, carried none of the romance that saw their first victory in 1954 generate such an impact.

On the contrary, the match that decided the destiny of the 1960 Word Cup - a rugged and spiteful slog between Britain and Australia in the mud at Odsal - did little to help the image of international Rugby League in the eyes of the national television audience that had, by that time, become an accepted (if not widely welcomed) part of the game.

As in the first two tournaments, no final was scheduled, with the winners of the World Cup being declared as the team which finished top of the table after the round-robin of matches had been completed.

With Great Britain and Australia viewed as the pre-tournament favourites, most predictions were that the deciding match would be when these two locked horns together, so - with a keen sense of drama by the fixture planner, RFL secretary Bill Fallowfield - this key encounter was left to the final weekend of the competition.

The contrast between the 1960 World Cup and the one we will be seeing later this year, could hardly be greater.

1960 WORLD CUP RESULTS

GREAT BRITAIN beat NEW ZEALAND 23-8
At Odsal Stadium, Bradford.
Crowd: 20,577

AUSTRALIA beat FRANCE 13-12
At Central Park, Wigan. Crowd: 20,278

GREAT BRITAIN beat FRANCE 33-7
At Station Road, Swinton. Crowd: 22,923

AUSTRALIA beat NEW ZEALAND 21-15
At Headingley, Leeds. Crowd: 10,773

GREAT BRITAIN beat AUSTRALIA 10-3
At Odsal Stadium, Bradford.
Crowd: 32,773

NEW ZEALAND beat FRANCE 9-0
At Central Park, Wigan. Crowd: 2,876

FINAL TABLE

	P	W	D	L	F	A	Pts
Great Britain	3	3	0	0	66	18	6
Australia	3	2	0	1	37	37	4
New Zealand	3	1	0	2	32	44	2
France	3	0	0	3	19	55	0

In 1960, all six matches in the tournament were staged in the Rugby League heartlands of Lancashire and Yorkshire. There was no thought of taking a game to London, or even experimenting a little by spreading the competition a tad wider across those traditional northern heartlands - like to Hull or to Cumbria, for example. Instead, only the established Test match venues of Wigan, Bradford, Leeds and Swinton were allocated games in the 1960 World Cup, with both Central

Park and Odsal Stadium actually staging two matches each.

Another point, which fans of today might find hard to believe, but on each of the three Saturdays (no midweek games like in the 1954 and 1957 tournaments) on which World Cup games were played, the normal full programme of Rugby League club fixtures was also staged.

And only two referees were employed to take control of the six games - Eric 'Sergeant Major' Clay, from Castleford, and Frenchman Edovard Martung, a Police Inspector from Bordeaux.

Each of the four competing nations was allowed a squad of 18 players for the duration of the 1960 World Cup tournament, with Great Britain captained by Wigan centre Eric Ashton.

Britain were top dog over the Australians going into the competition, having retained the Ashes so dramatically on the sensational 1958 Lions tour (Alan Prescott's tour) and successfully retained them on home soil against the Kangaroos in 1959.

That 1959 Ashes series had left the Aussies feeling badly done to, and less than happy about referee Clay.

The British team was able to recall a couple of the heroes (who, with the passing of time have become legends) of the 1958 Lions tour - Alex Murphy and Vince Karalius. Both had missed the 1959 Ashes series and, as events were to unfold, the 1960 World Cup triumph - and beating the Australians to achieve it - was to be the only really big moment for them both in international football in their own country.

In fact the recall of Karalius, along with forwards like Derek Turner, Jack Wilkinson and Hunslet's Brian Shaw, allied to the fact that the Aussies had virtually the same pack who felt so aggrieved at losing in the Ashes Tests just 12 months before (a pack including less than delicate flowers like Noel Kelly, Dud Beattie, Rex Mossop, Elton Rasmussen and Brian Hambly) - and you can see why that battle at Odsal was to be described as somewhat 'rugged'.

The tournament got off to a great start, with 20,000 plus crowds at both the opening fixtures. Great Britain defeated New Zealand fairly comfortably, 23-8, at Odsal Stadium, although the biggest talking point surrounded Billy Boston. The Wigan winger was declared not fit enough to play at the start of the World Cup, so in Britain's first two games, against New Zealand and France, the Warrington pair of Bobbie Greenhalgh and Jim Challinor wore the number two jersey. But, Billy - all 15 stones of him - was to return for the decider against Australia with devastating effect.

Whilst Eric Ashton was leading his men to that first-up win against the Kiwis, back at his home ground, Central Park, Australia and France were locked in a titanic battle. The Aussies got home by just one point, 13-12, thanks largely to the touches of individual brilliance provided by Reg Gasnier and Johnny Raper.

The French had put everything into their monumental effort against the Australians in their opening game, and found they couldn't raise their game to

Things get heated between Great Britain and France at Station Road, Swinton

similar heights in the following weeks against Great Britain and New Zealand.

France were captained in the 1960 World Cup by big second-rower Jean Barthe, a famous rugby union international who was equally successful after changing codes.

Amongst a new breed of player, the French still had one survivor from their famous 1951 touring team - Jackie Merquey, who played stand-off in all three of their 1960 World Cup games.

While Great Britain always seemed to have the measure of the French on home soil - and duly beat them 33-7 before a near 23,000 crowd at Station Road, Swinton - the Australians always found France to be much tougher opponents, and the green and golds were mighty relieved to get that one-point victory over the Tricolours at Wigan.

The Aussies had another close encounter before they managed to beat New Zealand, 21-15, at Headingley, thus setting up their match against Great Britain as the World Cup decider - a World Cup Final in everything but name - and 33,026 paid receipts of £9,113, to see it on a wet and murky afternoon at Bradford's Odsal Stadium.

But if those fans came to see the flowing, exciting football for which Rugby League was famous, they went home disappointed. One newspaper report commented: "Great Britain, with this win against the Aussies, lifted the World Cup, but the real winner in the disappointing forward slog was the mud. It beat all attempts to make this match worthy of the meeting of the two best teams in the world.

"It reduced movement to a slow tempo - fitfully the football came to the surface with three excellent tries - two for the British and one for the Aussies. But most times tempers were fretfully near the boil; almost every tackle for 20 minutes in the second-half had a neat slug packed into it.

"Three times the game boiled over into a brawling, milling mass of men. These Aussies do not stand on ceremony and are not the men for half measures, but I thought they would have had enough common sense to know that the British would not duck a battle. Certainly not with such men as Jack Wilkinson, Vincent Karalius and Derek Turner in the pack. These are men of raw courage and rare stamina. In the second-half when the Aussies looked like they would get on top, it was this trio that kept the forward battle going Britain's way."

Skipper Eric Ashton had won the toss for Great Britain, and he knew it was a good toss to win, because he was able to make the Australians play the first half with driving rain and a stiff wind blowing into their faces.

As well as bringing Billy Boston in on the right wing, Great Britain also had Saints' Austin Rhodes replacing Eric Fraser at full-back. And as a measure of Britain's first-half territorial superiority, with the wind and rain at their backs, Rhodes had no less than seven shots at goal, of which he successfully landed two.

The fireworks started after Australia's young star centre, Reg Gasnier, just managed to duck and avoid a viscious stiff-arm attempt. Soon after, British winger Mick Sullivan was flattened on the touchline and several forwards had a flare-up.

But Great Britain could still play some football, and Boston proved that the risk in playing him would pay dividends as he pushed off Brian Carlson and used every ounce of his strength to score in the corner. Austin Rhodes kicked a gem of a conversion from the touchline.

Soon after, Mick Sullivan came back to the fray to finish off a break by Karalius and Murphy.

With a 10-nil interval, and the mud beginning to take its toll, Great Britain looked in control, as the second half deteriorated in the Odsal gloom. Tempers did not improve as flare-ups continued, with referee Martung having a hard job to keep control.

Ten minutes from the end, Australia scored a consolation try by winger Carlson after a long run by Tony Brown.

Eddie Waring commented: "The mud was the winner in a match where the best players, like Gasnier for instance, were never seen."

Another famous British journalist of the time, Phil King of 'The People', was more stinging in his criticism. He reported: "The World Cup came deservedly back to Great Britain. But if Rugby League folk think the televising of the fantastic second-half niggle was a good advert for the game, they must surely be the most optimistic salesmen in the world."

Meanwhile, on the same afternoon as Odsal's war of attrition, over at Central Park, New Zealand and France fought out their own battle to avoid the wooden spoon. The Kiwis won, 9-nil, in front of only 2,876 spectators, who paid £661 in receipts.

Everyone else was at home watching Eric Ashton and his men lift the World Cup.

1968

The fourth Rugby League World Cup in 1968 brought several significant changes from the previous three tournaments.

For the first time, a World Cup Final was scheduled, to be contested by the top two teams in the league table after all countries had played each other.

And, just as it had done in the first World Cup in 1954 when an unscheduled play-off had to be hastily arranged, the large crowd at the Final ensured a financial profit was made.

Also for the first time, 1968 saw the tournament divided between two countries rather than hosted totally by one.

As France, Australia and England had hosted the first three World Cups, it was really New Zealand's turn to stage the fourth tournament, but it was felt that New Zealand alone could not generate crowds big enough to meet the costs of staging a World Cup, so the tournament was largely Australian based, with just two matches played in Auckland.

And, something else of great significance, the 1968 World Cup was the first to be played under limited tackle rules - in this case, it was the old four-tackle rule. Many Australian critics blamed the four-tackle rule for what they perceived to be sub-standard football compared to what they had seen in years gone by in matches between the Aussies and Great Britain and France.

There had been a gap of eight years since the previous World Cup in 1960, and this fourth tournament had originally been scheduled to be played in 1965. But that was called off by the Australians, who claimed it would be a flop because the French were not up to standard, their opinion having been formed after France had lost all three Tests against the Aussies on their disappointing 1964 tour and thus, for the first time, had been beaten in a Test series in Australia.

After France had beaten the 1967 Kangaroos, the Aussies deemed them to be back up to international standard, and so the World Cup went ahead in ' 68.

Great Britain were defending the trophy won on home soil in 1960, but they had just lost the Ashes again for the third consecutive series after the 1967 Kangaroos went home successful.

So the British had plenty to prove, and they brought in many new players for the 1968 World Cup team, which would be captained by Leeds full-back Bev Risman after Neil Fox had withdrawn through injury.

The selectors left out several experienced Test men who had done duty in the 1967 Ashes series. With hindsight, that was a selection policy Great Britain may have regretted, particularly the non-selection of their Ashes captain, Hull KR's Bill Holliday, whom the Aussies rated the best forward they had encountered on their tour.

Instead, the British World Cup team introduced several new forwards like John Warlow, Mick Clark, Ray French and Charlie Renilson.

Great Britain's campaign got off to a bad start when their high hopes nose-dived in the opening game against Australia.

This was the game everybody wanted to see, and the game everybody predicted would ultimately be the World Cup Final. 62,256 people packed the Sydney Cricket Ground full of anticipation.

But, instead of the rugged battle they had been used to between the two old enemies throughout the history of Test football, they got an uninspiring spectacle ruined by the haphazard panic football created by the four-tackle rule, and a referee who insisted on doing everything by the book, rather than letting the game flow as had been the custom in Anglo-Australian Tests.

New Zealand referee John Percival's strict application of the laws was certainly not appreciated by the British, as Australia's Aboriginal full-back Eric Simms a South Sydney legend kicked five penalties.

One Australian writer commented: "No team in a World Championship should be able to gather 10 points without doing more than merely kicking the ball over the cross-bar from relatively easy positions." (Note this man had obviously never seen a rugby union match!)

"I wouldn't criticise Percival in the sense that I felt he was leaning a little one way far from it but he was dogmatic to the 'nth' degree, and much of Britain's characteristic play soon faded from the scene."

Great Britain lost 25-10, despite Australia only scoring three tries to two.

And whilst the British pack had looked very disappointing compared to the Lions packs the Aussie crowds were used to, everybody anticipated Great Britain would have the chance to improve and take their revenge in the World Cup Final.

But they bargained without a huge quagmire of Carlaw Park mud in Auckland, and a French side displaying the most dogged defence ever seen from a team wearing the famous 'Tricolour' jerseys.

France, having suffered the indignity of being told they weren't up to standard for a World Cup in 1965, were determined to show the passion for Rugby League that still burned in their country.

They had beaten New Zealand in Auckland more convincingly than the 15-10 scoreline suggested only five penalties by big winger Ernie Wiggs keeping the Kiwis in the game but few people expected them to repeat that against a Great Britain team smarting from the defeat against Australia, and knowing they must beat the French to qualify for the Final.

In terrible conditions, the British looked the better team on attack, and tried manfully to handle the greasy ball adventurously, but they came up against a remarkably consistent French defence. France won 7-2, and were in the Final. As the

Aussies had comfortably beaten New Zealand in Brisbane, that left the third of the round-robin games as merely academic exercises.

Australia and France just went through the motions at Lang Park, knowing they would meet just two days later in the one that really counted, the Final, in Sydney.

Meanwhile, Great Britain and New Zealand were playing for the pride of avoiding the wooden spoon.

As it was, Great Britain played some sparkling football to wallop the Kiwis 38-14, with winger Clive Sullivan scoring a hat-trick of tries.

And so, the first 'official' World Cup Final was between Australia and France.

In a tough and dour struggle, the Aussies won 20-2, without ever seriously being tested.

The French defended with great determination but, unlike previous 'Tricolour' touring teams, had little to offer in attack, using the kicking skills of stand-off Jean Capdouze to generate most of their points. Aussie critics were of the opinion they had never seen a French side that lacked penetration as much as this one. Not that it bothered the Australian team; they bathed in the glory of carrying the huge World Cup trophy around the Sydney Cricket Ground.

Their captain, Johnny Raper, had been an inspiration. He controlled the Aussie game from dummy-half in the Final, and was ably assisted by another great back-rower Ron Coote, who achieved the remarkable feat for a forward of scoring a try in all four of Australia's games in the 1968 World Cup.

The Aussies were coached by Harry Bath, and had played flashes of brilliant attacking football, both in the lead-up games and in the Final.

The tournament saw the continued emergence of Arthur Beetson, destined to become a legend of Australian Rugby League. Arthur had made his Test debut in the last match of the 1966 series against Great Britain, and was a massive figure in the 1968 World Cup.

A teenager called Bob Fulton made his debut for Australia in the third game of the '68 World Cup, and retained his place for the Final.

Meanwhile, another young Australian called Johnny Rhodes was voted the star of the tournament, but it proved to be his only moments in the green and gold in

THE 1968 WORLD CUP FINAL

AUSTRALIA beat FRANCE 20-2.
Monday 10 June, 1968
at Sydney Cricket Ground

AUSTRALIA: Simms, Williamson, Langlands, Greaves, Rhodes, Fulton, Smith, Wittenberg, Jones, Beetson, Thornett, Raper (C), Coote. *Sub used:* Rasmussen
Tries: Williamson (2), Greaves, Coote.
Goals: Simms 4

FRANCE: Cros, Pelerin, J Gruppi, Lecompte, Ledru, Capdouze, Garrigues, Sabatie, Begou, Ailleres (C), De Nadai, Marracq, Clar
Goal: Capdouze

Referee: John Percival (New Zealand)
Attendance: 54,290

1968 WORLD CUP RESULTS

AUSTRALIA beat GREAT BRITAIN 25-10
At Sydney. Crowd: 62,256

FRANCE beat NEW ZEALAND 15-10
At Auckland. Crowd: 18,000

AUSTRALIA beat NEW ZEALAND 31-12
At Brisbane. Crowd: 23,608

FRANCE beat GREAT BRITAIN 7-2
At Auckland. Crowd: 15,760

AUSTRALIA beat FRANCE 37-4
At Brisbane. Crowd: 32,662

GREAT BRITAIN beat NEW ZEALAND 38-14
At Sydney. Crowd: 14,105

FINAL TABLE

	P	W	D	L	F	A	Pts
Australia	3	3	0	0	93	26	6
France	3	2	0	1	26	49	4
Great Britain	3	1	0	2	50	46	2
New Zealand	3	0	0	0	36	84	0

international football.

There was some controversy after the World Cup Final when the French team walked off and ignored the presentation ceremony. It was claimed the French were very angry at refereeing decisions in the Final, also controlled by Kiwi John Percival, but, no doubt, communication and language problems also contributed to the mix-up, as they invariably do.

For Great Britain, the bitterness of having lost their title without having played in the Final was not easily accepted by a very disappointed team.

In a nutshell, the 1968 World Cup tournament was summed up for them by well known Rugby League writer 'D'Artagnan', who said: "They failed, among other things, to adapt to the referee's disciplinary requirements in the first game against Australia, and they adopted the wrong tactics under the wet conditions against France. Thereafter, they settled down to play some attractive football in their remaining World Cup game against New Zealand, and the tour fixtures in Queensland. If only the settling down process had come earlier!"

Britain's outstanding players in the 1968 World Cup were rated to be half-backs Roger Millward and Tommy Bishop.

Australia was getting its first look at the teenaged Millward, who was destined to come back and beat them, and Bishop was named as one of the very best players in the tournament.

Despite the fact that the hoped for Great Britain v Australia Final failed to materialise, and the unfortunate state of affairs that saw Australia play France just two days before the same teams met in the Final, the 1968 World Cup made a substantial profit for all the competing nations.

In true Rugby League decision-making fashion, it was immediately announced by the International Board that the next World Cup would be one year later, in 1969, jointly staged in England and France.

But, as nobody will be surprised to know, it wasn't.

1970

THE fifth Rugby League World Cup tournament, which began with such a sense of optimism for Great Britain, ended in bitter disappointment for them.

It also ended amid unsavoury scenes in a Headingley final which did little to promote the image of the game as a whole.

The Headingley final would be the last time that the great Malcolm Reilly would ever wear a Great Britain shirt. Reilly would soon emigrate to Australia to play with Manly, and was an absentee from future Test series and World Cups played against Australia.

The 1970 competition, coming some 16 years after the first World Cup, saw two very significant innovations for Rugby League.

First was the introduction of a sponsor.

Secondly, and a direct result of the emergence of a sponsor, was the introduction of a new trophy.

The 1970 tournament also gave us the first World Cup games to be played under floodlights, and the first full internationals to be staged on Sundays in England.

The world of sponsorship, which rapidly became such an integral part of all major sports, was only beginning to open up back in 1970, when it was announced that the teams in the World Cup Series would be playing to win the V & G Trophy.

Those initials stood for the Vehicle & General group of insurance companies. Sadly, becoming one of Rugby League's first major sponsors didn't appear to do them too much good because, just a few years later, the company went bust!

And, in a significant pointer of things to come in British Rugby League, respect for tradition was quickly pushed out of the window in the rush to pander to sponsors. The original World Cup trophy, borne with pride by the winning captains in the first four World Cup tournaments, was replaced by a rather puny little cup bearing the sponsor's name.

The new trophy was to be won outright by the winning team, never to be seen again.

In the meantime it took fully 30 years for the magic of the original World Cup to be restored, as it was presented to the winning captain in the 2000 competition for the first time since Australia's Johnny Raper proudly carried it around the Sydney Cricket Ground in 1968.

Mind you, we did have an excuse for not using the original trophy for a large part of those 30 years, because it was stolen from the Aussies' hotel during the

Mick Shoebottom jumps for joy as Syd Hynes crosses to score against Australia

1970 tournament and did not resurface for a quarter of a century, when it was found, by chance, on a rubbish tip in Bradford.

As a precursor to the introduction of a sponsor, television had definitely arrived in Rugby League, and the BBC covered all the Saturday and Sunday games live, plus highlights of the two Wednesday night matches.

It was ten years since the north of England had previously staged the World Cup, and Great Britain were very confident they could repeat the feat of the victorious 1960 team.

Although the Australians were the Cup holders, having won it on home soil in 1968, just three months before the 1970 World Cup the British had won the Ashes back from the Aussies on the last great Lions tour.

Great Britain's superiority in the two deciding Tests in Sydney suggested Australia had little hope of turning the tables in the World Cup. But the one enforced change to Britain's first choice team proved to be highly significant.

Roger Millward, so important in the Ashes win, was injured. His place at stand-off was taken by Mick Shoebottom, moving up from full-back, where the goal-kicking Ray Dutton came in.

How Great Britain were to miss Millward's attacking flair as they struggled unsuccessfully to break the Australian defence in the 1970 World Cup Final.

Quite the most remarkable thing about the 1970 competition was that Australia went home crowned as World Champions, having won only one of their three qualifying games. The Aussies finished level on points with both France and New Zealand, who also won one match apiece, whilst Great Britain stood unbeaten at the top of the table. Only a better points scoring difference, achieved by virtue of their big win over the Kiwis at Wigan in the opening game, gave the Australians a place in the Final.

How Great Britain must have wished the old World Cup format of first past the post and no Final, which was used in the first three tournaments, had been in operation in 1970.

The key match, inevitably, was seen as the Great Britain versus Australia encounter.

This was Britain's opening game in the competition, whilst the Aussies were backing up three days after beating New Zealand.

In a tight and intense game, Great Britain won 11-4 at Headingley, with just one try, from Britain's centre Syd Hynes, breaking the defensive deadlock.

That win boosted everybody's confidence that Great Britain, again captained by Frank Myler, would carry on from where they left off on the Lions tour and add the World Cup to their achievements.

And the British duly completed a 100 per cent record by beating France, in a very tight encounter under floodlights in the rain at Castleford, the first full international to be played at Wheldon Road, and New Zealand, more easily, in a much more open and entertaining match at Swinton.

It was the French, more than anybody, who had cause to count themselves unfortunate not to reach the World Cup Final in 1970. Only by incurring the wrath

THE GOD SQUAD

THE AUSTRALIAN squad for the 1970 World Cup featured the only clergyman to have played international Rugby League for any country.

Father John Cootes was a Roman Catholic priest from Newcastle who was one of a select few of his profession who had been ordained by the Pope at the Vatican. Indeed, he had played Rugby Union in Rome while studying for the priesthood.

The World Cup was the highlight of a brief stay in the international limelight. Father Cootes had made his Test debut on the 1969 tour of New Zealand and retained his international jersey when the British Lions visited Australia the following year before he was named in Australia's 19-man squad for the Cup.

He was the focus of British media attention, especially when starting each day by saying mass at St Mary's Parish Church in Bradford.

"I'm a priest, that's what I do," he explained to an interviewer from the BBC. Father Cootes even rated a full-page story in the Daily Sketch newspaper.

He was no slouch on the field, topping the World Cup tryscoring lists with five touchdowns - two each against New Zealand and France and another in Australia's 12-7 victory over Great Britain in the brutal final at Headingley. And he scored Australia's only try when the tourists beat France 7-2 in an international at Perpignan on the way home.

This was his international farewell.

He later quit the priesthood and worked for a time as a television sports reporter before setting up a furniture business which he still runs today.

of English referees Billy Thompson and Fred Lindop, who were the only two officials involved in the tournament, did France manage to lose by conceding penalty goals against both New Zealand and Great Britain.

Against the Kiwis at Hull, France had only themselves to blame, as they missed numerous chances, as well as seeing New Zealand full-back Don Ladner kick five goals, before going down by one point, 16-15. This was the game in which the little French winger Serge Marsolan thrilled the Boulevard crowd by scoring a 100-yard try that started behind his own goal-line.

And the French showed that their reaching the 1968 World Cup Final was no fluke when they pushed Great Britain - featuring almost the same team that had just won the Ashes - all the way at Castleford. In a try-less game, it took three penalties from full-back Ray Dutton to give Britain their 6-nil win.

Four days later, France shocked Australia, and most other observers, when the beat the Aussies 17-15 at Odsal Stadium, with the brilliant Marsolan registering another two tries and Capdouze in fine form with the boot.

The Australians had plenty of humble-pie to eat after that defeat, and there were some embarrassed faces around as it was learned that, because of a better points difference, the green and golds would still get a place in the World Cup Final, and not France. How the French must have been kicking themselves for that one point loss against New Zealand.

It meant that, after all, we got the World Cup Final everyone expected, with Great Britain lining up against Australia at Headingley on November 7, 1970.

All form suggested it would be Britain's Cup, but instead it turned out to be one of Australia's finest hours.

The game turned into a cross between chess and trench-warfare, as Great Britain's pack of hard men, including Tony Fisher, Cliff Watson and Malcolm Reilly, put too much emphasis on the tough stuff instead of playing the football they had shown in previous games.

Great Britain dominated the play, but the try that would have turned the game for them in the second-half continued to elude them.

"Our form was a great disappointment," said British coach Johnny Whiteley.

THE 1970 WORLD CUP FINAL

AUSTRALIA beat GREAT BRITAIN 12-7.
Saturday November 7, 1970
at Headingley, Leeds

AUSTRALIA: Eric Simms, Lionel Williamson, John Cootes, Paul Sait, Mark Harris, Bob Fulton, Billy Smith, John O'Neill, Ron Turner, Bob O'Reilly, Bob McCarthy, Ron Costello, Ron Coote. Subs: Ray Branighan, Elwyn Walters.
Tries: Williamson, Cootes.
Goals: Simms 3

GREAT BRITAIN: Ray Dutton, Alan Smith, Syd Hynes, Frank Myler, John Atkinson, Mick Shoebottom, Keith Hepworth, Dennis Hartley, Tony Fisher, Cliff Watson, Jimmy Thompson, Doug Laughton, Malcolm Reilly. *Subs:* Chris Hesketh, Bob Haigh.
Try: Atkinson
Goals: Dutton, Hynes

Referee: Fred Lindop (England)
Attendance: 18,776

1970 WORLD CUP RESULTS

AUSTRALIA beat NEW ZEALAND 47-11
At Wigan. Crowd: 9,586

GREAT BRITAIN beat AUSTRALIA 11-4
At Headingley, Leeds. Crowd: 15,084

NEW ZEALAND beat FRANCE 16-15
At the Boulevard, Hull. Crowd: 3,824

GREAT BRITAIN beat FRANCE 6-0
At Castleford. Crowd: 8,958

GREAT BRITAIN beat NEW ZEALAND 27-17
At Swinton. Crowd: 5,609

FRANCE beat AUSTRALIA 17-15
At Bradford. Crowd: 6,215

FINAL TABLE

	P	W	D	L	F	A	Pts
Great Britain	3	3	0	0	44	21	6
Australia	3	1	0	2	66	39	2
France	3	1	0	0	32	37	2
New Zealand	3	1	0	0	44	89	2

Malcolm Reilly and Mick Shoebottom put a stop to this Australian attack during the 1970 World Cup Final

"We had our best chance just after the interval, but we let Australia off the hook three times. We lost all our composure. We even started niggling and that's something we have never gone in for."

Reilly was a magnificent hard working loose forward, But it was a rare error by him that gave Australia the initiative just before half-time. In possession, Reilly had the ball snatched from his grasp in a tackle by his opposite number, Aussie skipper Ron Coote, who swooped rapidly to put centre John Cootes (no relation) over for a try.

Father John Cootes was actually a Catholic priest, a rarity which provoked plenty of media interest from people who were amazed than a man of the cloth could be involved at such a high level in such a tough, physical contact sport. The amazement grew several notches as the second-half of the 1970 World Cup Final erupted into a niggling, spiteful clash, with plenty of fists and boots flying.

Australia, with Bobby Fulton in

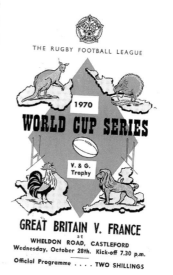

THE RUGBY FOOTBALL LEAGUE

1970

WORLD CUP SERIES

V. & G. Trophy

GREAT BRITAIN V. FRANCE
at
WHELDON ROAD, CASTLEFORD
Wednesday, October 28th. Kick-off 7.30 p.m.

Official Programme . . . . TWO SHILLINGS

commanding form, and a pack of forwards who wrote their names into the folklore of Aussie Rugby League that day - among them Ron Coote, John 'Lurch' O'Neill, Bob 'Bear' O'Reilly and Bobby McCarthy - held on to win 12-7.

As Britain's frustration grew, the niggle increased, erupting into fisticuffs several times. Eventually, referee Lindop decided enough was enough, and centre Syd Hynes and Aussie scrum-half Billy Smith were sent-off. They walked off arm in arm, moments after being caught slugging punches at each other. Such was the nature of Anglo-Aussie Rugby League in those days.

Not so amusing, however, were the incidents which came at the end of the game, which were sparked when Australian full-back Eric Simms, elated at the victory, went to shake hands with Great Britain winger John Atkinson - nowadays a member of the RFL Disciplinary Committee - and was greeted with a punch.

The brawling scenes shown on television brought a torrent of bad publicity for Rugby League, the most vitriolic being the 'Daily Mail', which howled that the innocent youth of our country should be protected from seeing such loutish behaviour, and provided a banner headline saying 'Get these thugs off our TV screens.'

It seemed at the time a grossly over-the-top reaction if one was to look closely at some of things happening elsewhere in the world of sport. But, as ever, Rugby League was an easy target, and a dog every chinless-wonder liked to kick.

A couple of months earlier, when the Great Britain team had produced such wonderful skills and sporting drama as they won back the Ashes, the same media had been blissfully ignoring Rugby League completely.

Billy Smith of Australia and Great Britain's Syd Hynes leave the field after being sent off for fighting during the 1970 World Cup Final

1972

Great Britain's Clive Sullivan receives the 1972 World Cup

It was 1954 all over again as Great Britain scored a memorable triumph to win the sixth World Cup tournament in 1972.

And, fittingly, the inspirational captain of the first British World Cup winners in France 18 years before, Dave Valentine, was present among the small band of Great Britain supporters to see them do it in an epic final at Lyon.

The similarities between 1954 and 1972 were uncanny, not just the fact that the tournament was again staged in France and played at many of the same stadiums - stadiums which also went on to host numerous games in the 1998 soccer world cup - but also because Great Britain once again crossed the channel with the "no hoper" tag around their necks.

Australia were defending the world crown they had won two years earlier in that infamous battle of Headingley, whilst Great Britain - just as in 1954 - had a new crop of players eager to rebuild an international reputation which had taken a battering soon after the memorable Ashes triumph by the 1970 Lions.

The omens had not looked good for Britain as the famous 1970 team broke up after its disappointment in the World Cup final of that year.

Twelve months later, against New Zealand, a new look British team flopped embarrassingly, enabling the Kiwis to win a Test series on British soil for the first time since Baskerville's original pioneers, the "All Golds," way back in 1908.

It was going to require a remarkable up-turn in the level of performance by the Great Britain team for them to win the 1972 World Cup, and there's little doubt the Australians - who had little knowledge of the quality of the new breed of players in the British team - went into the tournament over-confident and believing they couldn't lose.

But Britain got the up-turn they needed, thanks to the introduction of virtually a whole new team of players who rapidly established their reputations as internationals of the highest quality.

So much so that the Aussies, who'd never heard of them before, were falling over themselves to sign the British stars to follow in the footsteps of Malcolm Reilly, who had already departed for Manly. Among the men the Australian clubs were to get were Phil Lowe, Mick Stephenson and Brian Lockwood.

The victorious team of 1972 retained only one player from the 1970 World Cup Final, Leeds winger John Atkinson.

Roger Millward, who would have been a first choice, was again absent through injury, leaving Dennis O'Neill and David Topliss seemingly to battle for the number six jersey - although, as things turned out, it was the 18 year old John Holmes who emerged at stand-off to become one of Great Britain's 1972 World Cup heroes.

BIG LITTLE MEN

TWO of the lightest players ever to pull on the green and gold for Australia have featured in World Cup finals.

Scrum-half Dennis Ward was 8st 10lb (55.2kg) when he was called into Canterbury-Bankstown's lower-grade ranks in 1962. By the time he reached first-grade he weighed 9st 10lb (61.6kg) and when he played for Australia in the 1972 World Cup in France he was still only 10st 4lb (65.2kg).

Only fractionally heavier was John Kolc, the Parramatta half-back who played in the 1977 World Championship final. Kolc was only 5ft 3ins (1.6m) tall and weighed 10st 8lb (67kg).

But there was no doubting the size of their hearts.

The British clinched the World Cup after a tension-packed Final against Australia at the Stade de Gerland in Lyon.

It was the very same stadium in which Valentine's men had shocked the Aussies in their opening game of the first World Cup in 1954.

Skipper Clive Sullivan lifted the cup for Great Britain after a 10-all draw, after extra-time, saw the British declared winners on a countback because they had most league points from the qualifying matches.

Great Britain's George Nicholls on the attack against Australia

Effectively, the 1972 World Cup was won by Britain at Perpignan in their opening match against the Aussies.

It was widely quoted how the British boys had arrived in the Catalan city to see the super-fit, super-confident Aussies strolling around, looking awesomely invincible.

But reputations counted for nothing as a Great Britain pack, anchored by the veteran Terry Clawson - who also proved to be a valuable goal-kicker throughout the tournament - marshalled by clever hooker Stephenson from Dewsbury, and featuring a mighty back-three of Lowe, Lockwood and George Nicholls, outsmarted Arthur Beetson and his men.

107

The British won a superb nine-try thriller at the Stade Gilbert Brutus, 27-21, much to the joy of the Catalan crowd who got behind the underdogs as they knocked the confident Aussies out of their stride.

The World Cup tournament had kicked off the night before Britain's crucial triumph over Australia, as the hosts, France, emerged 20-9 winners over New Zealand in the famous Velodrome Stadium in Marseille. Both teams scored three tries, but the French got home on goal kicks leaving the Kiwis feeling badly done to and most observers fairly confident that neither of these two would be contesting the Final a couple of weeks later.

From Perpignan, Great Britain's road to the final took them first to Grenoble, in the shadow of the Alps, where they comfortably beat France 13-4.

Second-rower Lowe was the star, but it was a performance that largely left coach Jim Challinor unimpressed, and he was anxious to see his team smarten up for their third game, against New Zealand.

The British travelled back to the southwest, to the picturesque town of Pau, for the game with the Kiwis. And, boy did coach Challinor get his wish. Great Britain played sensational attacking rugby, breaking all kinds of records, as they swept New Zealand aside 53-19. It had a local crowd of over 7,000 in raptures - Pau was not an established Rugby League town, in fact now there is no League played in the area.

Widnes stand-off O'Neill had played in the opening two wins over Australia and France, but coach Challinor decided to give the Leeds teenager Holmes a run against the Kiwis. And with big prop Clawson also rested, Holmes was handed the goal-kicking role to go with the number six jersey.

The result was a piece of history, as Holmes scored two tries and ten goals to set a then international world record of 26 points. It also meant that he could not be left out of the team for the World Cup Final.

The Australians, meanwhile, had been locked in a tense battle with New Zealand, before edging home 9-5.

This match was played under lights in Paris, at the newly renovated Parc des Princes (venue of the first World Cup Final in 1954) and a crowd reported at 8,000 turned out in the French capital. That left the Aussies having to beat France to qualify for the Final, which they did easily, running up a 31-9 win over the hosts in Toulouse.

That set up the Great Britain versus Australia Final that was to etch its way in Rugby League folklore.

Sadly, in a poor piece of planning, the Final was played in the city of Lyon, a long way from the rugby heartlands of the south of France. And, with the French not involved, public interest was minimal with the result that one of the most epic games in international Rugby League history was played out in front of a vast almost empty stadium, containing little more than 4,000 spectators.

Any lack of atmosphere in the stands did not dampen the electricity on the pitch as both teams ripped into each other.

Powerful Aussie backs like Bob Fulton and big Mark Harris were met head-on by Britain's centre pairing of Chris Hesketh and John Walsh, and in the forwards

Aussie giants like Beetson, O'Neill and O'Reilly found Clawson, Nicholls and company standing firm like granite. Behind them was the brilliant little halfback Steve Nash, controlling the rucks and tackling everything that moved.

Prop "Lurch" O'Neill galloped 30 yards to score at the corner and Australia looked in control as half-time approached. Then came one of the most famous incidents in Rugby League folklore, as loose forward Nicholls hit the huge centre Harris with a massive tackle as he headed for the line. The ball jolted loose, and British skipper Clive Sullivan swooped to pick it up and sprint 80 yards down the touchline to score and put his team level. It was a wonderful moment.

And, in the second-half, Britain came back again after the Aussies had gone ahead 10-5.

Just seven minutes from full-time, Sullivan found a gap, passed to Lockwood who wrong-footed the defence to send hooker Stephenson over. Finger-nails were being bitten, but Clawson showed nerves of steel to slot over the equalising conversion.

The game was not without controversy, and the Aussies still swear to this day they had a perfectly good try disallowed by the French referee Georges Jameau, after Dennis Ward had put a kick up for captain-coach Langlands to run on to. Langlands dived, caught the ball on the full with spectacular ability, and touched down - only to be ruled offside by Monsieur Jameau.

With the scores locked at 10-all, 20 minutes of extra-time was played.

In pouring rain, in front of near deserted terraces, the tension was almost unbearable for those in the respective camps. After looking like a fighter on the ropes as the Aussies pounded them earlier in the game, the British boys rose to the challenge and grew stronger and more confident with every minute of the extra-time period.

At the end of it, the scores were still tied-up at 10-10, and that meant the World Cup belonged to Clive Sullivan and his brave British team. Australian coach Harry Bath and his team had no complaints. "We knew the rules," said Bath. "We had our chances but we didn't take them. We lost the series at Perpignan."

It was to be the last time Great Britain would send the Aussies home with their Kangaroo tails well and truly between their legs.

THE 1972 WORLD CUP FINAL

GREAT BRITAIN 10 AUSTRALIA 10
(After extra-time)
Saturday 11 November, 1972 at Lyon

GREAT BRITAIN: Charlton, Sullivan, Hesketh, Walsh, Atkinson, Holmes, Nash, Clawson, Stephenson, Jeanes, Lowe, Lockwood, Nicholls. *Sub who came on:* Irving.
Tries: Sullivan, Stephenson
Goals: Clawson 2

AUSTRALIA: Langlands, Grant, Harris, Starling, Branighan, Fulton, Ward, O'Neill, Walters, O'Reilly, Beetson, Stevens, Sullivan.
Tries: O'Neill, Beetson
Goals: Branighan 2

Referee: G Jameau (France)
Attendance: 4,231

1972 WORLD CUP RESULTS

FRANCE beat NEW ZEALAND 20-9
At Marseille. Crowd: 20,748

GREAT BRITAIN beat AUSTRALIA 27-21
At Perpignan. Crowd: 6,324

AUSTRALIA beat NEW ZEALAND 9-5
At Parc des Princes, Paris. Crowd: 8,000

GREAT BRITAIN beat FRANCE 13-4
At Grenoble. Crowd: 5,321

GREAT BRITAIN beat NEW ZEALAND 53-19
At Pau. Crowd: 7,500

AUSTRALIA beat FRANCE 31-9
At Toulouse. Crowd: 10,332

FINAL TABLE

	P	W	D	L	F	A	Pts
Great Britain	3	3	0	0	93	44	6
Australia	3	2	0	1	61	41	4
France	3	1	0	2	33	53	2
New Zealand	3	0	0	0	33	82	0

1975

In 1975 Rugby League staged its fourth World Cup in seven years.

Not content with having too much of a good thing, the game's authorities also decided to abandon the high-profile, condensed format that had served the World Cup so well since its inception.

Strictly speaking, the 1975 competition was not called the World Cup, instead it was christened the World Championship, and games were spread out over a period that lasted from March to November.

It was the first tournament to be staged in both hemispheres, and it was also the first Rugby League World Cup to involve more than the original four senior international playing nations of Britain, Australia, New Zealand and France. The fifth team was Wales, which meant England competed in its own right, rather than as Great Britain.

The inclusion of the Welsh team came on the back of a resurgence in the number of Welshmen playing Rugby League, and followed an emotional return by Wales earlier in 1975 to play a match on their own soil for the first time in 24 years, when they beat France at Swansea in the European Championship.

Hindsight was to reveal that the Welsh would play a key role in deciding the destiny of the 1975 World Championship.

Remarkably, despite being ongoing for almost nine months, the 1975 competition did not feature a play-off. Instead, Australia were crowned World Champions after finishing top of the table, despite failing to beat England, either home or away.

The English team, coached by Alex Murphy - it was Alex's one stab at coaching the national team as he was never given the Great Britain job - and captained by Roger Millward, had the measure of the Aussies both times they met.

On the first occasion, at the Sydney Cricket Ground, the world's top two teams drew 10-all, in front of the tournament's biggest crowd of 33,858.

The England team was a good one, coming on the back of a relatively successful Lions tour the year before, and with new stars like George Fairbairn, Keith Fielding, Les Dyl and Steve Norton combining with experienced internationals like John Walsh, Steve Nash and George Nicholls (all World Cup winners in 1972) plus, of course, Roger Millward himself.

England were very unlucky to drop a point as the Aussies scored one of their tries by winger Chris Anderson, who coached the Australians in the twelfth World Cup in 2000, from what almost everyone thought had been a forward pass.

Even New Zealand referee John Percival admitted he had been mistaken and had missed the forward pass when he saw the replays on television the next day.

The game featured a remarkable incident in which the giant Australian centre Mark Harris was put out of the game after just twelve minutes, with his nose badly broken in a high tackle by tiny scrum-half Steve Nash. England later lost skipper Millward with an injury. And it was his replacement, Ken Gill, who teamed up with Nash to score a superbly -created equalising try four minutes from the end.

Whilst the Aussies cruised to comfortable victories against the other three nations - Wales, France and New Zealand - England came unstuck twice on the Antipodean section of the tournament. As well as drawing with Australia, England also finished level with New Zealand in Auckland, and it was to prove to be a very valuable point lost.

But even that paled into insignificance compared to England's defeat by Wales at Lang Park, Brisbane. The Welsh scuppered English chances of winning the world title by beating them 12-7 in what was described as a vicious, bad-tempered clash. It seemed like the Welsh had been saving everything for this grudge match against the old enemy, played in pouring rain on foreign soil far away from home, in front of only 6,000 spectators.

Whilst the Welsh team had some skilful backs like David Watkins, Bill Francis and Clive Sullivan, it was their rugged pack, with Jim Mills, Tony Fisher, Bobby Wanbon and John Mantle - fired up by coach Les Pearce - who turned on the rough stuff

DUAL LEADERSHIP

ONLY a select few individuals have captained their country in a World Cup and later returned to the fray as coach.

The legendary French full-back Puig Aubert was skipper of the side that went down to Great Britain in the final of the inaugural tournament in 1954. And he was coach of the French side that played in the 1975 World Championships.

David Watkins was captain of Wales in the 1975 tournament and two years later was back as coach of the Great Britain side led by Roger Millward, who had also captained England in 1975.

That great Australian centre-cum-full-back Graeme Langlands was skipper of his country in the 1972 tournament. He missed what could have been the winning try in the final when French referee George Jameau ruled him offside as he raced through to regather a kick and touch down - although film of the incident seemed to show him behind the kicker.

Langlands started the 1975 World Series as captain-coach of Australia. But after suffering injury, he held the coaching reins from the sideline while Arthur Beetson led the Australians on the field.

and knocked England out of their stride. Ironically, the try that finally cost England the title was scored against them by none other than Clive Sullivan, Great Britain's World Cup hero and captain just three years before.

FRANCE beat WALES 14-7
At Toulouse. Crowd 7,563

ENGLAND beat FRANCE 20-2
At Headingley, Leeds. Crowd 10,842

AUSTRALIA beat NEW ZEALAND 36-8
At Brisbane. Crowd: 10,000

WALES beat ENGLAND 12-7
At Brisbane. Crowd 6,000

AUSTRALIA beat WALES 30-13
At Sydney. Crowd 25,386

NEW ZEALAND beat FRANCE 27-0
At Christchurch. Crowd 2,500

NEW ZEALAND and ENGLAND drew 17-17
At Auckland. Crowd 12,000

AUSTRALIA beat FRANCE 26-6
At Brisbane. Crowd 9,000

AUSTRALIA and ENGLAND drew 10-10
At Sydney. Crowd 33,858

NEW ZEALAND beat WALES 13-8
At Auckland. Crowd 9,368

ENGLAND beat WALES 22-16
At Warrington. Crowd 5,034

AUSTRALIA beat NEW ZEALAND 24-8
At Auckland. Crowd 20,000

ENGLAND beat FRANCE 48-2
At Bordeaux. Crowd 1,581

FRANCE and NEW ZEALAND drew 12-12
At Marseille. Crowd 18,000

AUSTRALIA beat WALES 18-6
At Swansea. Crowd 11,112

ENGLAND beat NEW ZEALAND 27-12
At Bradford. Crowd 5,937

AUSTRALIA beat FRANCE 41-2
At Perpignan. Crowd 10,440

ENGLAND beat AUSTRALIA 16-13
At Wigan. Crowd 9,393

WALES beat NEW ZEALAND 25-24
At Swansea. Crowd 2,645

WALES beat FRANCE 23-2
At Salford. Crowd 2,247

FINAL TABLE

	P	W	D	L	F	A	Pts
Australia	8	6	1	1	198	69	13
England	8	5	2	1	167	84	12
Wales	8	3	0	5	110	130	6
New Zealand	8	2	2	4	121	149	6
France	8	1	1	6	40	204	3

Both New Zealand and France were disappointing in the 1975 competition. The French defended solidly, although their attack looked uninspired in the first half of the tournament.

But when things returned to Europe in the northern hemisphere autumn, the wheels fell off for a French team wracked by internal fallouts and forced to played many young newcomers. France copped two big hidings on home soil against both England and Australia, although they did manage a draw against the Kiwis in a match, as in the 1972 World Cup, played as a curtain-raiser to a soccer match in Marseille.

England's lost points 12,000 miles away against Wales, meant that when the two top nations came face to face in the second half of the tournament, even an English victory over Australia would not be enough to clinch the title.

But that didn't stop the two teams producing by far the best match of the competition, England clinching an epic 16-13 victory at Central Park, Wigan.

The Australian team that came to Europe for the second half of the tournament was quite different to the one that had done duty on home soil, and drawn 10-10 with England in Sydney. Gone were household names like Langlands, Fulton, and Coote, and into their places came a host of Eastern Suburbs players on the back of the Roosters' superb Grand Final victory.

Coached by Jack Gibson and captained by Arthur Beetson, Easts played sparkling football to set the Aussie competition alight, and joining Artie in the Australian team in Europe were fellow Roosters like John Brass, Ian Schubert, John Peard, Johnny Mayes, and a certain John Quayle.

The 19 year old Schubert had enjoyed a meteoric rise to fame, and his flowing blonde locks became a familiar sight as he bounded in for try hat-tricks against both Wales and England.

But even Schubert's super efforts were not enough to deny an England team that rose to the challenge magnificently at Wigan. The win left everybody to ponder on what might have been, had it not been for Wales.

The Welsh themselves were involved in the most controversial match of the tournament, when they took on New Zealand at Swansea the day after England's thrilling win against the Aussies.

Wales beat New Zealand 25-24 in a match that by then meant little to the eventual outcome of the tournament. Unfortunately the game is remembered for one piece of disgraceful violence, when Welsh prop Jim Mills trampled over the face of his opposite number John Greengrass in the last minute of the game.

Mills was banned for life by the New Zealand Rugby League, and had to

A familiar sight in the 1975 World Cup - Ian Schubert touches down for an Australian try

withdraw from the 1977 tournament, to be played in Australia and New Zealand.

Sadly, the new format had been a financial disaster, and RFL Secretary Bill Fallowfield declared that Wales would never again enter a World Cup as a standalone team. In fact it was 1995 before a Welsh team entered the tournament again.

FOOTNOTE: *After England beat Australia at Wigan, and the Aussies received the World Championship trophy without having beaten England, a special challenge match was hastily arranged between the two nations eleven days after England's epic win at Central Park.*

The extra game was billed as a friendly, but everybody knew the Aussies were determined to get square and prove themselves worthy winners of the world title.

In the event, a considerably changed England team were no match for the much more motivated Australians, who won 25-nil at Headingley. A distasteful feature of this match was Aussie scrum-half Tom Raudonikis's brutal treatment of Roger Millward, which eventually erupted into a brawl resulting in both Millward and Raudonikis being sent off by referee Lindop. It was the only time Millward was ever sent off in his long and distinguished career.

1977

It was hard to fathom the logic of Rugby League's leaders as the game embarked on its fifth World Cup tournament in the space of nine years in 1977.

Only two years before, the 1975 World Championship, spread across both hemispheres and nine months, had proved to be a financial and promotional flop. This, at least, ensured the 1977 tournament - the eighth in the game's history - reverted to the original tried and trusted formula of the four established Test playing nations gathering together for a quick-fire competition spread over a few weeks.

It was to be a repeat of the fourth World Cup, played in 1968, in that games were staged in both Australia and New Zealand, with the final scheduled for the Sydney Cricket Ground.

There was, however, to be no repeat of the 1975 competition, in which Wales played such a significantly dramatic, albeit hardly positive, role. The two nations were competing under the Great Britain banner once again yet, ironically, with the Welsh coach David Watkins at the helm.

In the months leading up to the 1977 World Cup, England had finished last in the European Championship, having lost to both Wales and France. The Welsh had ground out a 6-2 result in a poor game at Headingley, only to lose to France in Toulouse. The French then produced a spectacular victory over England at Carcassonne to clinch the title and leave English coach Peter Fox's hopes of leading the British team to the World Cup in tatters. Politics demanded that Fox be left at home and Watkins was appointed.

By his own admission, Watkins was no coach. He was put in charge of the Welsh team merely as a symbolic figurehead, and he made one famous quote about his time with the 1977 Great Britain team when he said: "How can I tell people like Roger Millward how to play the game?"

Millward was the British captain as they flew out to New Zealand with many question marks hanging over their heads. They didn't quite have the 'no hoper' tag endured, and later celebrated, by the victorious World Cup teams of 1954 and 1972. But with plenty of newcomers to international football, nobody was quite sure how this team would cope with the pressure of playing in Australia and New Zealand.

And, significantly, although England had lost to Wales, resulting in Watkins being made Great Britain coach, only one member of the Welsh team was included in the 1977 World Cup squad. That was Wigan's Yorkshire-born and bred Bill Francis.

A trio of established British internationals did return however. George

Nicholls, Jimmy Thompson and Steve Nash were back in the fold, and Peter Fox was quick to point out that these were men he had wanted in his England team earlier in the year, only to be denied by the selectors.

There's no doubt that the presence of Reg Parker as manager proved to be a masterstroke for the 1977 World Cup squad. Reg, a former Barrow player and then a Blackpool Borough director, had been an effective manager of the 1974 Lions tour, so he knew the ropes. He was also able to influence team selection enough to ensure this British team got the right type of eager and ambitious players.

Among these were forwards Len Casey and Peter Smith, both winning their first Great Britain honours. Then there was a trio of men whose selections were directly due to Reg Parker and who proved to be the outstanding figures in the 1977 World Cup team. They were Leeds prop Steve Pitchford, a late call-up after his sensational Lance Todd trophy winning display at Wembley that year, and the Cumbrian back-rowers Eddie Bowman and Phil Hogan.

Only two of Great Britain's pack in 1977 - George Nicholls and Jimmy Thompson - had been capped before the World Cup. And the new boys took the Australians by surprise, stepping into the sizeable shoes of forwards like Phil Lowe, Brian Lockwood, Doug Laughton, Steve Norton, Mal Reilly and company, who were all unavailable.

The 22-year-old Barrow loose forward Hogan produced a man-of-the-match display in his Great Britain debut, as Millward's men mastered both the Carlaw Park mud in Auckland and a French challenge that they knew would be tough.

France had gone to the World Cup on a high, having thrashed England earlier in the year, but with Hogan running magnificently, despite the atrocious conditions, behind a dominant pack, ably orchestrated by experienced halves Millward and Nash, the British won convincingly 23-4. Full-back George Fairbairn had a dream day, kicking seven goals from eight attempts, despite the greasy ball.

Nothing went right for France, and their hopes of repeating their feat in 1968, of beating Great Britain and reaching the World Cup Final, were dashed. They

THE 1977 WORLD CUP FINAL

AUSTRALIA beat GREAT BRITAIN 13-12
Saturday, 25 June at Sydney Cricket Ground

AUSTRALIA: Graham Eadie, Alan McMahon, Mick Cronin, Russell Gartner, Mark Harris, John Peard, John Kolc, Greg Veivers, Nick Geiger, Terry Randall, Arthur Beetson (Capt.), Ray Higgs, Greg Pierce. Sub (used): Dennis Fitzgerald.
Tries: McMahon, Gartner, Kolc.
Goals: Cronin 2

GREAT BRITAIN: George Fairbairn, Stuart Wright, John Holmes, Les Dyl, Bill Francis, Roger Millward (Capt.), Steve Nash, Jimmy Thompson, Keith Elwell, Steve Pitchford, Len Casey, Eddie Bowman, Phil Hogan. Subs: Ken Gill, Peter Smith.
Tries: Pitchford, Gill
Goals: Fairbairn 3

Referee: Billy Thompson (England);
Attendance: 24,457

1977 WORLD CUP RESULTS

AUSTRALIA beat NEW ZEALAND 27-12
At Auckland. Crowd: 18,000

GREAT BRITAIN beat FRANCE 23-4
At Auckland. Crowd: 10,000

AUSTRALIA beat FRANCE 21-9
At Sydney. Crowd: 13,321

GREAT BRITAIN beat NEW ZEALAND 30-12
At Christchurch. Crowd: 9,000

AUSTRALIA beat GREAT BRITAIN 19-5
At Brisbane. Crowd: 27,000

NEW ZEALAND beat FRANCE 28-20
At Auckland. Crowd: 8,000

FINAL TABLE

	P	W	D	L	F	A	Pts
Australia	3	3	0	0	67	26	6
Great Britain	3	2	0	1	58	35	4
New Zealand	3	1	0	2	52	77	2
France	3	0	0	3	33	72	0

started the game without their main attacking weapon, centre Jean-Marc Bourret, and their frustrations were complete when, late in the game, forward Jean-Pierre Sauret crossed the line, only to have his try disallowed by the referee and be asked to play the ball inches short. Then the referee penalised him for playing the ball incorrectly!

With Australia the hottest of favourites to win the title in 1977, the major question centred around whether Great Britain could rise to the challenge of both France and New Zealand, to set up the Final all the Aussies wanted to see. And with France safely negotiated, Millward's men travelled to New Zealand's South Island to play the Kiwis at Christchurch.

It was a vital game, with the winners almost certain to progress to the World Cup Final, and the Kiwis were very confident after putting up a good show, despite losing 27-12, to the Aussies in their opening match.

But New Zealand reckoned without the brilliance of Millward and Nash, and new boy Hogan, who thrived on the platform set by Nicholls, Thompson and Bowman, to streak away to a stunning 30-12 victory.

That meant Great Britain, as they crossed the Tasman to Australia, knew they were already through to the World Cup Final, although they still had to play the Aussies in their third qualifying game.

Australia, meanwhile, had safely negotiated France at the Sydney Cricket Ground in a match refereed by England's Billy Thompson. The French put up a strong effort, despite losing their star Bourret with a recurrence of his leg injury early in the first half.

Australia got home 21-9, with two sparkling tries from full-back Graham Eadie finally dousing the French hopes. France were later to be penalised out of their game against New Zealand in Auckland, scoring four tries apiece, but Chris Jordan kicking eight goals for the Kiwis in a 28-20 scoreline.

Great Britain flew to Brisbane, where they met the Aussies in front of the biggest crowd of the tournament, which exceeded that of the Final a week later. The British went into this game as favourites, following their superb display against New Zealand and Australia's lacklustre show against France. And, true to form, the British were on top throughout the first half, with the barrel-like Pitchford ripping the Aussie defence open time after time. Eddie Bowman had set up a try for Millward six minutes before half-time, Great Britain led and were looking good.

Disaster struck just before the interval, when hooker David Ward was injured. He tried bravely to continue but, eventually, had to leave the field, leaving Great Britain struggling to win any scrum possession in the second half. Eventually the pressure told, with the brilliant Eadie again chiming in with two tries from full-back, as Australia won 19-5. It had been a tough encounter, but few people didn't regard the Aussies as hot favourites for the World Cup as they went into the final in Sydney seven days later.

Such was the Australian public's over-confidence, and the overkill of having five World Cups in just nine years, an attendance of less than 25,000 turned out at the Sydney Cricket Ground. But they saw a thrilling finale to the tournament.

The 1977 World Cup Final will be remembered as one of the great hard-luck stories for Britain. They eventually lost by just one point, in a game made famous for a controversial incident involving referee Billy Thompson, who called back British winger Stuart Wright when he was in the clear and heading for a try under the posts. Instead of playing advantage, the referee had whistled for a penalty to Great Britain, and the chance was gone.

Australia had led 10-7 at half-time, after Great Britain had lost key forward Phil Hogan with injury. The experienced George Nicholls had already pulled out just before the kick-off suffering from a virus, but with debutant hooker Keith Elwell winning the scrums, and the handling skills of Millward, Nash and Bowman causing problems, and the barnstorming Pitchford breaking the Aussie defence, the British did everything but win.

In the dying moments, Fairbairn had a penalty shot to win the game, but his attempt fell short, and with it went Great Britain's World Cup hopes.

Australian captain Arthur Beetson reckoned this torrid affair was 'the toughest game against Britain since the 1970 World Cup Final', and there's no doubt that the British team of 1977 had done their country proud against crippling odds.

"They played like heroes," said manager Reg Parker, whilst coach Watkins claimed a moral victory, saying "both our tries came from our own ball skills; two of Australia's were from our mistakes."

It had, indeed, been a great effort by Roger Millward and his team. Most outstanding of all had been scrum-half Steve Nash. The pocket battleship played in every minute of every single match on the tour, without ever being replaced. Great Britain had played an additional seven tour games in Australia and New Zealand, as well as the four World Cup matches.

And, there was no doubt that Britain's display in the 1977 World Cup brought a new air of confidence to the game. A new era of a return to full international tours was on the horizon, and a new international transfer ban had just been announced. That was bad news for several of the 1977 team, who had plenty of offers from Australian clubs, but the ban meant no longer would Great Britain be deprived of many of their best players, as they had been in the first half of the seventies.

The 1977 Great Britain World Cup coach David Watkins was one man delighted and excited by the prospect of seeing all the best British players turning out for their country again.

"I doubt whether Australia will beat Great Britain for the next six years," said Watkins in 1977.

"They may never beat them again."

How wrong could someone be?

1985-88

AFTER 1977 the Rugby League World Cup went into hibernation, as the game's international administrators returned to staging full Lions, Kangaroos and Kiwi tours.

Rather than do the obvious thing of slotting a high profile World Cup tournament into each four-yearly cycle, after a gap of eight years Rugby League's international brainstrust came up with the novel idea of re-introducing the World Cup, but spreading it over a three year period.

The plan was for each of the now five Test playing nations (by this time Papua New Guinea had been accepted into the fold) to play each other both home and away, with one chosen Test match of an already existing series designated as a World Cup qualifying game.

Points would be awarded for these games, and a league table would be compiled over the three-year period. At that point the top two countries in the league would play off in a World Cup Final.

The logic behind this scheme was to give additional meaning to the final Test of a series, designating it as a World Cup qualifier, and giving additional impetus to what could otherwise be a dead rubber.

The long drawn out tournament had plenty of critics, for obvious reasons. But it still managed to produce some memorable moments, and culminated in a spectacular climax.

Of course, it could just as easily have done that over a period of three weeks, rather than three years, but that's another story.

This ninth World Cup both began and ended in the city of Auckland, providing New Zealand Rugby League with one its most famous, and then its most infamous, occasions.

The Kiwis kicked off the tournament by beating Australia 18-0 at Carlaw Park, in the third Test of their 1985 series.

New Zealand had lost the previous two Tests very narrowly, and controversially, both to last-minute tries by John Ribot.

But when the same two teams lined up three years later in the same city for the final of the same competition, things were very, very different.

The personnel of both Australian and New Zealand teams had changed a lot. Their respective coaches, and even the way the game was played, had moved on considerably too, and the venue was vastly different, as public interest in the League code in New Zealand was building dramatically to the high that would

118

culminate with the birth of the Auckland Warriors.

But an awful lot of football had to be played in various countries before the Kiwis and the Aussies were to emerge at Auckland's Eden Park for the 1988 World Cup Final.

Great Britain got their first taste of the tournament with a hard -fought draw against New Zealand at Elland Road, Leeds in November 1985.

It was an emotional moment, as a late penalty goal by Lee Crooks levelled the scores at six apiece, and enabled Britain to share the series, as well as the World Cup points, with the Kiwis.

Maurice Bamford was Great Britain's coach then, as he steadily rebuilt the prestige of the national team following the disasters of the 1982 Ashes series and 1984 Lions tour.

But the British got a shock when they travelled to Avignon to play France in their first away game in the World Cup.

The Kiwis had won 22-0 in France, and Great Britain expected to triumph just as comfortably, but ended up being grateful to get a point from another draw against a young French side coached by Tas Baitieri.

Emerging youngsters Patrick Entat and Gilles Dumas made their Test debuts in that 10-all draw. Dumas, playing at full-back, scored all his team's points, and if he had kicked a pretty straight-forward penalty shot in the dying minutes France would have been celebrating a victory in the competition they invented.

LONE APPEARANCE IN FINAL

ANDREW Farrar made just one appearance in Australia's colours - in the 1988 World Cup final. The big centre won his spot in the international line-up after a blockbusting display as Canterbury scored a 24-12 win over Balmain in the ARL Premiership grand a fortnight earlier.

Although he played a dominant role in Australia's World Cup success at Auckland's Eden Park, Farrar never played for Australia again. He is remembered by British fans for a season with Wigan in 1992-93.

But that achievement at Avignon in February 1986 was as good as it got for France in this World Cup. Twelve months later their game was thrust into crisis with serious financial problems, and their League's president was thrown out of office.

The financial crisis meant France could not afford to tour down-under, and thus were unable to fulfil their away fixtures in Australia, New Zealand and Papua New Guinea.

Instead, those three nations were all automatically awarded two points in lieu towards the World Cup table. Great Britain had already played and beaten France at Leeds before the French crisis blew up.

Papua New Guinea made its World Cup debut in this 1985-88 tournament and, remarkably, achieved a momentous victory in their opening game against New Zealand. Just 12 months earlier the Kiwis had been on a high, thrashing the Aussies,

Great Britain's Tony Myler (6) congratulates Joe Lydon on a successful conversion against Australia at Wigan in 1986. The celebrations proved to be in vain as the Aussies went on to win 24-15

and the defeat in Port Moresby marked the end of Graham Lowe's reign as New Zealand's coach.

Despite putting up a much improved performance in the third Test of the 1986 Ashes series, Great Britain still lost their home World Cup qualifier with Australia, in an exciting match played at Wigan, which was only decided late in the game, with a controversial obstruction try being awarded to Dale Shearer and a piece of Wally Lewis magic.

That meant Britain's hopes of qualifying for the World Cup Final rested on the results of their southern hemisphere Lions tour of 1988.

Everybody knew that Australia would make the Final, and Great Britain were given the huge incentive of knowing that the Aussies, despite being first past the post, were prepared to give up home advantage to play the Final at Wembley Stadium if Britain qualified to be their opposition.

Papua New Guinea was safely negotiated in Port Moresby, and then Great

Britain gave their World Cup Final hopes a massive, if unexpected, boost by beating Australia 26-12 in the third Test of the 1988 series.

The Ashes had already been lost again in disappointing fashion, but the British boys won a famous victory against the Aussies in that final Test. It was Britain's first Test win over Australia in 10 years, and it just happened to be the World Cup designated match. It was a tremendous result for new Great Britain coach Malcolm Reilly, with two-try hero Henderson Gill being just one player to cement his reputation in front of the sceptical Australians.

And so, despite the drawn out process of a qualifying tournament spread over three years, everything bubbled up into a sudden death, winner takes all, shoot out between New Zealand and Great Britain, just one week after the Lions' famous victory in Sydney.

Conditions in the cold and wet of Christchurch on New Zealand's South Island could hardly have contrasted more with the pleasant Sydney sunshine, as the Lions and Kiwis slugged out a titanic battle in the mud.

In the end, New Zealand won, controversially, by just two points, after two key tries by Gary Freeman, who came off the substitutes' bench to win the game for the Kiwis.

Their 12-10 win left the Great Britain team bitterly disappointed, and the British game as a whole deflated, as they saw what would have been a huge occasion at Wembley slither away in the Christchurch mud.

THE 1988 WORLD CUP FINAL

AUSTRALIA beat NEW ZEALAND 25-12
9 October, 1988 at Eden Park, Auckland

AUSTRALIA: Garry Jack, Dale Shearer, Andrew Farrar, Mark McGaw, Michael O'Connor, Wally Lewis, Allan Langer, Paul Dunn, Benny Elias, Steve Roach, Paul Sironen, Gavin Miller, Wayne Pearce. *Subs:* Terry Lamb, David Gillespie.
Tries: Langer 2, Shearer, Miller.
Goals: O'Connor 4. Field goal: Elias

NEW ZEALAND: Gary Mercer, Tony Iro, Kevin Iro, Dean Bell, Mark Elia, Gary Freeman, Clayton Friend, Peter Brown, Wayne Wallace, Adrian Shelford, Mark Graham, Kurt Sorensen, Mark Horo. *Subs:* Shane Cooper, Sam Stewart.
Tries: T Iro, K Iro
Goals: Brown 2

Referee: Graham Ainui (Papua New Guinea)
Attendance: 47,363

Instead, it was Rugby League in New Zealand that was destined to have its place in the sun as, for the first time, the Kiwis took part in a World Cup Final.

Public interest in the Final, scheduled after the end of the domestic Australian season in early October, was immense in New Zealand.

The country had never been so crazy about Rugby League, and the decision to stage the game at Auckland's Eden Park, the city's traditional rugby union venue, was a measure of League's growing status.

The attendance of 47,363 at Eden Park was the biggest crowd ever to watch a Rugby League match in New Zealand.

And the game made history by having a neutral referee - Graham Ainui - from Papua New Guinea.

Sadly for the home nation, amid all the hype and hysteria, so foreign to the League code in New Zealand, everybody forgot about the football, and the 1988 World Cup Final turned into a huge anti-climax for the Kiwis' new audience.

The New Zealand team was totally overawed by the occasion, too many of them seemed to want to fight rather than play football, and a superb Australian

1985-88 WORLD CUP RESULTS

NEW ZEALAND beat AUSTRALIA 18-0
At Auckland. Crowd: 19,000

GREAT BRITAIN drew with NEW ZEALAND 6-6
At Elland Road, Leeds. Crowd: 22,209

NEW ZEALAND beat FRANCE 22-0
At Perpignan. Crowd: 5,000

FRANCE drew with GREAT BRITAIN 10-10
At Avignon. Crowd: 5,000

AUSTRALIA beat NEW ZEALAND 32-12
At Sydney. Crowd: 22,811

PAPUA NEW GUINEA beat NEW ZEALAND 24-22
At Port Moresby. Crowd: 15,000

AUSTRALIA beat PAPUA NEW GUINEA 62-12
At Port Moresby. Crowd: 17,000

AUSTRALIA beat GREAT BRITAIN 24-15
At Wigan. Crowd: 20,169

AUSTRALIA beat FRANCE 52-0
At Carcassonne. Crowd: 3,000

GREAT BRITAIN beat FRANCE 52-4
At Headingley, Leeds. Crowd: 6,567

GREAT BRITAIN beat PAPUA NEW GUINEA 42-0
At Wigan. Crowd: 9,121

FRANCE beat PAPUA NEW GUINEA 21-4
At Carcassonne. Crowd: 5,000

GREAT BRITAIN beat PAPUA NEW GUINEA 42-22
At Port Moresby. Crowd: 12,077

GREAT BRITAIN beat AUSTRALIA 26-12
At Sydney. Crowd: 15,994

NEW ZEALAND beat PAPUA NEW GUINEA 66-14
At Auckland. Crowd: 8,392

NEW ZEALAND beat GREAT BRITAIN 12-10
At Christchurch. Crowd: 8,525

AUSTRALIA beat PAPUA NEW GUINEA 70-8
At Wagga Wagga. Crowd: 11,685

FINAL TABLE

	P	W	D	L	F	A	Pts
Australia ●	7	5	0	2	252	91	12
New Zealand ●	7	4	1	2	158	86	11
Great Britain	8	4	2	2	203	90	10
PNG ●	7	1	0	6	84	325	4
France	5	1	1	3	35	140	3

● *Awarded two points in lieu of France's non-fulfilment of fixtures in the southern hemisphere.*

team blitzed them with early points.

The Aussies had the game won well before half-time, leaving the huge crowd stunned.

This was a very different Australian team to the one which had lost so embarrassingly (for them) against Great Britain in Sydney a couple of months earlier.

With the Aussies now out of season, gone were the political selections based on State of Origin results, and in their place was an Australian team based very much on the power of the Sydney clubs, in particular the Grand Finalists Canterbury and Balmain.

Apart from skipper Wally Lewis, only two Queenslanders were in the World Cup Final team. New scrum-half Alfie Langer replaced the injured Peter Sterling, and winger Dale Shearer retained his place.

In contrast, the Australian team beaten by Great Britain in July 1988 had contained no less than nine Queenslanders plus Lewis.

Captain Wally had mixed feelings on the 1988 World Cup Final, as he saw his team win an emphatic victory, but in the process he suffered a broken arm.

Lewis sustained the injury midway through the first half, and whilst he continued for a while despite his obvious discomfort, he didn't do an Alan Prescott and stay on the field for the full 80 minutes. He didn't need to.

With Gavin Miller giving a man-of-the-match display, Ben Elias and Wayne Pearce inspirational, and the brilliant Terry Lamb slotting effortlessly into Wally 's stand-off role, Australia cruised home 25-12.

The World Cup was Australia's once again, for the sixth time in nine competitions.

The new format may not have been what Rugby League really needed, but it had eventually provided the game in New Zealand with the biggest day in its history, and the Aussies with one of their most satisfying and deserved victories.

1989-92

THE tenth Rugby League World Cup was, like the previous tournament, spread across three years and both hemispheres.

And, also like its predecessor, it produced a magnificent event as its climax.

When Great Britain and Australia marched out at Wembley for the World Cup Final on October 24, 1992, international Rugby League in this country reached its peak.

Things just couldn't have got any better, as the biggest crowd ever to watch an international match in Britain - 73,631 - packed into the nation's most famous stadium. The Rugby League boys were playing in a World Cup Final in the very same place as Bobby Moore, Geoff Hurst and company had lifted that other World Cup one summer's day in 1966.

The very fact that the game was played at Wembley was the key. Rugby League had finally broken the ice and staged a major international occasion in the national stadium two years earlier, when Great Britain had scored a famous victory over the Australians in the first Test of the 1990 Ashes series.

Contrary to the negative thinking of the doubters, that match had been a huge success at the gate, proving that Rugby League could present itself on a national stage, and no longer had to hide its considerable wares in the north of England.

A World Cup Final was a one-off big event that everybody could relate to, far more than a three-match Ashes series, which was more for the traditionalists, something the instant-fix mentality created by the tabloids couldn't really concentrate on long enough to appreciate.

In addition, of course, another very important factor was the air of expectancy surrounding Great Britain's team. There was very real confidence that Britain were going to beat the Australians this time, and win the World Cup. They'd proved in the recent past that they could beat the Aussies in a one-off match, but couldn't quite sustain it over a three-match series. And the Wembley World Cup Final was to be a one-off.

Great Britain's confidence, and public expectancy, had grown because of the two most recent Ashes series.

The first, played at home in 1990, included that famous win at Wembley, and then the epic Manchester Test in which only Ricky Stuart's injury time break and Mal Meninga's shoulder charge on Carl Gibson saved the Aussies.

Britain's new, very real competitiveness was confirmed two years later on the Lions tour to Australia, in which a tough first Test defeat in Sydney was followed by

Great Britain's David Hulme and referee Greg McCallum stand over a prone Martin Offiah during the Lions' 10-6 victory over the Kiwis at Wigan in 1989

a sensational victory in Melbourne, setting up a decider in Brisbane. A very intense battle was fought out under the Lang Park floodlights, before Mal Meninga's Aussie team emerged victors by just six points, two tries to one.

Not since Chris Hesketh led his 1974 Lions to Australia had Great Britain gone so close to regaining the Ashes as they had in both 1990 and 1992. It was the pinnacle of the rebirth of the British national team, supervised and inspired by coach Malcolm Reilly, and, if Britain couldn't get the Ashes, the World Cup title in 1992 would be a very nice consolation prize.

Thousands of British fans had followed the team in Australia in the summer of 1992, and as autumn came around they couldn't wait to get another crack at the Aussies at Wembley.

The Australians themselves, despite having capacity crowds at all three Ashes Tests in 1992 - the first time since 1974 a series against Great Britain had provoked the same kind of feverish public interest down-under as it always did in the old days - were more than happy to give up the home advantage they could have claimed for the chance to stage the final at Wembley.

Australia's right to home advantage came because they finished top of the league table, following the completion of the three year home-and-away series of World Cup qualifiers.

The Aussies had a 100 per cent record, with eight wins out of eight.

Great Britain finished level on points with New Zealand, and only got into the World Cup Final on a better points for-and-against record. It was tough luck on the Kiwis, but sweet revenge for the British, who had themselves been edged out of the previous World Cup Final in 1988 so narrowly by New Zealand.

As the World Cup qualifying period of 1989-1992 evolved, once again the clashes between Great Britain and New Zealand proved to be crucial. Both were very closely contested by two very evenly matched teams, and both were won narrowly by the respective home teams.

Great Britain beat the Kiwis at Wigan in 1989 by 10 points to six, after an epic battle. The victory brought much joy for Malcolm Reilly's men, not only because two World Cup points had been won, but more so because it clinched their first major series win over either Australia or New Zealand since the 1979 Lions had beaten the Kiwis on their own soil.

Great Britain managed to retain their whip-hand over the Kiwis by winning the 1990 series in New Zealand, a victory against all expectations after so many front-line international players had declined the tour.

Inspired by captain Garry Schofield, the British had wrapped up the series in the first two Tests, before they travelled to the South Island for the third, which was the World Cup qualifier.

New Zealand scraped home to a 21-18 win, thanks largely to six goals by Matthew Ridge and a boob by Martin Offiah, when he dropped the ball over the line in the act of touching down for what would, as things turned out, have been a decisive try. Offiah's mistake did not go down well with coach Reilly, who recognised that it could, in the final wash-up, cost Great Britain a place in the World Cup Final. Thankfully, it didn't.

With Australia reigning supreme in all their games against Great Britain and New Zealand, despite having to negotiate some pretty competitive opposition, there was no doubt that the British and the Kiwis were very much on an

1989-92 WORLD CUP RESULTS

AUSTRALIA beat NEW ZEALAND 22-14
At Auckland. Crowd: 15,000

GREAT BRITAIN beat NEW ZEALAND 10-6
At Wigan. Crowd: 20,346

NEW ZEALAND beat FRANCE 34-0
At Carcassonne. Crowd: 4,208

GREAT BRITAIN beat PAPUA NEW GUINEA 40-8
At Port Moresby. Crowd: 5,969

AUSTRALIA beat FRANCE 34-2
At Parkes, NSW. Crowd: 12,384

NEW ZEALAND beat GREAT BRITAIN 21-18
At Christchurch. Crowd: 3,133

NEW ZEALAND beat PAPUA NEW GUINEA 18-10
At Port Moresby. Crowd: 10,000

AUSTRALIA beat GREAT BRITAIN 14-0
At Elland Road, Leeds. Crowd: 32,500

AUSTRALIA beat FRANCE 34-10
At Perpignan. Crowd: 3,428

GREAT BRITAIN beat FRANCE 45-10
At Perpignan. Crowd: 3,965

NEW ZEALAND beat FRANCE 32-10
At Christchurch. Crowd: 2,000

FRANCE beat PAPUA NEW GUINEA 20-18
At Goroka. Crowd: 11,485

AUSTRALIA beat NEW ZEALAND 40-12
At Brisbane. Crowd: 29,139

AUSTRALIA beat PAPUA NEW GUINEA 40-6
At Port Moresby. Crowd: 14,500

GREAT BRITAIN beat PAPUA NEW GUINEA 56-4
At Wigan. Crowd: 4,193

FRANCE beat PAPUA NEW GUINEA 28-14
At Carcassonne. Crowd: 1,440

GREAT BRITAIN beat FRANCE 36-0
At Hull. Crowd: 5,250

AUSTRALIA beat GREAT BRITAIN 16-10
At Brisbane. Crowd: 32,313

NEW ZEALAND beat PAPUA NEW GUINEA 66-10
At Auckland. Crowd: 3,000

AUSTRALIA beat PAPUA NEW GUINEA 36-14
At Townsville. Crowd: 12,470

FINAL TABLE

	P	W	D	L	F	A	Pts
Australia	8	8	0	0	236	68	16
Great Britain	8	5	0	3	215	79	10
New Zealand	8	5	0	3	203	120	10
France	8	2	0	6	80	247	4
PNG	8	0	0	8	84	304	0

even keel together on the second rung of the world Rugby League ladder.

Further down it lay France and Papua New Guinea.

The French had a much better record in the 1989-1992 World Cup compared to the previous tournament. At least this time they were able to complete all their fixtures in the southern hemisphere, and they performed relatively well against both Australia and New Zealand, avoiding the hammerings most people had predicted.

France's spirited display against the Australians, on a freezing cold night in the New South Wales country town of Parkes, came on the back of their famous victory over Great Britain at Headingley in April 1990.

The French had the consolation of winning their World Cup game in Papua New Guinea a year later, despite their 1991 squad being nowhere near as good as the 1990 team. As both Great Britain and New Zealand knew only too well, it wasn't always easy to win in the heat and humidity of Papua New Guinea.

But despite taking the Frenchmen to the hostile environment of Goroka, the Kumuls could not beat a 'Tricolours' team superbly led by prop Thierry Buttignol and guided by half-backs Patrick Entat and Pascal Fages.

France managed a double over Papua New Guinea, leaving the Kumuls without a single point in the World Cup table. They did, however, enjoy one of their finest moments in international Rugby League by giving Australia a real run for their money in a Test play in North Queensland, at Townsville, in the aftermath of the Lions tour to Australia in 1992.

The Aussies won 36-14, rather than by the predicted massacre, and the game was best remembered for a superb display and solo try by Kumuls scrum-half Aquila Emil. In the Australian team for that Test, and scorer of two tries, was the big winger Graham Mackay, who is currently playing with the Leeds Rhinos.

THE 1992 WORLD CUP FINAL

AUSTRALIA beat GREAT BRITAIN 10-6
24 October, 1992 at Wembley Stadium

AUSTRALIA: Tim Brasher, Willie Carne, Steve Renouf, Mal Meninga, Michael Hancock, Brad Fittler, Allan Langer, Glenn Lazarus, Steve Walters, Mark Sargent, Paul Sironen, Bob Lindner, Brad Clyde. *Subs:* David Gillespie, Kevin Walters, John Cartwright.
Try: Renouf.
Goals: Meninga 3

GREAT BRITAIN: Joe Lydon, Alan Hunte, Gary Connolly, Garry Schofield, Martin Offiah, Shaun Edwards, Deryck Fox, Kevin Ward, Martin Dermott, Andy Platt, Denis Betts, Phil Clarke, Ellery Hanley. Subs: John Devereux, Alan Tait, Kelvin Skerrett, Richie Eyres.
Goals: Fox 3

Referee: Dennis Hale (New Zealand)
Attendance: 73,631

Things were very different for Australia as they stepped into the cauldron of Wembley for the World Cup Final on October 24. The exhibition match attitude, and sunshine and hard ground of Townsville, had been replaced by a dull, damp English autumn day, and a lush turf made slippery by the drizzle. In addition, they faced a Great Britain team pumped up by their own self-belief, and the urgings of the massive 73,000-plus crowd.

For the first time, Wembley was a virtual sell-out for an international Rugby League match, and the atmosphere was much more like the Challenge Cup Final in which the winner was going to take all.

In the event, it all proved to be a disappointment for the British. The letdown was intensified because they went so very close to victory, and were left to rue chances missed and mistakes made.

Australian skipper Mal Meninga celebrates his side's 1992 success

Australia retained the World Cup with a 10-6 win, after a close - many critics described it as dour - encounter of the toughest kind. There was little flowing football, as both teams had their defences planned to perfection. Instead, it became like a game of chess, thought out in an environment of intense physical contact in which only the toughest could survive.

Great Britain's pack was magnificent, superbly prompted by scrum-half Deryck Fox, who also kept his team ahead on the scoreboard with three penalty-goals. But there was little creative attack from the British, and coach Malcolm Reilly later admitted it had been a mistake to play Shaun Edwards at stand-off.

There was a controversial incident early in the game, when hooker Martin Dermott hit Australia's key man, Brad Fittler, with a high shot. It was later discovered that Fittler had sustained a broken jaw in the incident, but he bravely played on. Aussie critics were livid that referee Dennis Hale had allowed Dermott to stay on the field.

The deciding moment of the 1992 World Cup Final came late in the second-half, when a mistake by ex-rugby union man John Devereux, on the field as a substitute, allowed Aussie centre Steve Renouf - playing his first match in the green and gold - to get around him on the outside and score the only try of the game. It was the only time in the match Britain's defence had been found wanting, and that one mistake proved crucial.

That meant it was Mal Meninga who lifted the 1992 World Cup, leaving Great Britain so frustrated that they had gone so, so close to glory.

But it had been a wonderful occasion for Rugby League, at last on show on the biggest stage of all.

Steve Walters evades the challenge of Shaun Edwards

Bob Lindner meets Denis Betts head on (LEFT) and
Allan Langer races away from the chasing Andy Platt (RIGHT)

Gary Connolly and a determined Deryck Fox stop Brad Fittler in his tracks

Glenn Lazarus takes on Kevin Ward, Martin Dermott and Denis Betts

Brad Fittler moves in on the flying Allan Hunte

Phil Clarke swamped by the Australian defence

1995 CENTENARY WORLD CUP

THE 1995 Rugby League World Cup, the eleventh in the eventful history of the competition, was staged in Britain as the focal point of the game's Centenary celebrations.

It was the first World Cup tournament for 18 years in which all the nations would come together in one place at one time for a festival of Rugby League.

And it was the biggest gathering of nations in the game's 100 year history.

For a sport that for so long had seen its World Cup contested by just four established countries, the prospect of ten nations taking part was dreamlike.

Adding icing to the cake for internationalists was a secondary tournament for Emerging Nations, in which a further seven countries took part.

The 1995 World Cup had a major sponsor, the Halifax Building Society, and another new trophy, despite the fact that the original World Cup, which went missing in 1970, had by this time been recovered.

The Halifax Centenary World Cup was a silver trophy manufactured by the famous London jewellers Tiffany's, and was reported to have cost some £10,000.

The tournament, once the players got to work on the field, turned out to be a huge success.

Staged throughout an unusually warm and sunny October, bigger than expected crowds flocked to see the variety of nations in action, creating a wonderfully uplifting atmosphere of celebration.

Sadly, that was more than the Rugby League's own Centenary efforts had managed to achieve, resulting in the build-up to the 1995 World Cup being plagued by controversies and months of public pessimism.

It seemed that Rugby League fans, so used to seeing their game kicked around and mismanaged, had developed their own self-doubts about the game's ability to attract public interest in such an ambitious international event.

**England winger Jason Robinson crashes past the challenge of
Australian fullback Tim Brasher and the corner flag to score in the
1995 opening game at Wembley, and ABOVE: shows his delight**

Fiji's Joe Dakuitoga on the burst against South Africa at Keighley
BELOW: The Fijian squad perfom their version of the Haka

Most of the public criticism was aimed at the RFL's chief executive Maurice Lindsay, who had also taken on the role as World Cup tournament director at a time when he had quite enough on his plate in the aftermath of the announcement of Rupert Murdoch's attempted take-over of the game, causing the Super League war to rage in Australia.

Lindsay managed to fend off the criticisms by insisting that the players would make the World Cup a success by their performances on the field. And, as ever, the players didn't let anybody down.

The tournament was played out against the background of the game's civil war in Australia, and effectively was the last throw of the dice for the old Australian Rugby League as they saw the rest of the world submerged by Super League.

It was a cruel irony that, as all the other nations deserted the ARL and opted to take the money from Murdoch instead, it was almost exclusively thanks to the efforts of the ARL (notably their creation of the World Sevens and their work in the South Pacific islands) that the 1995 World Cup was able to include, for the first time, fully fledged teams from Tonga, Fiji, Western Samoa and South Africa.

The biggest casualty of the 'war' was the Australian team itself.

The ARL stuck rigidly to a policy of not choosing any players who had aligned themselves with Super League, meaning almost a whole team of the biggest stars in the Australian game were left at home.

The one star who stayed loyal to the ARL, Brad Fittler, captained a team of

> ## RECORD SCORES
>
> *THE 1995 and 2000 World Cups featured a pointscoring frenzy that saw several Australasians earn a place in the record books.*
>
> *When Australia beat South Africa 86-6 at Gateshead in 1995, Newcastle Knights' scrum-half Andrew Johns made an incredible international debut, scoring two tries and booting 11 goals for a personal tally of 30 points.*
>
> *This equalled the world's best in an international clash set by Michael O'Connor who scored four tries and kicked seven goals in Australia's 70-8 Test victory over Papua New Guinea in 1988.*
>
> *Johns' 11 goals equalled the previous world record shared by New Zealand's Des White (in a 1952 Test against Australia) and Kangaroo Rod Wishart (against France in 1994).*
>
> *Australia's 86 points was also a record score for Test or World Cup encounters.*
>
> *Five years later, also at Gateshead, Australia's Mat Rogers topped Johns' pointscoring with 34 (four tries and nine goals) as Fiji went down 66-8.*
>
> *A day later, as New Zealand crushed the Cook Islands 84-10, stand-off Tasesa Lavea booted 12 goals for a new world best. He also scored two tries, but his 32 points couldn't quite match Rogers' record.*
>
> *But both records lasted only a few days. Australia inflicted a world record 110-4 defeat on Russia. And Ryan Girdler scored 46 of the points (three tries and 17 goals).*

1995 WORLD CUP RESULTS

GROUP ONE

ENGLAND beat AUSTRALIA 20-16
At Wembley; Crowd: 41,271

FIJI beat SOUTH AFRICA 52-6
At Keighley; Crowd: 4,845

AUSTRALIA beat SOUTH AFRICA 86-6
At Gateshead; Crowd: 9,191

ENGLAND beat FIJI 46-0
At Wigan; Crowd: 26,263

AUSTRALIA beat FIJI 66-0
At Huddersfield; Crowd: 7,127

ENGLAND beat SOUTH AFRICA 46-0
At Leeds; Crowd: 14,014

GROUP ONE TABLE

	P	W	D	L	F	A	Pts
England	3	3	0	0	112	16	6
Australia	3	2	0	1	168	26	4
Fiji	3	1	0	2	52	118	2
South Africa	3	0	0	0	12	184	0

GROUP TWO

NEW ZEALAND beat TONGA 25-14
At Warrington; Crowd: 8,083

PAPUA NEW GUINEA and TONGA drew 28-28
At Hull; Crowd: 5,121

NEW ZEALAND beat PAPUA NEW GUINEA 22-6
At St Helens; Crowd: 8,679

GROUP TWO TABLE

	P	W	D	L	F	A	Pts
New Zealand	2	2	0	0	47	30	4
Tonga	2	0	1	1	52	53	1
PNG	2	0	1	1	34	50	1

GROUP THREE

WALES beat FRANCE 28-6
At Cardiff; Crowd: 10,250

WESTERN SAMOA beat FRANCE 56-10
At Cardiff; Crowd: 2,173

WALES beat WESTERN SAMOA 22-10
At Swansea; Crowd: 15,385

GROUP THREE TABLE

	P	W	D	L	F	A	Pts
Wales	2	2	0	0	50	16	4
W Samoa	2	1	0	1	66	32	2
France	2	0	0	2	16	84	0

SEMI-FINALS

ENGLAND beat WALES 25-10
At Old Trafford, Manchester. Crowd: 30,042

AUSTRALIA beat NEW ZEALAND 30-20
(After extra-time. 80 mins score: 20-20)
At McAlpine Stadium, Huddersfield.
Crowd: 16,608

players who knew they were perceived as second-stringers.

But, with coach Bob Fulton at the helm, these Aussies developed a real siege mentality that increased as the tournament progressed and the pressure mounted.

Fulton didn't win himself many friends in England, but he could certainly put this Australian team's eventual victory in the 1995 World Cup down as his greatest coaching achievement against all the odds.

England, coached by Phil Larder and with Shaun Edwards as captain (until he was injured), knew they would never get a better chance to beat Australia and win the World Cup.

It didn't matter to the English players or fans that these weren't Australia's first choice men. They were still Aussies, and they were still wearing the famous green and gold uniforms.

And England got off to the flying start they wanted by beating the Aussies in the opening game at Wembley.

Despite all the negative vibes about lack of public interest, slavishly whipped up by rugby union propagandists in the media, a crowd of over 41,000 were at Wembley to see ex-Supreme Diana Ross provide the pre-match entertainment (as she had done at the launch of the soccer World Cup in Chicago the previous year). England's victory in the opener, one of the few games that was televised by the BBC, had a galvanising and positive effect which set up the rest of the World Cup tournament.

Any lingering doubts were joyously swept away the following day by two wonderful exhibitions of Rugby League in matches involving some of the "new" nations.

At a packed Cougar Park in Keighley, the sensational attacking skills of the Fijians had the crowd in raptures as they swept past the South Africans.

And at Warrington, Tonga and New Zealand fought out a match that will live in the memory as one of the best games of Rugby League ever seen.

**Tongan forward Solomon Haumono looks for support during his side's
thrilling 24-25 loss against New Zealand at Wilderspool**

**Kiwi pair Stephen Kearney and Mark Horo congratulate Tonga's
Duane Mann on a fine performance**

**Wales' John Devereux on the charge
against France at Cardiff
INSET: Australia's John Hopoate
takes on South Africa's
Berend Alkema at Gateshead**

Tonga were outstanding in their debut full international, and led New Zealand 24-12 with just ten minutes to go.

It took a last minute equaliser, followed by an injury-time field goal by skipper Matthew Ridge, to save the Kiwis' blushes, as Tonga lost so cruelly, 25-24.

From then on, nobody had any doubts that the 1995 World Cup was going to be a great tournament, as the football flowed and the excitement mounted.

The competition was split into three pools. The one staged in South Wales involving the Welsh, Western Samoa and France, was christened the "group of death," and it did prove to be the toughest of the lot.

The Welsh, skippered by Jonathan Davies, having his last fling in Rugby League, knew they faced an epic against the mighty Samoans, coached by Graham Lowe and another nation making their debut on the big stage in Rugby League.

Wales had to get past France first, and they did so with some difficulty in a tough game in front of over 10,000 at Ninian Park.

The poor French really drew the short straw and, after taking a physical battering from the big Welsh pack, had to back up just three days later against the even more awesome looking Samoans.

France weren't given any chance, and it set up the showdown between Wales and Western Samoa at Swansea.

Papua New Guinea's Adrian Lam evades the challenge of Tonga's George Mann at The Boulevard, Hull

It was one of the regrets of the 1995 World Cup that League fans in the north of England never got the chance to see the Samoans in action, either live or on television.

But over 15,000 Welshmen in the capacity crowd at the Vetch Field did, as one of the fiercest battles in recent times was fought out in an incredible atmosphere.

Wales won 22-10 in one of the most memorable matches in the history of Welsh Rugby League.

That meant Jonathan Davies and his team met England in the first semi-final of the World Cup at Manchester's Old Trafford.

With one side of the stadium closed due to building works, the 30,000 crowd was a capacity figure as, at last, British Rugby League had its own domestic international rivalry presented on the big stage.

England, carefully guided by Bobbie Goulding, who had replaced the injured Edwards, won comfortably enough to progress to the final at Wembley.

This Old Trafford semi-final proved to be Jonathan Davies' last game in Rugby League.

24 hours later, Australia and New Zealand fought out another epic in the second semi at Huddersfield's new McAlpine Stadium.

A remarkable comeback by the Kiwis brought them level at 20-all when, in the last minute, Matthew Ridge's drop-goal attempt shaved the wrong side of the post.

The Aussies emerged 30-20 winners after extra-time, ready to do battle with England at Wembley again.

How English supporters would have cheered had Ridge's goal gone over! But they still travelled to Wembley with plenty of confidence that this battling Aussie team was there for the taking.

Iestyn Harris touches down against Western Samoa at Swansea

**New Zealand's Jason Williams tackled by Papua New Guinea's
Joshua Kouoru at St Helens**

**Western Samoa's Va'aiga Tuigamala held up by French duo
Hadj Boudebza and Patrick Entat (7) at Cardiff**

1995 WORLD CUP SEMI FINALS

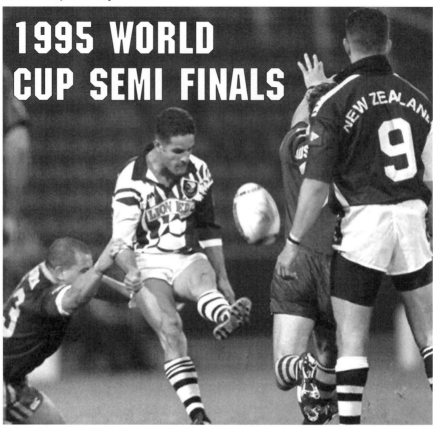

New Zealand's Matthew Ridge attempts the famous last minute drop goal to try and break the 20-20 deadlock between the Kiwis and the Aussies. The ball sailed inches wide, extra time was played, and Terry Hill raced in for the match-winning try (BELOW)

England's Kris Radlinski held up by Wales duo Jonathan Davis (on ground) and Paul Moriarty

THE WORLD CUP FINAL

ENGLAND 8 ....AUSTRALIA 16

Played at Wembley Stadium, Saturday 28th October 1995

Missed chances, some straight down the line refereeing decisions by Stuart Cummings (in situations where other English referees might well have seen things differently), and the remarkable resilience of the Australians, superbly prompted by Andrew Johns in the unaccustomed role of hooker, led to another World Cup disappointment for England.

Gary Connolly was making his first appearance in the tournament, following a bout of pneumonia, and he replaced Nick Pinkney in the centre, with Pinkney dropping to the bench. Chris Joynt also came into the squad on the bench, while Dean Sampson and Simon Haughton dropped out of the squad that had beaten Wales. The Australians made no changes from the squad that had seen off New Zealand in the semi-final.

The game was tense and tight. The Aussies took a sixth-minute lead, after Andrew Johns kicked through to the line for Rod Wishart to touch down, and from then on they never looked like losing in a game that lacked many exciting incidents.

Down 10-4 at the break, England threatened to come back when Paul Newlove scored after making a powerful charge from the play-the-ball on 44 minutes, bringing the score back to 10-8. But it was Australia who would complete the scoring, with a try to Tim Brasher on 67 minutes, goaled again by Johns.

AUSTRALIA: Tim Brasher, Rod Wishart, Mark Coyne, Terry Hill, Brett Dallas, Brad Fittler, Geoff Toovey, Dean Pay, Andrew Johns, Mark Carroll, Steve Menzies, Gary Larson, Jim Dymock. Subs. Jason Smith, Robbie O'Davis, Matthew Johns, Nik Kosef.
Tries: Wishart, Brasher.
Goals: A Johns 4

ENGLAND: Kris Radlinski, Jason Robinson, Gary Connolly, Paul Newlove, Martin Offiah, Tony Smith, Bobbie Goulding, Karl Harrison, Lee Jackson, Andy Platt, Denis Betts, Phil Clarke, Andy Farrell. Subs. Nick Pinkney, Barrie-Jon Mather, Mick Cassidy, Chris Joynt.
Try: Newlove. **Goals:** Goulding 2

Referee: Stuart Cummings (England)
Attendance: 66,540

The Aussies held out to win 16-8 in front of a 66,540 crowd - not bad for a tournament that the media tried to tell us nobody was interested in.

Brad Fittler received the Halifax World Cup from HRH Prince Edward, as a disappointed Maurice Lindsay looked on, beaten by the ARL's boys.

But the whole tournament had been a triumph for Rugby League, totally destroying the millstone of the game's old parochial image, as nations from all around the world gathered to play the game with such obvious enjoyment.

Such was the spirit of the competition that not a single player was sent off for the duration of the whole tournament.

And crowds of over 26,000 at Wigan and 14,000 at Leeds for England's night games against Fiji and South Africa respectively could never have been predicted beforehand by even the most optimistic pundits.

Andrew Johns was named the outstanding player of the 1995 World Cup. Yet, remarkably, he couldn't find a place in the official World XIII named after the tournament, losing out to Papua New Guinea captain Adrian Lam for the scrum-half slot, and England's Lee Jackson for the hooking role.

Brett Dallas, Jim Dymock, Dean Pay and Jason Smith enjoy the moment

WORLD CUP RECORDS

TROPHY WINS:
8 by Australia; 3 by Great Britain

HIGHEST SCORE AND WIDEST MARGIN:
Australia 110 v. Russia 4 at Hull
4 November 2000

BIGGEST ATTENDANCE:
73,631 Great Britain v. Australia at
Wembley (Final) *24 October 1992*

MOST TRIES IN A MATCH:
4 by Keith Fielding (England) v. France at
Bordeaux *11 October 1975*
4 by Dale Shearer (Australia) v. France at
Carcassonne *13 December1986*
4 by Michael O'Connor (Australia) v
Papua New Guinea at Wagga Wagga
20 July 1988
4 by Mat Rogers (Australia) v. Fiji at
Gateshead *1 November 2000*
4 by Wendell Sailor (Australia) v. Russia
at Hull *4 November 2000*

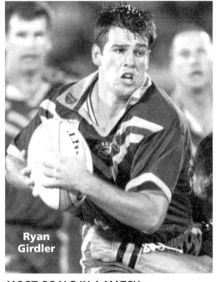

Ryan Girdler

MOST GOALS IN A MATCH:
17 Ryan Girdler (Australia) v. Russia at
Hull *4 November 2000*

MOST POINTS IN A MATCH:
46 by Ryan Girdler (Australia) v. Russia
at Hull *4 November 2000*

Tim Brasher takes on Phil Clarke

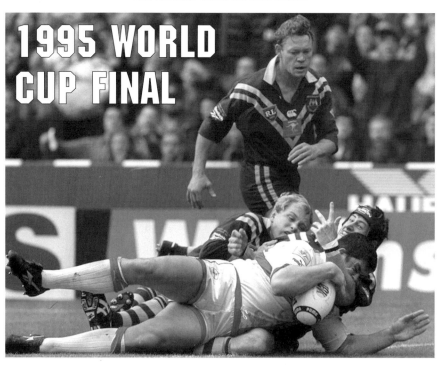

**Andy Farrell grounded by Australian duo Geoff Toovey and
Steve Menzies as Rod Wishart moves in**

A rampaging Andy Farrell tries to break free from the clutches of Gary Larson

Jubilant Australian captain Brad Fittler lifts the World Cup at Wembley in 1995 and (BELOW) the Australia squad celebrate their success

3
WORLD CUP
STATISTICS

AUSTRALIA

DATE	FIXTURE	RESULT	GROUP	ATT
28/10/00	England	W22-2	1st	33,758

t:Sailor(2),Gidley,MacDougall g:Rogers(3)

| 1/11/00 | Fiji | W66-8 | 1st | 4,197 |

t:Rogers(4),Kennedy(2),Girdler(2),Barrett,Hindmarsh,MacDougall, Gidley g:Rogers(9)

| 4/11/00 | Russia | W110-4 | 1st | 3,044 |

t:Sailor(4),Girdler(3),Barrett(2),Croker(2),Hindmarsh(2), MacDougall,Fletcher,Webcke,Tallis,Johns,Gidley g:Girdler(17)

| 11/11/00 | Samoa (QF) | W66-10 | N/A | 5,404 |

t:Fletcher(3),Johns(2),Hill(2),MacDougall(2),Girdler,Fittler,Sailor g:Rogers(9)

| 19/11/00 | Wales (SF) | W46-22 | N/A | 8,124 |

t:Fittler(2),Lockyer(2),Kimmorley,Sailor,Fletcher,Gower,Kennedy g:Lockyer(4),Girdler

| 25/11/00 | New Zealand (F) | W40-12 | N/A | 44,329 |

t:Sailor(2),Gidley,Hindmarsh,Lockyer,Fittler,Barrett g:Rogers(6)

	APP(S)	TRIES	GOALS	FG	PTS
Trent Barrett	2(2)	4	0	0	16
Darren Britt	(3)	0	0	0	0
Jason Croker	1(3)	2	0	0	8
Brad Fittler	5	4	0	0	16
Bryan Fletcher	5	5	0	0	20
Matthew Gidley	6	4	0	0	16
Ryan Girdler	5	6	18	0	60
Craig Gower	2(1)	1	0	0	4
Scott Hill	5(1)	2	0	0	8
Nathan Hindmarsh	1(3)	4	0	0	16
Andrew Johns	5	3	0	0	12
Robbie Kearns	4(2)	0	0	0	0
Ben Kennedy	1(2)	3	0	0	12
Brett Kimmorley	5	1	0	0	4
Darren Lockyer	5	3	4	0	20
Adam MacDougall	4(2)	5	0	0	20
Mat Rogers	4	4	27	0	70
Wendell Sailor	5	10	0	0	40
Jason Stevens	1(3)	0	0	0	0
Gorden Tallis	5	1	0	0	4
Michael Vella	2(1)	0	0	0	0
Shane Webcke	5(1)	1	0	0	4

ENGLAND

DATE	FIXTURE	RESULT	GROUP	ATT
28/10/00	Australia	L2-22	3rd	33,758

g:Farrell

| 1/11/00 | Russia | W76-4 | 2nd | 5,736 |

t:Sinfield(3),Rowley(2),Peacock(2),Long(2),Hay,Walker,Pryce, Stephenson,Deacon g:Farrell(5),Long(5)

| 4/11/00 | Fiji | W66-10 | 2nd | 10,052 |

t:Peacock(3),Wellens(2),Rogers(2),Hay,Smith,Farrell,Naylor, Radlinski g:Farrell(9)

| 11/11/00 | Ireland (QF) | W26-16 | N/A | 15,405 |

t:Senior,Peacock,Smith,Walker g:Farrell(5)

| 18/11/00 | New Zealand (SF) | L6-49 | N/A | 16,032 |

t:Smith g:Farrell

	APP(S)	TRIES	GOALS	FG	PTS
Paul Anderson	2(2)	0	0	0	0
Paul Deacon	4	1	0	0	4
Andy Farrell	5	1	21	0	46
Stuart Fielden	3(2)	0	0	0	0
Darren Fleary	1(2)	0	0	0	0
Mike Forshaw	3	0	0	0	0
Andy Hay	2(1)	2	0	0	8
Harvey Howard	2(3)	0	0	0	0
Sean Long	4(1)	2	5	0	18
Adrian Morley	2	0	0	0	0
Scott Naylor	3(1)	1	0	0	4
Jamie Peacock	2(2)	6	0	0	24
Leon Pryce	2	1	0	0	4
Kris Radlinski	4	1	0	0	4
Darren Rogers	3	2	0	0	8
Paul Rowley	3	2	0	0	8
Paul Sculthorpe	1	0	0	0	0
Keith Senior	4	1	0	0	4
Kevin Sinfield	1(2)	3	0	0	12
Tony Smith	3(1)	3	0	0	12
Stuart Spruce	1(1)	0	0	0	0
Francis Stephenson	2	1	0	0	4
Chev Walker	4(1)	2	0	0	8
Paul Wellens	4(1)	2	0	0	8

FIJI

DATE	FIXTURE	RESULT	GROUP	ATT
29/10/00	Russia	W38-12	2nd	2,187

t:Vunivalu(3),Tuqiri(2),Kuruduadua,Sovatabua g:Tuqiri(5)

| 1/11/00 | Australia | L8-66 | 3rd | 4,197 |

t:Cakacaka,Tuqiri

| 4/11/00 | England | L10-66 | 3rd | 10,052 |

t:Navale,Tuqiri g:Vunivalu

	APP(S)	TRIES	GOALS	FG	PTS
Jimi Bolakoro	1	0	0	0	0
Tabuinatoga Cakacaka	3	1	0	0	4
Jone Kuruduadua	2	1	0	0	4
Josefa Lasagavibau	(2)	0	0	0	0
Sam Marayawa	3	0	0	0	0
Roger Matakamikamica	(1)	0	0	0	0
Mesake Navugona	(1)	0	0	0	0
Eparama Navale	3	1	0	0	4
Seteriki Rakabula	1	0	0	0	0
Fred Robart	3	0	0	0	0
Stephen Smith	2	0	0	0	0
Waisale Sovatabua	3	1	0	0	4
Semi Tadulala	2	0	0	0	0
Amani Takayawa	(2)	0	0	0	0
Josese Tamani	2	0	0	0	0
Farasiko Tokarei	(3)	0	0	0	0
Kalaveti Naisoro					
Tuiabayaba	3	0	0	0	0
Lote Tuqiri	3	4	5	0	26
Nikotimo Vakararawa	1	0	0	0	0
Etuate Vakatawa	3	0	0	0	0
Atunaisa Vunivalu	3	3	1	0	14
Peceli Vuniyayana	(2)	0	0	0	0
Peceli Wawavanua	1(1)	0	0	0	0

RUSSIA

DATE	FIXTURE	RESULT	GROUP	ATT
29/10/00	Fiji	L12-38	4th	2,187

t:Iliassov,Rullis g:Jiltsov,Mitrofanov

| 1/11/00 | England | L4-76 | 4th | 5,736 |

g:Mitrofanov(2)

| 4/11/00 | Australia | L4-110 | 4th | 3,044 |

t:Donovan

	APP(S)	TRIES	GOALS	FG	PTS
Viatcheslav Artachine	(1)	0	0	0	0
Robert Campbell	3	0	0	0	0
Rinat Chamsoutdinov	1	0	0	0	0
Craig Cygler	2	0	0	0	0
Matthew Donovan	2	1	0	0	4
Andrei Doumalkine	1	0	0	0	0
Aaron Findlay	2	0	0	0	0
Roustem Garifoulline	1	0	0	0	0
Igor Gavriline	3	0	0	0	0
Michael Giorgas	(1)	0	0	0	0
Robert Iliassov	3	1	0	0	4
Igor Jiltsov	(2)	0	1	0	2
Pavel Kalachkine	(3)	0	0	0	0
Kirillin Koulemine	1	0	0	0	0
Andrei Kuchumov	1	0	0	0	0
Alexander Lysenkov	3	0	0	0	0
Mikhail Mitrofanov	3	0	3	0	6
Victor Netchaev	(2)	0	0	0	0
Andre Olar	3	0	0	0	0
Vadim Postnikov	(2)	0	0	0	0
Maxim Romanov	3	0	0	0	0
Ian Rubin	3	0	0	0	0
Joel Rullis	3	1	0	0	4
Petr Sokolov	2	0	0	0	0

COOK ISLANDS

DATE	FIXTURE	RESULT	GROUP	ATT
29/10/00	Wales	L6-38	3rd	5,017
t:Temata g:Piakura				
2/11/00	New Zealand	L10-84	4th	3,982
t:Noovao,Iro g:Piakura				
5/11/00	Lebanon	D22-22	4th	5,500
t:Berryman(2),Joe,Toa g:Berryman(2),Piakura				

	APP(S)	TRIES	GOALS	FG	PTS
Michael Andersson	1(2)	0	0	0	0
Steve Berryman	2	2	2	0	12
Craig Bowen	2(1)	0	0	0	0
Zane Clarke	3	0	0	0	0
Adam Cook	(2)	0	0	0	0
Tere Glassie	1(1)	0	0	0	0
Kevin Iro	3	1	0	0	4
Leroy Joe	3	1	0	0	4
Vaine Kino	(1)	0	0	0	0
Patrick Kuru	1(1)	0	0	0	0
Peter Lewis	2(1)	0	0	0	0
Meti Noovao	1	1	0	0	4
Tyrone Pau	2	0	0	0	0
Richard Piakura	3	0	3	0	6
Raymond Ruapuro	(1)	0	0	0	0
Anthony Samuel	3	0	0	0	0
Sonny Shepherd	(2)	0	0	0	0
Karl Temata	3	1	0	0	4
Jason Temu	3	0	0	0	0
Tiri Toa	1	1	0	0	4
Tangiia Tongia	2	0	0	0	0
George Tuakura	3	0	0	0	0

LEBANON

DATE	FIXTURE	RESULT	GROUP	ATT
29/10/00	New Zealand	L0-64	4th	2,496
No Scorers				
2/11/00	Wales	L22-24	3rd	1,497
t:Saleh(2),Coorey,S El Masri g:H El Masri(3)				
5/11/00	Cook Islands	D22-22	3rd	5,500
t:H El Masri(2),Touma,H Saleh g:H El Masri(3)				

	APP(S)	TRIES	GOALS	FG	PTS
Mohammed Abbas	2	0	0	0	0
Najjarin Bilal	1	0	0	0	0
Mohammed Chahal	1	0	0	0	0
Sami Chamoun	3	0	0	0	0
Michael Coorey	2	1	0	0	4
Raymond Daher	2	0	0	0	0
Fady El Chab	1	0	0	0	0
Hazem El Masri	3	2	6	0	20
Samer El Masri	2(1)	1	0	0	4
Moneh Elahmad	2	0	0	0	0
Eben Goddard	1	0	0	0	0
George Katrib	1(1)	0	0	0	0
Paul Khoury	2(1)	0	0	0	0
Joe Lichaa	1(2)	0	0	0	0
Darren Maroon	3	0	0	0	0
Charlie Nohra	(2)	0	0	0	0
Hassan Saleh	3	3	0	0	12
Nedol Saleh	1	0	0	0	0
Christopher Salem	1(2)	0	0	0	0
Anthony Semrani	2	0	0	0	0
Jason Stanton	2	0	0	0	0
Kandy Tamer	1(2)	0	0	0	0
Travis Touma	2(1)	1	0	0	4

NEW ZEALAND

DATE	FIXTURE	RESULT	GROUP	ATT
29/10/00	Lebanon	W64-0	1st	2,496
t:Talau(2),Barnett(2),Carroll(2),Vainikolo(2),Jones(2),Jellick,Swann g:Jones(6),H Paul(2)				
2/11/00	Cook Islands	W84-10	1st	3,982
t:Barnett(2),Vaealiki(2),Lavea(2),R Paul(2),N Vagana,Vainikolo, Cayless,Lauiti'iti,Puletua,Wiki,Pongia g:Lavea(12)				
5/11/00	Wales	W58-18	1st	17,612
t:Vainikolo(3),Barnett(2),Talau,H Paul,Wiki,Carroll,Lauiti'iti,N Vagana g:H Paul(5),Lavea(2)				
12/11/00	France (QF)	W54-6	N/A	5,158
t:R Paul(3),Rua,Pongia,Smith,Kearney,Talau,Blackmore g:H Paul(7)				
18/11/00	England (SF)	W49-6	N/A	16,032
t:Vainikolo(2),Talau(2),Kearney,Wiki,N Vagana,Swann g:H Paul(8) fg:H Paul				
25/11/00	Australia (F)	L12-40	N/A	44,329
t:Vainikolo,Carroll g:H Paul(2)				

	APP(S)	TRIES	GOALS	FG	PTS
Richie Barnett	6	6	0	0	24
Richie Blackmore	2	1	0	0	4
Tonie Carroll	4(1)	4	0	0	16
Nathan Cayless	2(4)	1	0	0	4
Brian Jellick	2	2	0	0	8
Stacey Jones	4(1)	2	6	0	20
Stephen Kearney	5(1)	2	0	0	8
Ali Lauiti'iti	1(1)	2	0	0	8
Tasesa Lavea	1(1)	2	14	0	36
Henry Paul	5	1	24	1	53
Robbie Paul	2(3)	5	0	0	20
Quentin Pongia	4(1)	2	0	0	8
Tony Puletua	1(1)	1	0	0	4
Matt Rua	4(1)	1	0	0	4
Craig Smith	5(1)	1	0	0	4
Richard Swain	6	0	0	0	0
Logan Swann	2(2)	2	0	0	8
Willie Talau	5	6	0	0	24
Joe Vagana	1(5)	0	0	0	0
Nigel Vagana	5	3	0	0	12
David Vaealiki	1	2	0	0	8
Lesley Vainikolo	5	9	0	0	36
Ruben Wiki	5(1)	3	0	0	12

WALES

DATE	FIXTURE	RESULT	GROUP	ATT
29/10/00	Cook Islands	W38-6	2nd	5,017
t:Tassell(3),Briers,Jenkins,Cunningham g:Harris(7)				
2/11/00	Lebanon	W24-22	2nd	1,497
t:Harris(2),Sterling,Cunningham,Davies g:Harris(2)				
5/11/00	New Zealand	L18-58	2nd	17,612
t:Briers,Atcheson,Farrell g:Harris(3)				
12/11/00	PN Guinea (QF)	W22-8	N/A	5,211
t:Critchley,Briers,Davies g:Harris(5)				
19/11/00	Australia (SF)	L22-46	N/A	8,124
t:Watson,Tassell,Briers g:Harris(4) fg:Briers(2)				

	APP(S)	TRIES	GOALS	FG	PTS
Paul Atcheson	3(2)	1	0	0	4
Lee Briers	5	4	0	2	18
Dean Busby	3	0	0	0	0
Garreth Carvell	(2)	0	0	0	0
Jason Critchley	5	1	0	0	4
Keiron Cunningham	4	2	0	0	8
Wes Davies	1(4)	2	0	0	8
John Devereux	(2)	0	0	0	0
Barry Eaton	(1)	0	0	0	0
Anthony Farrell	5	1	0	0	4
Iestyn Harris	5	2	21	0	50
Paul Highton	2(3)	0	0	0	0
Mick Jenkins	4	1	0	0	4
David Luckwell	(1)	0	0	0	0
Justin Morgan	5	0	0	0	0
Paul Moriarty	1(1)	0	0	0	0
Chris Morley	2(2)	0	0	0	0
Hefin O'Hare	1	0	0	0	0
Chris Smith	1(1)	0	0	0	0
Paul Sterling	4	1	0	0	4
Anthony Sullivan	5	0	0	0	0
Kris Tassell	4	4	0	0	16
Ian Watson	2(1)	1	0	0	4
David Whittle	3	0	0	0	0

151

FRANCE

PAPUA NEW GUINEA

DATE	FIXTURE	RESULT	GROUP	ATT
28/10/00	Papua N Guinea	L20-23	3rd	7,498

t:Hechiche(2),Benausse,Dekkiche g:Banquet(2)

| 1/11/00 | Tonga | W28-8 | 3rd | 10,288 |

t:Banquet,Sirvent,Dulac,Garcia,Jampy g:Banquet(4)

| 5/11/00 | South Africa | W56-6 | 2nd | 7,969 |

t:Jampy(3),Cassin(2),Banquet,Guisset,Sirvent,Tallec g:Banquet(10)

| 12/11/00 | New Zealand (QF) | L6-54 | N/A | 5,158 |

t:Sirvent g:Banquet

	APP(S)	TRIES	GOALS	FG	PTS
Frederic Banquet	4	2	17	0	42
Patrice Benausse	1	1	0	0	4
Laurent Carrasco	(4)	0	0	0	0
Jean-Emmanuel Cassin	4	2	0	0	8
Yacine Dekkiche	1	1	0	0	4
David Despin	(4)	0	0	0	0
Fabien Devecchi	4	0	0	0	0
Arnaud Dulac	4	1	0	0	4
Abderazak El Khalouki	(1)	0	0	0	0
Laurent Frayssinous	1	0	0	0	0
Jean-Marc Garcia	3	1	0	0	4
Jerome Guisset	4	1	0	0	4
Rachid Hechiche	4	2	0	0	8
Pascal Jampy	4	4	0	0	16
Julien Rinaldi	3	0	0	0	0
Jason Sands	2(2)	0	0	0	0
Claude Sirvent	3	3	0	0	12
Romain Sort	(3)	0	0	0	0
Gael Tallec	4	1	0	0	4
Frederic Teixido	3(1)	0	0	0	0
Vincent Wulf	4	0	0	0	0

DATE	FIXTURE	RESULT	GROUP	ATT
28/10/00	France	W23-20	2nd	7,498

t:Bai,Krewanty,Buko,Lam g:Wilshere(2),Buko fg:Lam

| 2/11/00 | South Africa | W16-0 | 1st | 4,313 |

t:Aila,Wilshere,Paiyo g:Wilshere(2)

| 6/11/00 | Tonga | W30-22 | 1st | 3,666 |

t:Gene(2),Mondo,Buko,Karl g:Wilshere(5)

| 12/11/00 | Wales (QF) | L8-22 | N/A | 5,211 |

t:Wilshere g:Wilshere(2)

	APP(S)	TRIES	GOALS	FG	PTS
Eddie Aila	4	1	0	0	4
Makali Aizure	(3)	0	0	0	0
Marcus Bai	4	1	0	0	4
David Buko	4	2	1	0	10
Stanley Gene	4	2	0	0	8
Raymond Karl	4	1	0	0	4
Alex Krewanty	(4)	1	0	0	4
Adrian Lam	4	1	0	1	5
Bruce Mamando	4	0	0	0	0
Michael Marum	1	0	0	0	0
Mark Mom	3(1)	0	0	0	0
Michael Mondo	3(1)	1	0	0	4
Duncan Naawi	4	0	0	0	0
Andrew Norman	(4)	0	0	0	0
Tom O'Reilly	4	0	0	0	0
Elias Paiyo	(3)	1	0	0	4
Lucas Solbat	1	0	0	0	0
Alfred Songoro	4	0	0	0	0
John Wilshere	4	2	11	0	30

SOUTH AFRICA

TONGA

DATE	FIXTURE	RESULT	GROUP	ATT
28/10/00	Tonga	L18-66	4th	7,498

t:Breytenbach,Barnard,Best g:Bloem(2),O'Shea

| 2/11/00 | Papua N Guinea | L0-16 | 4th | 4,313 |

No Scorers

| 5/11/00 | France | L6-56 | 4th | 7,969 |

t:de Villiers g:Bloem

	APP(S)	TRIES	GOALS	FG	PTS
Leon Barnard	3	1	0	0	4
Brian Best	3	1	0	0	4
Jamie Bloem	3	0	3	0	6
Jaco Booysens	3	0	0	0	0
Conrad Breytenbach	1	1	0	0	4
Francois Cloete	(2)	0	0	0	0
Archer Dames	3	0	0	0	0
Quinton de Villiers	3	1	0	0	4
Hercules Erasmus	3	0	0	0	0
Chris Hurter	1(1)	0	0	0	0
Justin Jennings	1(2)	0	0	0	0
Mark Johnson	3	0	0	0	0
Richard Louw	(1)	0	0	0	0
Hendrik Mulder	(3)	0	0	0	0
Corne Nel	(2)	0	0	0	0
Ian Noble	2	0	0	0	0
Tim O'Shea	1	0	1	0	2
Eugene Powell	3	0	0	0	0
Sean Rutgerson	3	0	0	0	0
Sean Skelton	1	0	0	0	0
Pierre Van Wyk	2	0	0	0	0
Jaco Webb	(1)	0	0	0	0

DATE	FIXTURE	RESULT	GROUP	ATT
28/10/00	South Africa	W66-18	1st	7,498

t:Vaikona(3),D Mann(2),W Wolfgramm,Liava'a, M Masella,Moala,E Mann,Lomi,L Kaufusi,Mason g:Moala(6),D Mann

| 1/11/00 | France | L8-28 | 2nd | 10,288 |

t:D Fisi'iahi,P Fisi'iahi

| 6/11/00 | Papua N Guinea | L22-30 | 3rd | 3,666 |

t:Moala(2),Mason,Vaikona g:Moala(3)

	APP(S)	TRIES	GOALS	FG	PTS
David Fisi'iahi	1(2)	1	0	0	4
Paul Fisi'iahi	(1)	1	0	0	4
Nuko Hifo	1	0	0	0	0
Phil Howlett	3	0	0	0	0
Lipina Kaufusi	3	1	0	0	4
Malupo Kaufusi	1	0	0	0	0
Brent Kite	1(1)	0	0	0	0
Paul Koloi	3	0	0	0	0
Talite Liava'a	2	1	0	0	4
Nelson Lomi	(3)	1	0	0	4
Andrew Lomu	1(1)	0	0	0	0
Duanne Mann	3	2	1	0	10
Esau Mann	3	1	0	0	4
Willie Manu	2(1)	0	0	0	0
Alfons Masella	1(1)	0	0	0	0
Martin Masella	3	1	0	0	4
Willie Mason	3	2	0	0	8
Fifita Moala	3	3	9	0	30
Tevita Vaikona	3	4	0	0	16
Greg Wolfgramm	2	0	0	0	0
Willie Wolfgramm	1(1)	1	0	0	4

IRELAND

DATE	FIXTURE	RESULT	GROUP	ATT
28/10/00	Samoa	W30-16	1st	3,207

t:Joynt,Ricketson,Eagar,Carney,Prescott g:Prescott(5)

| 1/11/00 | Scotland | W18-6 | 1st | 1,782 |

t:Sheridan,Withers g:Prescott(5)

| 4/11/00 | Aotearoa Maori | W30-16 | 1st | 3,164 |

t:Forster,Carney,Barnhill,Withers,Sheridan g:Prescott(5)

| 11/11/00 | England (QF) | L16-26 | N/A | 15,405 |

t:Withers(2),Martyn g:Prescott(2)

	APP(S)	TRIES	GOALS	FG	PTS
David Barnhill	1(3)	1	0	0	4
David Bradbury	(1)	0	0	0	0
Liam Bretherton	(2)	0	0	0	0
Kevin Campion	4	0	0	0	0
Brian Carney	4	2	0	0	8
Gavin Clinch	1(1)	0	0	0	0
Michael Eagar	3	1	0	0	4
Mark Forster	3	1	0	0	4
Ian Herron	1	0	0	0	0
Chris Joynt	4	1	0	0	4
Johnny Lawless	1(2)	0	0	0	0
Tommy Martyn	3	1	0	0	4
Jamie Mathiou	(2)	0	0	0	0
Barrie McDermott	4	0	0	0	0
Terry O'Connor	4	0	0	0	0
Steve Prescott	4	1	17	0	38
Luke Ricketson	4	1	0	0	4
Ryan Sheridan	4	2	0	0	8
Paul Southern	(3)	0	0	0	0
Liam Tallon	(1)	0	0	0	0
Danny Williams	3(1)	0	0	0	0
Michael Withers	4	4	0	0	16

 # AOTEAROA MAORI

DATE	FIXTURE	RESULT	GROUP	ATT
29/10/00	Scotland	W17-16	2nd	2,008

t:Toopi(2),Kidwell g:Ngamu(2) fg:Ngamu

| 1/11/00 | Samoa | L16-21 | 2nd | 4,107 |

t:Matthews,Nelson,Rauhihi g:Goodwin(2)

| 4/11/00 | Ireland | L16-30 | 3rd | 3,164 |

t:Nelson,Te Rangi,Koopu g:Perenara,Ngamu

	APP(S)	TRIES	GOALS	FG	PTS
James Cook	1	0	0	0	0
Luke Goodwin	1	0	2	0	4
Terry Hermansson	2(1)	0	0	0	0
Sean Hoppe	2	0	0	0	0
David Kidwell	2(1)	1	0	0	4
Toa Kohe-Love	2(1)	0	0	0	0
Wairangi Koopu	2	1	0	0	4
Kyle Leuluai	1(1)	0	0	0	0
Odell Manuel	2	0	0	0	0
Steve Matthews	1	1	0	0	4
Jared Mills	1	0	0	0	0
Martin Moana	(3)	0	0	0	0
Chris Nahi	(2)	0	0	0	0
Boycie Nelson	1(1)	2	0	0	8
Gene Ngamu	2	0	3	1	7
Tawera Nikau	3	0	0	0	0
Henry Perenara	2	0	1	0	2
Paul Rauhihi	3	1	0	0	4
Tahi Reihana	1(2)	0	0	0	0
Jeremy Smith	1	0	0	0	0
Tyran Smith	3	0	0	0	0
Hare Te Rangi	2	1	0	0	4
Clinton Toopi	3	2	0	0	8
Paul Whatuira	1	0	0	0	0

 # SAMOA

DATE	FIXTURE	RESULT	GROUP	ATT
28/10/00	Ireland	L16-30	4th	3,207

t:Leauma,Milford,Betham g:Geros(2)

| 1/11/00 | Aotearoa Maori | W21-16 | 3rd | 4,107 |

t:Fa'afili(2),W Swann,Milford g:Poching(2) fg:W Swann

| 5/11/00 | Scotland | W20-12 | 2nd | 1,579 |

t:Leauma(2),Solomona,Milford g:Laloata(2)

| 11/11/00 | Australia (QF) | L10-66 | N/A | 5,404 |

t:Solomona,Leauma g:Laloata

	APP(S)	TRIES	GOALS	FG	PTS
Henry Aau Fa'afili	3	2	0	0	8
Monty Betham	4	1	0	0	4
Max Fala	(3)	0	0	0	0
Joe Galuvao	2	0	0	0	0
Simon Geros	1(1)	0	2	0	4
Fa'rvae Kalolo	(1)	0	0	0	0
Shane Laloata	2	0	3	0	6
Mark Leafa	1(3)	0	0	0	0
Bryan Leauma	4	4	0	0	16
Philip Leuluai	1(2)	0	0	0	0
Peter Lima	2	0	0	0	0
Francis Meli	2(1)	0	0	0	0
Loa Milford	4	3	0	0	12
Fred Petersen	1	0	0	0	0
Willie Poching	4	0	2	0	4
Frank Puletua	4	0	0	0	0
Jerry Seu Seu	4	0	0	0	0
David Solomona	4	2	0	0	8
Anthony Swann	4	0	0	0	0
Willie Swann	3(1)	1	0	1	5
Albert Talapeau	1	0	0	0	0
Tony Tatupu	1(3)	0	0	0	0

 # SCOTLAND

DATE	FIXTURE	RESULT	GROUP	ATT
29/10/00	Aotearoa Maori	L16-17	3rd	2,008

t:Penny,Maiden,Bell g:Mackay,Crowther

| 1/11/00 | Ireland | L6-18 | 4th | 1,782 |

t:Arnold g:Crowther

| 5/11/00 | Samoa | L12-20 | 4th | 1,579 |

t:Vowles,Rhodes g:Crowther(2)

	APP(S)	TRIES	GOALS	FG	PTS
Danny Arnold	2	1	0	0	4
Geoff Bell	3	1	0	0	4
Scott Cram	3	0	0	0	0
Matt Crowther	2(1)	0	4	0	8
Matt Daylight	3	0	0	0	0
Lee Gilmour	3	0	0	0	0
Nathan Graham	(1)	0	0	0	0
Daniel Heckenberg	3	0	0	0	0
Richard Horne	3	0	0	0	0
Dale Laughton	3	0	0	0	0
Scott Logan	3	0	0	0	0
Graham Mackay	1	0	1	0	2
David Maiden	(3)	1	0	0	4
Wayne McDonald	(3)	0	0	0	0
Lee Penny	1	1	0	0	4
Andrew Purcell	2	0	0	0	0
Scott Rhodes	1(1)	1	0	0	4
Danny Russell	3	0	0	0	0
Darren Shaw	(3)	0	0	0	0
Adrian Vowles	3	1	0	0	4

2000 EMERGING NATIONS

GROUP ONE

USA 52 ....**CANADA 10**
At Court Place Farm, Oxford, Monday 13 November 2000
Attendance: 500
USA: T - Balachandran, Vassilakopoulos, Duncan 2, Niu, Warren 2, Broussard, Fabri, Sheridan, G - Simon 6
Canada: T - Whale, Van der Hoek, G - De Snayer

CANADA 6 ....**ITALY 66**
At Cougar Park, Keighley, Wednesday 15 November 2000
Attendance: 1,028
Canada: T - Coussons; G - Weiler
Italy: T - Trimboli 2, Schifilitti 2, D'Arro, Barbaro, Ienco 2, Napolitano 2, Di Paoli, Frare, A Dal Santo; G - Frare 7

ITALY 40 ....**USA 16**
At the New Shay, Halifax, Friday 17 November 2000
Attendance: 1,487
Italy: T - Riolo, Frare 2, Ienco 2, Mancuso, A Capovilla; G - Albertini 4, Ienco 2.
USA: T - O'Neill, Duncan, Retchless; G - Duncan

GROUP TWO

BARLA GB & IRELAND 60 ....**MOROCCO 2**
At Lionheart Stadium, Featherstone, Monday 13 November 2000
Attendance: 769
BARLA: T - Jackson 2, Cooper, 2, Davidson, Morton 2, Innes 2, O'Neill, Shaw, Halmshaw, G - Jackson 4, Innes 2.
Morocco: G - Martinez

MOROCCO 12 ....**JAPAN 8**
At New Craven Park, Hull, Wednesday 15 November 2000
Attendance: 1,488
Morocco: T- El Arf, G - Martinez 4
Japan: T - Kunemura, G - Inose 2

BARLA GB & IRELAND 54 ....**JAPAN 0**
At Copeland Stadium, Whitehaven, Friday 17 November 2000
Attendance: 1,007
BARLA: T - Lynn 2, Newby, Jones, Innes 2, G Fletcher 2, Shaw, McHugh, O'Neil, G - Newby 5

GROUP ONE TABLE

	P	W	D	L	F	A	Pts
Italy	2	2	0	0	106	22	4
USA	2	1	0	1	68	50	2
Canada	2	0	0	2	16	118	0

GROUP TWO TABLE

	P	W	D	L	F	A	Pts
BARLA GB & Ireland	2	2	0	0	114	2	4
Morocco	2	1	0	1	14	68	2
Japan	2	0	0	2	8	66	0

PLAY-OFFS

CANADA 28 ....**JAPAN 12**
At Robin Park, Wigan, Monday 20 November 2000
Attendance: 500
Canada: T - Demetriou 3, Whale, McKenzie; G - Weiler 2, De Snayer 2
Japan: T - Williamson, Nakashima; G - Okamura 2
(Canada finish 5th)

UNITED STATES 50...**MOROCCO 10**
At Robin Park, Wigan, Monday 20 November 2000
Attendance: 500
USA: T - Sheridan 2, Broussard, O'Neill, Retchless 2, Duncan 2, Hollingsworth; G - Duncan 6, Niu
Morocco: T - El Arf, Fakir; G - Martinez
(USA finish 3rd)

2000 EMERGING NATIONS FINAL

BARLA GB & IRELAND 20 ....**ITALY 14**
At Ram Stadium, Dewsbury, Monday 20 November 2000
Attendance: 1,601; **Referee:** Robert Connolly (England)
BARLA: T - Fletcher, McHugh, Birdsall; G - Jackson 4
Italy: T - Riolo, A Capovilla, Bulgarelli; G - Albertini
BARLA: Dave Hedgecock, Steve Morton, Phil O'Neil (c), Darrell Cooper, Wayne McHugh, Darren Jones, Terry Lynn, Stuart Dancer, Marc Jackson, Terry Halmshaw, Brian Newby, Ian Devlin, Scott Fletcher. Subs: Rob Shaw, Paul Davidson, Phil Sherwen, Paul Birdsall.
Italy: Darren Albertini, Charlie Ienco, Ian Schifilitti, Dainan Mancuso, David Riolo, John Frare, Michael Mantelli, Paul Dalsanto, Darren Capovilla, Brendan Di Paoli, Mark Sessarago, Adam Capovilla. Subs: Patrick Trimboli, Carlo Napolitano, Anthony Dalsanto, Pete Magnone

2000 WOMENS WORLD SERIES

GREAT BRITAIN & IRELAND 12 ....**NEW ZEALAND 22**
At Orrell, Tuesday, November 7 2000
Great Britain: T - Gilmour, Land; G - Dobek 2
New Zealand: T - Witehera, Te Amo 2, Niha, Wrigley; G Hina

AUSTRALIA 6 ....**NEW ZEALAND10**
At South Leeds Stadium, Hunslet, Friday, November 10 2000
Australia: T - Norris; G - Shaw
New Zealand: T - Johnstone, Witehera; G - Hina

GREAT BRITAIN & IRELAND 14 ....**AUSTRALIA 10**
At Ram Stadium, Dewsbury, Tuesday, November 14 2000
Great Britain: T - Banks, Gilmour, Dobek; G - Dobek
Australia: T - Jarrett, Murphy; G - Shaw

PLAY-OFF ONE

NEW ZEALAND 50..**AUSTRALIA 6**
At Ram Stadium, Dewsbury, Friday November 17 2000
New Zealand: T - O'Carroll 2, Mariu 2, Howard, Logopati, Driscoll, Te Amo, Presland, White; G - Hina 4, Mariu
Australia: T - Fanning; G - Shaw

PLAY-OFF TWO

GREAT BRITAIN & IRELAND 4 ....**AUSTRALIA 0**
At The Jungle, Castleford, Tuesday November 21 2000
Great Britain: G - Dobek 2

FINAL

NEW ZEALAND 26..........................**GREAT BRITAIN & IRELAND 4**
At Wilderspool Stadium, Warrington, Friday 24 November 2000
New Zealand: T - Hina 2, Te Amo 2, Presland; G - Hina 2, Mariu
Great Britain: T - Land
New Zealand: Kat Howard, Sharlene Johnson, Michelle Driscoll, Selena Te Amo, Stacey O'Carroll, Trish Hina, Laura Mariu , Nicole Presland, Tracy Wrigley, Louise Avaiki, Rachel White, Nadene Conlon, Tasha Davie. Subs: Miriama Niha, Leah Witehira, Somma Te Kahu, Hanu Wainohu
Great Britain: Joanne Hewson, Dani Titterington, Allison Kitchin, Natalie Gilmour, Teresa Bruce, Brenda Dobek, Wendy Charnley, Paula Tunnicliffe, Shelley Land, Lisa Macintosh, Jane Bank, Rebecca Stevens, Sally Milburn. Subs: Sam Bailey, Michelle Handley, Sarah Roper, Gemma Walsh

WORLD CUP 2000 QUALIFYING TOURNAMENT

MEDITERRANEAN GROUP

ITALY 16 ....**LEBANON 36**
at Stade Jean Laffon, Perpignan, Thursday 11th November, 1999
Italy: T - Riolo, Barbaro, Salafia; G - Salafia 2
Lebanon: T - Coorey, Lambert, Salem 2, Chalal, Daher; G - H El Masri 6

ITALY 34 ....**MOROCCO 0**
at Stade de Minimes, Toulouse, Sunday 14th November, 1999
Italy: T - Riolo 3, Margheritini, Napoli, Di Paolo; G - Margheritini 5

LEBANON 104..**MOROCCO 0**
at Parc Des Sports, Avignon, Wednesday 17th November, 1999
Lebanon: T - Salem 5, H El Masri 4, Lambert, Chalal 3, Khoury, Touma, N Saleh, Coorey, Chehade; G - H El Masri 16

MEDITERRANEAN GROUP TABLE

	P	W	D	L	F	A	Pts
Lebanon	2	2	0	0	140	16	4
Italy	2	1	0	1	50	36	2
Morocco	2	0	0	2	0	138	0

PACIFIC GROUP

UNITED STATES 54 ....**JAPAN 0**
at Disney's Wide World of Sports, Orlando, Tuesday 9th November, 1999
United States: T- Craig, Balachandran, Broussard 3, Mains, Matautia, Niu, Sheridan, Fabri, Faimalo; G - Niu 4, David Bowe

JAPAN 14 ....**CANADA 0**
at Disney's Wide World of Sports, Orlando, Thurs 11th Nov, 1999
Japan: T - Bannister, Ueda, Kanemura; G - Tateyama

UNITED STATES 68 ....**CANADA 0**
at Disney's Wide World of Sports, Orlando, Monday 15th November, 1999
United States: T - Fabri, Sheridan 3, Broussard 3, Warren 2, Mains, Matautia 2, Faimalo; G - Niu 7, Bowe

PACIFIC GROUP TABLE

	P	W	D	L	F	A	Pts
USA	2	2	0	0	122	0	4
Japan	2	1	0	1	14	54	2
Canada	2	0	0	2	0	82	0

FINAL

UNITED STATES 8 ....**LEBANON 62**
at Disney's Wide World of Sports, Orlando, Sunday 21st November, 1999
United States: T - Mains; G - Niu 2
Lebanon: T - Coorey 3, Khoury 2, Chehade, Chalal, Lambert, Touma, H El Masri, Salem; G - H El Masri 9

WORLD CUP
RECORDS 1954 - 1995

1954

FRANCE 22 ....**NEW ZEALAND 13**
At Parc de Princes, Paris, Saturday, October 30, 1954
Attendance: 13,240; **Referee:** Cyril Appleton (England)
France: T - Contrastin, Delaye, Crespo, Audobert;
G - Puig Aubert 5
New Zealand: T - Edwards, Eastlake, McKay; G - Bond 2
France: Puig Aubert (c), Vincent Cantoni, Jackie Merquey, Antoine
Jiminez, Raymond Contrastin, Claude Teisseire, Gilbert Benausse,
Francois Rinaldi, Jean Audoubert, Joseph Krawzyk, Guy Delaye,
Jean Pambrun, Joseph Crespo.
New Zealand: Doug Anderson, Jim Edwards, Cyril Eastlake (c),
George Menzies, Ron McKay, Bill Sorensen, Bill McLennan, Lory
Blanchard, Cliff Johnson, John Bond, John Yates, Lenny Eriksen.

GREAT BRITAIN 28 ....**AUSTRALIA 13**
At Stade de Gerland, Lyon, Sunday, October 31, 1954
Attendance: 10,250; **Referee:** Rene Guidicelli (France)
Great Britain: T - Brown 2, Jackson 2, Kitchen, Rose;
G - Ledgard 5
Australia: T- Wells 2, Kearney; G - Pidding 2
Great Britain: Jim Ledgard, David Rose, Phil Jackson, Mick
Sullivan, Frank Kitchen, Gordon Brown, Gerry Helme, Bob
Coverdale, Sam Smith, John Thorley, Don Robinson, Basil Watts,
Dave Valentine (c).
Australia: Clive Churchill (c), Noel Pidding, Alex Watson, Harry
Wells, Ian Moir, Ken McCaffery, Keith Holman, Roy Bull, Ken
Kearney, Duncan Hall, Brian Davies, Norm Provan, Peter Diversi.

AUSTRALIA 34 ....**NEW ZEALAND 15**
At Marseilles, Sunday, November 7, 1954
Attendance: 20,000; **Referee:** Rene Guidicelli (France)
Australia: T - Watson 3, Hawick, Bull, Kearney, O'Shea, Diversi;
G - Pidding 5
New Zealand: T - Eriksen; G - McKay 6
Australia: Clive Churchill (c), Noel Pidding, Alex Watson, Harry
Wells, Denis Flannery, Bob Banks, Greg Hawick, Roy Bull, Ken
Kearney, Brian Davies, Kel O'Shea, Mick Crocker, Peter Diversi.
New Zealand: Nev Denton, Jim Edwards, Cyril Eastlake (c), Ron
McKay, George Menzies, Bill Sorensen, Lenny Eriksen, Bill
McLennan, Lory Blanchard, Cliff Johnson, Jock Butterfield, John
Yates, Alister Atkinson.

FRANCE 13 ....**GREAT BRITAIN 13**
At Toulouse, Sunday, November 7, 1954
Attendance: 37,471 *(French record)*
Referee: Cyril Appleton (England)
France: T - Contrastin 2, Krawzyk; G - Puig Aubert 2
Great Britain: T - Rose, Brown, Helme; G - Ledgard 2
France: Puig Aubert (c), Vincent Cantoni, Jackie Merquey, Antoine
Jiminez, Raymond Contrastin, Gilbert Benausse, Joseph Crespo,
Francois Rinaldi, Jean Audoubert, Joseph Krawzyk, Guy Delaye,
Jean Pambrun, Roger Guilhem.
Great Britain: Jim Ledgard, David Rose, Phil Jackson, Albert
Naughton, Mick Sullivan, Gordon Brown, Gerry Helme, Bob
Coverdale, Sam Smith, John Thorley, Don Robinson, Basil Watts,
Dave Valentine (c).

FRANCE 15 ....**AUSTRALIA 5**
At Nantes, Thursday, November 11, 1954
Attendance: 13,000; **Referee:** Cyril Appleton (England)
France: T - Merquey, Contrastin, Cantoni; G - Puig Aubert 3
Australia: T - O'Shea; G - Pidding
France: Puig Aubert (c), Vincent Cantoni, Jackie Merquey, Claude
Teissiere, Raymond Contrastin, Antoine Jiminez, Joseph Crespo,

Francois Rinaldi, Jean Audoubert, Joseph Krawzyk, Armand Save,
Jean Pambrun, Gilbert Verdie
Australia: Clive Churchill (c), Noel Pidding, Alex Watson, Greg
Hawick, Denis Flannery, Bob Banks, Keith Holman, Roy Bull, Ken
Kearney, Brian Davies, Kel O'Shea, Mick Crocker, Peter Diversi.

GREAT BRITAIN 26 ....**NEW ZEALAND 6**
At Bordeaux, Thursday, November 11, 1954
Attendance: 14,000; **Referee:** Rene Guidicelli (France)
Great Britain: T - Kitchen 2, Brown, Rose, Jackson, Ledgard;
G - Ledgard 4
New Zealand: G - McKay 3
Great Britain: Jim Ledgard, David Rose, Phil Jackson, Mick
Sullivan, Frank Kitchen, Gordon Brown, Gerry Helme, Bob
Coverdale, Sam Smith, John Thorley, Don Robinson, Basil Watts,
Dave Valentine (c).
New Zealand: Ian Grey, Jim Edwards, Cyril Eastlake (c), Ron
McKay, Jim Austin, Bill Sorensen, Lenny Eriksen, Bill McLennan,
Lory Blanchard, John Bond, Jock Butterfield, George McDonald,
Alister Atkinson.

FINAL TABLE

	P	W	D	L	F	A	Pts
Great Britain	3	2	1	0	67	32	5
France	3	2	1	0	50	31	5
Australia	3	1	0	2	52	58	2
New Zealand	3	0	0	3	34	82	0

FINAL

FRANCE 12 ....**GREAT BRITAIN 16**
At Parc de Princes, Paris, Saturday, November 13, 1954
Attendance: 30,368; **Referee:** Cyril Appleton (England)
France: T - Cantoni, Contrastin; G - Puig Aubert 3
Great Britain: T - Brown 2, Rose, Helme; G - Ledgard 2
France: Puig Aubert (c), Vincent Cantoni, Jackie Merquey, Claude
Teissiere, Raymond Contrastin, Antoine Jiminez, Joseph Crespo,
Francois Rinaldi, Jean Audoubert, Joseph Krawzyk, Armand Save,
Jean Pambrun, Gilbert Verdie.
Great Britain: Jim Ledgard, David Rose, Phil Jackson, Albert
Naughton, Mick Sullivan, Gordon Brown, Gerry Helme, Bob
Coverdale, Sam Smith, John Thorley, Don Robinson, Basil Watts,
Dave Valentine (c).

THE 1954 SQUADS

AUSTRALIA *(Coach: Vic Hey)*

	M	T	G	Pts
Bob Banks (Toowoomba)	2	-	-	-
Roy Bull (Manly-Warringah)	3	1	-	3
Clive Churchill (South Sydney) (c)	3	-	-	-
Mick Crocker (Parramatta)	2	-	-	-
Brian Davies (Brisbane Brothers)	3	-	-	-
Peter Diversi (North Sydney)	3	1	-	3
Denis Flannery (Ipswich)	2	-	-	-
Duncan Hall (Brisbane Wests)	1	-	-	-
Greg Hawick (South Sydney)	2	1	-	3
Keith Holman (Western Suburbs)	2	-	-	-
Ken Kearney (St George)	3	2	-	6
Ken McCaffery (Toowoomba)	1	-	-	-
Ian Moir (South Sydney)	1	-	-	-
Kel O'Shea (Ayr)	2	2	-	6
Noel Pidding (Maitland)	3	-	8	16
Norm Provan (St George)	1	-	-	-
Alex Watson (Brisbane Wests)	3	3	-	9
Harry Wells (Wollongong)	2	2	-	6

FRANCE *(Coaches: Jean Duhau & Rene Duffort)*

	M	T	G	Pts
Jean Audobert (Lyon)	4	1	-	3
Gilbert Benausse (Carcassonne)	2	-	-	-
Vincent Cantoni (Toulouse)	4	2	-	6
Andre Carrere (Villeneuve)a	-	-	-	-
Raymond Contrastin (Bordeaux)	4	5	-	15
Joseph Crespo (Lyon)	4	1	-	3
Guy Delaye (Avignon)	2	1	-	3
Roger Guilhem (Carcassonne)	1	-	-	-
Antoine Jiminez (Villeneuve)	4	-	-	-
Joseph Krawzyck (Lyon)	4	1	-	3
Jackie Merquey (Avignon)	4	1	-	3
Jean Pambrun (Marseille)	4	-	-	-
Francois Rinaldi (Marseille)	4	-	-	-
Puig Aubert (XIII Catalan) (c)	4	-	13	26
Armand Save (Bordeaux)	2	-	-	-
Claude Teissiere (Carcassonne)	3	-	-	-
Gilbert Verdie (Albi)	2	-	-	-
Maurice Voron (Lyon)	-	-	-	-

GREAT BRITAIN *(Coach: Joe Egan ●)*

	M	T	G	Pts
Billy Banks (Huddersfield)	-	-	-	-
Harry Bradshaw (Huddersfield)	-	-	-	-
Gordon Brown (Leeds)	4	6	-	18
Bob Coverdale (Hull)	4	-	-	-
Gerry Helme (Warrington)	4	2	-	6
Phil Jackson (Barrow)	4	3	-	9
Frank Kitchen (Leigh)	2	3	-	9
Jim Ledgard (Leigh)	4	1	13	29
Albert Naughton (Warrington)	2	-	-	-
Don Robinson (Wakefield Trinity)	4	-	-	-
David Rose (Leeds)	4	4	-	12
Ron Rylance (Huddersfield)	-	-	-	-
Sam Smith (Hunslet)	4	-	-	-
Mick Sullivan (Huddersfield)	4	-	-	-
John Thorley (Halifax)	4	-	-	-
Dave Valentine (Huddersfield) (c)	4	-	-	-
Basil Watts (York)	4	-	-	-
Johnny Whiteley (Hull)	4	-	-	-

● *pre-tournament only - no coach in France*

NEW ZEALAND *(Coach: Jim Amos)*

	M	T	G	Pts
Doug Anderson (Auckland)	1	-	-	-
Alister Atkinson (Canterbury)	2	-	-	-
Jim Austin (Auckland)	1	-	-	-
Lory Blanchard (Canterbury)	3	-	-	-
John Bond (Canterbury)	2	-	2	4
Jock Butterfield (Canterbury)	2	-	-	-
Nev Denton (Auckland)	1	-	-	-
Cyril Eastlake (Auckland) (c)	3	1	-	3
Jim Edwards (Auckland)	3	1	-	3
Lenny Eriksen (Auckland)	3	1	-	3
Ian Grey (Auckland)	1	-	-	-
Cliff Johnson (Auckland)	2	-	-	-
George McDonald (Waikato)	1	-	-	-
Ron McKay (Taranaki)	3	1	9	21
Bill McLennan (West Coast)	3	-	-	-
George Menzies (West Coast)	2	-	-	-
Bill Sorensen (Auckland)	3	-	-	-
John Yates (Auckland)	2	-	-	-

1957

AUSTRALIA 25 ....**NEW ZEALAND 5**
At Brisbane Cricket Ground, Saturday, June 15, 1957
Attendance: 29,636; **Referee:** Vic Belsham (New Zealand)
Australia: T - Provan, Carlson, O'Shea, Moir, Wells; G - Barnes 5
New Zealand: T - Johnson; G - Sorensen
Australia: Keith Barnes, Ian Moir, Harry Wells, Dick Poole (c), Brian Carlson, Greg Hawick, Keith Holman, Brian Davies, Ken Kearney, Bill Marsh, Norm Provan, Kel O'Shea, Brian Clay.
New Zealand: Pat Creedy, Vern Bakalich, Bill Sorensen, Ron Ackland, Tom Hadfield, George Menzies, Sel Belsham, Henry Maxwell, Jock Butterfield, Bill McLennan, John Yates, Cliff Johnson (c), Rex Percy.

GREAT BRITAIN 23 ....**FRANCE 5**
At Sydney Cricket Ground, Saturday, June 15, 1957
Attendance: 50,007; **Referee:** Darcy Lawler (Australia)
Great Britain: T - Sullivan 2, Boston, Stevenson, Jackson; G - Jones 4
France: T - Merquey; G - Benausse
Great Britain: Glyn Moses, Billy Boston, Phil Jackson, Alan Davies, Mick Sullivan, Lewis Jones, Jeff Stevenson, Alan Prescott (c), Tommy Harris, Syd Little, Jack Grundy, Geoff Gunney, Derek Turner.
France: Andre Rives, Guy Husson, Antoine Jiminez, Jackie Merquey (c), Maurice Voron, Gilbert Benausse, Rene Jean, Rene Ferrero, Nick Appelian, Gabriel Berthomieu, Armand Save, Augustin Parent, Jean Rouqueirol.

AUSTRALIA 31 ....**GREAT BRITAIN 6**
At Sydney Cricket Ground, Monday, June 17, 1957
Attendance: 57,955; **Referee:** Vic Belsham (New Zealand)
Australia: T - McCaffery 2, Moir 2, O'Shea, Wells, Clay; G - Carlson 4, Davies
Great Britain: G - Jones 3
Australia: Brian Carlson, Ian Moir, Harry Wells, Dick Poole (c), Alex Watson, Brian Clay, Ken McCaffery, Brian Davies, Ken Kearney, Bill Marsh, Norm Provan, Kel O'Shea, Don Schofield.
Great Britain: Glyn Moses, Billy Boston, Eric Ashton, Alan Davies, Mick Sullivan, Lewis Jones, Jeff Stevenson, Alan Prescott (c), Tommy Harris, Syd Little, Jack Grundy, Johnny Whiteley, Derek Turner.

NEW ZEALAND 10 ....**FRANCE 14**
At Brisbane Exhibition Ground, Monday, June 17, 1957
Attendance: 22,142; **Referee:** Darcy Lawler (Australia)
New Zealand: T - Sorensen, Hadfield; G - Creedy, Sorensen
France: T - Foussat 2; G - Benausse 4
New Zealand: Pat Creedy, Vern Bakalich, Bill Sorensen, Ron Ackland, Tom Hadfield, George Menzies, Sel Belsham, Henry Maxwell, Jock Butterfield, Bill McLennan, John Yates, Cliff Johnson (c), Rex Percy.
France: Andre Rives, Guy Husson, Jackie Merquey (c), Maurice Voron, Jean Foussat, Gilbert Benausse, Rene Jean, Henri Delhoste, Nick Appelian, Robert Medus, Gabriel Berthomieu, Augustin Parent, Jean Rouqueirol.

AUSTRALIA 26 ....**FRANCE 9**
At Sydney Cricket Ground, Saturday, June 22, 1957
Attendance: 35,158; **Referee:** Vic Belsham (New Zealand)
Australia: T - Carlson, Poole, O'Shea, Marsh; G - Carlson 7
France: T - Benausse; G - Benausse 3
Australia: Brian Carlson, Ian Moir, Harry Wells, Dick Poole (c), Alex Watson, Brian Clay, Ken McCaffery, Brian Davies, Ken Kearney, Bill Marsh, Norm Provan, Kel O'Shea, Don Schofield.
France: Andre Rives, Guy Husson, Antoine Jiminez (c), Jean Foussat, Maurice Voron, Gilbert Benausse, Rene Jean, Henri Delhoste, Nick Appelian, Rene Ferrero, Robert Medus, Augustin Parent, Francis Levy.

NEW ZEALAND 29 ....**GREAT BRITAIN 21**
At Sydney Cricket Ground, Tuesday, June 25, 1957
Attendance: 14,263; **Referee:** Darcy Lawler (Australia)
New Zealand: T - Hadfield, Turner, Menzies, McLennan, Riddell; G - Sorensen 7
Great Britain: T - Jackson, Jones, Sullivan, Little, Grundy; G - Jones 3
New Zealand: Pat Creedy, Reece Griffiths, George Turner, Bill Sorensen, Tom Hadfield, George Menzies, Sel Belsham, Henry Maxwell, Jock Butterfield, Bill McLennan, John Yates, Jim Riddell.
Great Britain: Glyn Moses, Eric Ashton, Phil Jackson, Lewis Jones, Mick Sullivan, Austin Rhodes, Jeff Stevenson, Alan Prescott (c), Tom McKinney, Syd Little, Jack Grundy, Geoff Gunney, Derek Turner.

FINAL TABLE

	P	W	D	L	F	A	Pts
Australia	3	3	0	0	82	20	6
Great Britain	3	1	0	2	50	65	2
New Zealand	3	1	0	2	44	60	2
France	3	1	0	2	28	59	2

No Final required. Australia won the Cup.

AUSTRALIA 20 ....**REST OF THE WORLD 11**
At Sydney Cricket Ground, Saturday, June 22, 1954
Attendance: 30,675; **Referee:** Vic Belsham (New Zealand)
Australia: T - Provan, Moir, Poole, Ritchie; G - Carlson 3; FG - Carlson
World: T - Benausse, Ashton, Merquey; G - Sorensen
Australia: Brian Carlson, Ian Moir, Harry Wells, Dick Poole (c), Ray Ritchie, Greg Hawick, Ken McCaffery, Brian Davies, Ken Kearney, Bill Marsh, Norm Provan, Kel O'Shea, Brian Clay.
World: Lewis Jones (GB), Maurice Voron (France), Jackie Merquey (France) (c), Bill Sorensen (NZ), Eric Ashton (GB), Gilbert Benausse (France), Sel Belsham (NZ), Cliff Johnson (NZ), Nick Appelian (France), Henry Maxwell (NZ), Geoff Gunney (GB), Jim Riddell (NZ), John Whiteley (GB).

THE 1957 SQUADS

AUSTRALIA *(Captain-coach: Dick Poole)*

	M	T	G	Pts
Keith Barnes (Balmain)	1	-	5	10
Brian Carlson (Blackall) ●	4	2	15	36
Brian Clay (St George)	4	1	-	3
Brian Davies (Brisbane Brothers)	4	-	1	2
Greg Hawick (Wagga Wagga)	2	-	-	-
Keith Holman (Western Suburbs)	1	-	-	-
Ken Kearney (St George)	4	-	-	-
Ken McCaffery (North Sydney)	3	2	-	6
Bill Marsh (Balmain)	4	1	-	3
Ian Moir (South Sydney)	4	4	-	12

Kel O'Shea (Western Suburbs)	4	3	-	9
Dick Poole (Newtown) (c)	4	2	-	6
Norm Provan (St George)	4	2	-	6
Ray Ritchie (Manly-Warringah)	1	1	-	3
Don Schofield (Cessnock)	2	-	-	-
Tom Tyquin (Brisbane Souths)	-	-	-	-
Alex Watson (Brisbane Wests)	2	-	-	-
Harry Wells (Western Suburbs)	4	2	-	6

● *sacked by club at start of World Cup*

GREAT BRITAIN *(Captain-coach: Alan Prescott)*

	M	T	G	Pts
Eric Ashton (Wigan)	3●	1	-	3
Billy Boston (Wigan)	2	1	-	3
Alan Davies (Oldham)	2	-	-	-
Phil Jackson (Barrow)	2	2	-	6
Jack Grundy (Barrow)	3	1	-	3
Geoff Gunney (Hunslet)	3●	-	-	-
Tommy Harris (Hull)	2	-	-	-
Lewis Jones (Leeds)	4●	1	10	23
Syd Little (Oldham)	3	1	-	3
Tom McKinney (St Helens)	1	-	-	-
Glyn Moses (St Helens)	3	-	-	-
Alan Prescott (St Helens) (c)	3	-	-	-
Ray Price (Warrington)	-	-	-	-
Austin Rhodes (St Helens)	1	-	-	-
Jeff Stevenson (Leeds)	3	1	-	3
Mick Sullivan (Huddersfield)	3	3	-	9
Derek Turner (Oldham)	3	-	-	-
Johnny Whiteley (Hull)	1	-	-	-

● *one match for Rest of the World*

FRANCE *(Coach: Jean Duhau)*

	M	T	G	Pts
Nick Appelian (Marseille)	4●	-	-	-
Gilbert Benausse (Carcassonne)	4●	2	8	22
Gabriel Berthomieu (Albi)	2	-	-	-
Henri Delhoste (XIII Catalan)	2	-	-	-
Rene Ferrero (Marseille)	2	-	-	-
Jean Foussat (Villeneuve)	2	2	-	6
Guy Husson (Albi)	3	-	-	-
Rene Jean (Avignon)	3	-	-	-
Antoine Jiminez (Villeneuve)	2	-	-	-
Francis Levy (XIII Catalan)	1	-	-	-
Robert Medus (XIII Catalan)	2	-	-	-
Jackie Merquey (c) (Avignon)	3●	2	-	6
Augustin Parent (Avignon)	3	-	-	-
Andre Rives (Albi)	3	-	-	-
Jean Rouqueirol (Avignon)	2	-	-	-
Arnaud Save (Bordeaux)	1	-	-	-
Gilbert Verdier (Albi)	-	-	-	-
Maurice Voron (Lyon)	4●	-	-	-

● *one match for Rest of the World*

NEW ZEALAND *(Coach: Bill Telford)*

	M	T	G	Pts
Ron Ackland (Auckland)	2	-	-	-
Vern Bakalich (Auckland)	2	-	-	-
Keith Bell (Auckland)	-	-	-	-
Sel Belsham (Auckland)	4●	-	-	-
Jock Butterfield (Canterbury)	2	-	-	-
Pat Creedy (Canterbury)	3	-	1	2
Tom Hadfield (Auckland)	3	2	-	6
Reece Griffiths (West Coast)	1	-	-	-
Cliff Johnson (Auckland) (c)	4●	1	-	3
Bill McLennan (West Coast)	3	1	-	3
Henry Maxwell (Auckland)	4●	-	-	-
George Menzies (West Coast)	3	1	-	3
Kevin Pearce (Canterbury)	-	-	-	-
Rex Percy (Auckland)	1	-	-	-
Jim Riddell (Auckland)	2●	1	-	3
Bill Sorensen (Auckland)	4●	1	10	23
George Turner (Auckland)	1	1	-	3
John Yates (Auckland)	3	-	-	-

● *one match for Rest of the World*

1960

GREAT BRITAIN 23 ....**NEW ZEALAND 8**
At Odsal Stadium, Bradford, Saturday, September 24, 1960
Attendance: 20,577; **Referee:** Edouard Martung (France)
Great Britain: T - Ashton, Davies, Myler, Murphy, McTigue;
G - Fraser 4
New Zealand: T - Hadfield, Cooke; G - Sorensen
Great Britain: Eric Fraser, Bobby Greenhough, Eric Ashton (c),
Alan Davies, Mike Sullivan, Frank Myler, Alex Murphy, Jack
Wilkinson, Tommy Harris, Brian McTigue, Johnny Whiteley, Vince
Karalius, Derek Turner.
New Zealand: Cyril Eastlake, Tom Hadfield, George Turner, Bill
Sorensen, Neville Denton, George Menzies, Keith Roberts, Cliff
Johnson (c), Jock Butterfield, Henry Maxwell, Ron Ackland, Trevor
Kilkelly, Mel Cooke.

AUSTRALIA 13 ....**FRANCE 12**
At Central Park, Wigan, Saturday, September 24, 1960
Attendance: 20,278; **Referee:** Eric Clay (Great Britain)
Australia: T - Raper, Kelly, Gasnier; G - Carlson 2
France: T - Gruppi 2; G - Lacaze 3
Australia: Brian Carlson, Ken Irvine, Reg Gasnier, Harry Wells,
Lionel Morgan, Tony Brown, Barry Muir (c), Dud Beattie, Noel
Kelly, Rex Mossop, Elton Rasmussen, Brian Hambly, Johnny
Raper.
France: Louis Poletti, Jacques Dubon, Claude Mantoulan, Roger
Rey, Raymond Gruppi, Jackie Merquey, Georges Fages, Aldo
Quaglio, Andre Casas, Angelo Boldini, Robert Eramouspe, Jean
Barthe (c), Andre Lacaze.

GREAT BRITAIN 33 ....**FRANCE 7**
At Station Road, Swinton, Saturday, October 1, 1960
Attendance: 22,923; **Referee:** Edouard Martung (France)
Great Britain: T - Rhodes 2, Davies 2, Wilkinson, Sullivan, Myler;
G - Fraser 6
France: T - Dubon; G - Lacaze 2
Great Britain: Eric Fraser, Jim Challinor, Austin Rhodes, Alan
Davies, Mike Sullivan, Frank Myler, Alex Murphy, Jack Wilkinson,
John Shaw, Brian McTigue, Brian Shaw, Vince Karalius, Johnny
Whiteley (c).
France: Louis Poletti, Jacques Dubon, Claude Mantoulan, Roger
Rey, Raymond Gruppi, Jackie Merquey, Joseph Guiraud, Aldo
Quaglio, Andre Casas, Robert Eramouspe, Jean.Barthe (c), Yves
Mezard, Andre Lacaze.

AUSTRALIA 21 ....**NEW ZEALAND 15**
At Headingley, Leeds, Saturday, October 1, 1960
Attendance: 10,773; **Referee:** Eric Clay (Great Britain)
Australia: T - Carlson 3, Gasnier, Wells; G - Carlson 3
New Zealand: T - Hadfield, Turner, Menzies; G - Eastlake 3
Australia: Keith Barnes (c), Ken Irvine, Reg Gasnier, Harry Wells,
Brian Carlson, Tony Brown, Barry Muir, Dud Beattie, Noel Kelly,
Gary Parcell, Rex Mossop, Brian Hambly, Johnny Raper.
New Zealand: Gary Phillips, Tom Hadfield, George Turner, Cyril
Eastlake, Neville Denton, George Menzies, Keith Roberts, Cliff
Johnson (c), Jock Butterfield, Henry Maxwell, Ron Ackland, Laurie
Oliff, Mel Cooke.

GREAT BRITAIN 10 ....**AUSTRALIA 3**
At Odsal Stadium, Bradford, Saturday, October 8, 1960
Attendance: 32,773; **Referee:** Edouard Martung (France)
Great Britain: T - Boston, Sullivan; G - Rhodes 2
Australia: T - Carlson
Great Britain: Austin Rhodes, Billy Boston, Eric Ashton (c), Alan
Davies, Mike Sullivan, Frank Myler, Alex Murphy, Jack Wilkinson,
John Shaw, Brian McTigue, Brian Shaw, Derek Turner, Vince
Karalius.
Australia: Keith Barnes (c), Ron Boden, Reg Gasnier, Harry Wells,
Brian Carlson, Tony Brown, Barry Muir, Dud Beattie, Noel Kelly,
Gary Parcell, Rex Mossop, Elton Rasmussen, Brian Hambly.

FRANCE 0 ....**NEW ZEALAND 9**
At Central Park, Wigan, Saturday, October 8, 1960
Attendance: 2,876; **Referee:** Eric Clay (Great Britain)
New Zealand: T - Reid; G - Eastlake 3
France: Louis Poletti, Jacques Dubon, Claude Mantoulan, Roger
Rey, Raymond Gruppi, Jackie Merquey, Georges Fages, Aldo
Quaglio, Andre Vadon, Aldo Boldini, Robert Eramouspe,
Jean.Barthe (c), Andre Lacaze.
New Zealand: Gary Phillips, Tom Hadfield, George Turner, Cyril
Eastlake, Reece Griffiths, George Menzies, Keith Roberts, Cliff
Johnson (c), Jock Butterfield, Tom Reid, Ron Ackland, Laurie Oliff,
Mel Cooke.

FINAL TABLE

	P	W	D	L	F	A	Pts
Great Britain	3	3	0	0	66	18	6
Australia	3	2	0	1	37	37	4
New Zealand	3	1	0	2	32	44	2
France	3	0	0	3	19	55	0

No Final required. Great Britain won the Cup.

GREAT BRITAIN 33 ....**REST OF THE WORLD 27**
At Odsal Stadium, Bradford, Monday, October 10, 1960
Attendance: 3,908; **Referee:** Edouard Martung (France)
Great Britain: T - Murphy 2, Myler 2, Ashton 2, Sullivan, Davies, B
Shaw; G - Rhodes 3
World: T - Menzies 3, Gruppi 2, Hadfield, Gourbal; G - Mantoulan
2, Eastlake
Great Britain: Austin Rhodes, Jim Challinor, Eric Ashton (c), Alan
Davies, Mike Sullivan, Frank Myler, Alex Murphy, Jack Wilkinson,
John Shaw, Brian McTigue, Brian Shaw, Derek Turner, Vince
Karalius.
World: Cyril Eastlake (NZ), Tom Hadfield (NZ), Ron Boden (Aust),
Claude Mantoulan (France), Raymond Gruppi (France), George
Menzies (NZ), Barry Muir (Aust), Cliff Johnson (NZ) (c), Bill
Rayner (Aust), Dud Beattie (Aust), Robert Eramouspe (France),
Yvon Gourbal (France), Brian Hambly (Aust).

World Cup Records

THE 1960 SQUADS

AUSTRALIA *(Captain-coach: Keith Barnes)*

	M	T	G	Pts
Keith Barnes (Balmain) (c)	2	-	-	-
Dud Beattie (Ipswich)	4●	-	-	-
Bob Bugden (St George)	-	-	-	-
Bill Rayner (Parramatta)	1●	-	-	-
Ron Boden (Parramatta)	2●	-	-	-
Brian Carlson (North Sydney)	3	4	5	22
Reg Gasnier (St George)	3	2	-	6
Brian Hambly (Parramatta)	4●	-	-	-
Ken Irvine (North Sydney)	2	-	-	-
Noel Kelly (Ipswich)	3	1	-	3
Lionel Morgan (Wynnum-Manly)	1	-	-	-
Rex Mossop (Manly-Warringah)	3	-	-	-
Barry Muir (Brisbane Wests)	4●	-	-	-
Gary Parcell (Ipswich)	3	-	-	-
Johnny Raper (St George)	2	1	-	3
Elton Rasmussen (Toowoomba)	1	-	-	-
Harry Wells (Western Suburbs)	3	1	-	3

● one match for Rest of the World

FRANCE *(Coaches: Rene Duffort & Jean Duhau)*

	M	T	G	Pts
Jean Barthe (Roanne) (c)	3	-	-	-
Angelo Boldini (Villeneuve)	2	-	-	-
Andre Casas (XIII Catalan)	2	-	-	-
Jacques Dubon (Villeneuve)	3	1	-	3
Robert Eramouspe (Roanne)	4●	-	-	-
George Fages (Albi)	2	-	-	-
Yvon Gourbal (XIII Catalan)	2●	1	-	3
Raymond Gruppi (Villeneuve)	4●	4	-	12
Joseph Guiraud (Limoux)	1	-	-	-
Andre Lacaze (Villeneuve)	3	-	5	10
Claude Mantoulan (Roanne)	4●	-	2	4
Andre Marty (Carcassonne)	-	-	-	-
Jackie Merquey (Villeneuve)	3	-	-	-
Yves Mezard (Avignon)	1	-	-	-
Louis Poletti (Carcassonne)	3	-	-	-
Aldo Quaglio (Roanne)	3	-	-	-
Roger Rey (Avignon)	3	-	-	-
Andre Vadon (Albi)	3	-	-	-

● one match for Rest of the World

GREAT BRITAIN *(Captain-coach: Eric Ashton)*

	M	T	G	Pts
Eric Ashton (Wigan) (c)	3●	3	-	9
Billy Boston (Wigan)	1	1	-	3
Jim Challinor (Warrington)	2●	-	-	-
Alan Davies (Oldham)	4●	3	-	9
Eric Fraser (Warrington)	2	1	10	23
Bobby Greenhough (Warrington)	1	-	-	-
Tommy Harris (Hull)	1	-	-	-
Vince Karalius (St Helens)	4●	-	-	-
Brian McTigue (Wigan)	4●	1	-	3
Alex Murphy (St Helens)	4●	3	-	9
Frank Myler (Widnes)	4●	4	-	12
Austin Rhodes (St Helens)	3●	2	5	16
Brian Shaw (Hunslet)	3●	1	-	3
John Shaw (Halifax)	3●	-	-	-
Mick Sullivan (Wigan)	4●	3	-	9
Derek Turner (Wakefield Trinity)	3●	-	-	-
Johnny Whiteley (Hull)	2	-	-	-
Jack Wilkinson (Wakefield Trinity)	4●	1	-	3

● one match for Rest of the World

NEW ZEALAND *(Coach: Travers Hardwick)*

	M	T	G	Pts
Ron Ackland (Auckland)	3	-	-	-
Jock Butterfield (Canterbury)	3	-	-	-
Mel Cooke (Canterbury)	3	1	-	3
Ron Cooke (Auckland)	-	-	-	-
Neville Denton (Auckland)	2	-	-	-
Cyril Eastlake (Auckland)	4●	-	7	14
Reece Griffiths (West Coast)	1	-	-	-
Tom Hadfield (Auckland)	4●	3	-	9
Cliff Johnson (Auckland) (c)	4●	-	-	-
Henry Maxwell (Auckland)	2	-	-	-
George Menzies (West Coast)	4●	4	-	12
Laurie Oliff (Auckland)	2	-	-	-
Gary Phillips (Auckland)	3	-	-	-
T om Reid (West Coast)	1	1	-	3
Keith Roberts (Canterbury)	3	-	-	-
Bill Sorensen (Auckland)	1	-	1	2
George Turner (Auckland)	3	1	-	3

● one match for Rest of the World

1968

AUSTRALIA 25 .... **GREAT BRITAIN 10**
At Sydney Cricket Ground, Saturday, May 25, 1968
Attendance: 62,256; **Referee:** John Percival (New Zealand)

Australia: T - Coote, Smith, Raper; G - Simms 8
Great Britain: T - Brooke, Sullivan; G - Risman 2
Australia: Eric Simms, John Rhodes, Johnny Greaves, Graeme Langlands, Johnny King, Tony Branson, Billy Smith, John Wittenberg, Fred Jones, Arthur Beetson, Dick Thornett, Ron Coote, Johnny Raper (c).
Great Britain: Bev Risman (c), Ian Brooke, Mick Shoebottom, Alan Burwell, Clive Sullivan, Roger Millward, Tommy Bishop, Cliff Watson, Kevin Ashcroft, Mick Clark, Bob Haigh, Ray French, Charlie Renilson.

NEW ZEALAND 10 ....**FRANCE 15**
At Carlaw Park, Auckland, Saturday, May 25, 1968
Attendance: 18,000; **Referee:** Col Pearce (Australia)
New Zealand: G - Wiggs 5
France: T - Capdouze; G - Capdouze 5, Garrigue
New Zealand: Roger Tait, Bob Mincham, Ray Sinel, Paul Schultz, Ernie Wiggs, James Bond (c), Gary Clarke, Oscar Danielson, Colin O'Neil, Gary Smith, Brian Lee, Kevin Dixon, Tony Kriletich. Replacement: Henry Tatana.
France: Jean-Pierre Cros, Daniel Pellerin, Jean-Pierre Lecompte, Michel Molinier, Andre Ferren, Jean Capdouze, Roger Garrigue, Christian Sabatie, Yves Begou, Georges Ailleres (c), Francis De Nadai, Henri Marracq, Jean-Pierre Clar.

AUSTRALIA 31 ....**NEW ZEALAND 12**
At Lang Park, Brisbane, Saturday, June 1, 1968
Attendance: 23,608; **Referee:** John Percival (New Zealand)
Australia: T - King 2, Rhodes, Coote, Jones; G - Simms 6; FG - Simms 2
New Zealand: T - Dunn, Schultz; G - Wiggs 3
Australia: Eric Simms, John Rhodes, Johnny Greaves, Graeme Langlands, Johnny King, Tony Branson, Billy Smith, John Wittenberg, Fred Jones, Elton Rasmussen, Dick Thornett, Ron Coote, Johnny Raper (c). Replacement: Bob Fulton (for Branson).
New Zealand: Doug Ellwood, Bob Mincham, Spencer Dunn, Paul Schultz, Ernie Wiggs, James Bond (c), Gary Clarke, Henry Tatana, Colin O'Neil, Gary Smith, Kevin Dixon, Brian Lee, Tony Kriletich. Replacement: Roger Tait (for Bond)

GREAT BRITAIN 2 ....**FRANCE 7**
At Carlaw Park, Auckland, Sunday, June 2, 1968
Attendance: 15,760; **Referee:** Col Pearce (Australia)
Great Britain: G - Risman
France: T - Ledru; G - Garrigue, Capdouze
Great Britain: Bev Risman (c), John Atkinson, Ian Brooke, Alan Burwell, Clive Sullivan, Roger Millward, Tommy Bishop, Cliff Watson, Peter Flanagan, Mick Clark, Bob Haigh, Arnold Morgan, Charlie Renilson. Replacement: John Warlow.
France: Jean-Pierre Cros, Daniel Pellerin, Jean-Pierre Lecompte, Michel Molinier, Jean-Rene Ledru, Jean Capdouze, Roger Garrigue, Christian Sabatie, Yves Begou, Georges Ailleres (c), Herve Mazard, Henri Marracq, Jean-Pierre Clar.

AUSTRALIA 37 ....**FRANCE 4**
At Lang Park, Brisbane, Saturday, June 8, 1968
Attendance: 32,662; **Referee:** John Percival (New Zealand)
Australia: T - Williamson 2, Fulton 2, Greaves, Smith, Coote; G - Simms 5; FG - Smith 3
France: G - Capdouze 2
Australia: Eric Simms, Brian James, John Rhodes, Johnny Greaves, Lionel Williamson, Bob Fulton, Billy Smith, John Wittenberg, Brian Fitzsimmons, Arthur Beetson, Dennis Manteit, Ron Coote, Johnny Raper (c).
France: Jean-Pierre Cros, Andre Ferren, Michel Molinier, Jacques Gruppi, Jean-Rene Ledru, Jean Capdouze, Marius Frattini, Christian Sabatie, Yves Begou, Nestor Serrano, Adolphe Alesina, Herve Mazard, Jean-Pierre Clar. Replacement: Francis De Nadai (for Sabatie).

GREAT BRITAIN 38 ....**NEW ZEALAND 14**
At Sydney Cricket Ground, Saturday, June 8, 1968
Attendance: 14,105; **Referee:** Col Pearce (Australia)
Great Britain: T - Sullivan 3, Brooke, Burwell 2, Shoebottom, Morgan; G - Risman 7
New Zealand: Schultz 2; G - Wiggs 4
Great Britain: Bev Risman (c), John Atkinson, Ian Brooke, Alan Burwell, Clive Sullivan, Roger Millward, Tommy Bishop, John Warlow, Peter Flanagan, Mick Clark, Ray French, Arnold Morgan, Charlie Renilson. Replacements: Mick Shoebottom and Cliff Watson.
New Zealand: Doug Ellwood, Bob Mincham, Spencer Dunn, Paul Schultz, Ernie Wiggs, Roger Tait, Eric Carson, Colin McMaster, Colin O'Neil, Gary Smith, Ray Sinel, Brian Lee, Tony Kriletich. Replacement: Kevin Dixon.

FINAL TABLE

	P	W	D	L	F	A	Pts
Australia	3	3	0	0	93	26	6
France	3	2	0	1	26	49	4
Great Britain	3	1	0	2	50	46	2
New Zealand	3	0	0	3	36	84	0

FINAL

AUSTRALIA 20 ....**FRANCE 2**
At Sydney Cricket Ground, Monday, June 10, 1968
Attendance: 54,290; **Referee:** John Percival (New Zealand)
Australia: T - Williamson 2, Greaves, Coote; G - Simms 4
France: G - Capdouze
Australia: Eric Simms, John Rhodes, Johnny Greaves, Graeme Langlands, Lionel Williamson, Bob Fulton, Billy Smith, John Wittenberg, Fred Jones, Arthur Beetson, Dick Thornett, Ron Coote, Johnny Raper (c). Replacement: Elton Rasmussen.
France: Jean-Pierre Cros, Daniel Pellerin, Jacques Gruppi, Jean-Pierre Lecompte, Jean-Rene Ledru, Jean Capdouze, Roger Garrigue, Christian Sabatie, Yves Begou, Georges Ailleres (c), Francis De Nadai, Henri Marracq, Jean-Pierre Clar.

THE 1968 SQUADS

AUSTRALIA *(Coach: Harry Bath)*

	M	T	G	Pts
Arthur Beetson (Balmain)	3	-	-	-
Tony Branson (St George)	2	-	-	-
Ron Coote (South Sydney)	4	4	-	12
Brian Fitzsimmons (Townsville)	1	-	-	-
Bob Fulton (Manly-Warringah)	3	2	-	6
Johnny Greaves (Canterbury-Bankstown)	4	2	-	6
Brian James (South Sydney)	1	-	-	-
Fred Jones (Manly-Warringah)	3	1	-	3
Johnny King (St George)	2	2	-	6
Graeme Langlands (St George)	3	-	-	-
Dennis Manteit (Brisbane Brothers)	1	-	-	-
Johnny Raper (St George) (c)	4	1	-	3
Elton Rasmussen (St George)	2	-	-	-
John Rhodes (Canterbury-Bankstown)	4	1	-	3
Eric Simms (South Sydney)	4	-	25	50
Billy Smith (St George)	4	2	3	12
Dick Thornett (Parramatta)	3	-	-	-
Lionel Williamson (Innisfail)	2	4	-	12
John Wittenberg (St George)	4	-	-	-

FRANCE *(Coach: Rene Lacoste)*

	M	T	G	Pts
Georges Ailleres (c) (Toulouse)	3	-	-	-
Adolphe Alesina (Carcassonne)	1	-	-	-
Yves Begou (Toulouse)	4	-	-	-
Jean Capdouze (XIII Catalan)	4	1	9	21
Jean-Pierre Clar (Villeneuve)	4	-	-	-
Jean-Pierre Cros (Albi)	4	-	-	-
Francis De Nadai (Limoux)	3	-	-	-
Andre Ferren (Toulouse)	2	-	-	-
Marius Frattini (Avignon)	1	-	-	-
Roger Garrigue (Saint-Gaudens)	3	-	2	4
Jacques Gruppi (Villeneuve)	2	-	-	-
Jean-Pierre Lecompte (Saint-Gaudens)	3	-	-	-
Jean-Rene Ledru (Marseille)	3	1	-	3
Henri Marracq (Saint-Gaudens)	3	-	-	-
Herve Mazard (Lezignan)	2	-	-	-
Michel Molinier (Saint-Gaudens)	3	-	-	-
Daniel Pellerin (Villeneuve)	3	-	-	-
Christian Sabatie (Villeneuve)	4	-	-	-
Nestor Serrano (Saint-Gaudens)	1	-	-	-

GREAT BRITAIN *(Coach: Colin Hutton)*

	M	T	G	Pts
Kevin Ashcroft (Leigh)	1	-	-	-
John Atkinson (Leeds)	2	-	-	-
Tommy Bishop (St Helens)	2	-	-	-
Ian Brooke (Wakefield Trinity)	3	2	-	6
Alan Burwell (Hull Kingston Rovers)	3	2	-	6
Mick Clark (Leeds)	3	-	-	-
Derek Edwards (Castleford)	-	-	-	-
Peter Flanagan (Hull Kingston Rovers)	2	-	-	-
Ray French (Widnes)	2	-	-	-
Bob Haigh (Wakefield Trinity)	2	-	-	-
Roger Millward (Hull Kingston Rovers)	3	-	-	-
Arnold Morgan (Featherstone Rovers)	3	1	-	3
Charlie Renilson (Halifax)	3	-	-	-
Bev Risman (Leeds) (c)	3	-	10	20
Mick Shoebottom (Leeds)	2	1	-	3
Clive Sullivan (Hull)	3	4	-	12
John Warlow (St Helens)	2	-	-	-
Cliff Watson (St Helens)	3	-	-	-
Chris Young (Hull Kingston Rovers)	-	-	-	-

NEW ZEALAND *(Coach: Des Barchard)*

	M	T	G	Pts
James Bond (Canterbury) (c)	2	-	-	-
Eric Carson (Auckland)	1	-	-	-
Gary Clarke (Canterbury)	2	-	-	-
Oscar Danielson (Auckland)	1	-	-	-
Kevin Dixon (West Coast)	3	-	-	-
Spencer Dunn (Canterbury)	2	1	-	3
Doug Ellwood (Auckland)	2	-	-	-
Tony Kriletich (Auckland)	3	-	-	-
Brian Lee (Auckland)	3	-	-	-
Colin McMaster (West Coast)	1	-	-	-
Bob Mincham (Auckland)	3	-	-	-
Colin O'Neil (Wellington)	3	-	-	-
Dave Parkinson (Waikato)	-	-	-	-
Paul Schultz (Auckland)	3	3	-	9
Ray Sinel (Auckland)	2	-	-	-
Gary Smith (Wellington)	3	-	-	-
Roger Tait (Auckland)	3	-	-	-
Henry Tatana (Auckland)	2	-	-	-
Ernie Wiggs (Auckland)	3	-	12	24

1970

AUSTRALIA 47...**NEW ZEALAND 11**
At Central Park, Wigan, Wednesday, October 21, 1970
Attendance: 9,805; **Referee:** Billy Thompson (Great Britain)
Australia: T - Cootes 2, Branighan, Fulton, Smith, McCarthy, Coote, Turner, Simms; G - Simms 9; FG - Simms
New Zealand: T - Smith; G - Ladner; FG - Ladner 3
Australia: Eric Simms, Ray Branighan, John Cootes, Bob Fulton, Lionel Williamson, Denis Pittard, Billy Smith, Bob O'Reilly, Elwyn Walters, John O'Neill, Pail Sait, Bob McCarthy, Ron Coote (c). Replacement: Ron Turner (for Coote).
New Zealand: Don Ladner, Bob McGuinn, Roy Christian (c), Bernie Lowther, Mocky Brereton, Gary Woollard, Graham Cooksley, Doug Gailey, Colin O'Neil, Eddie Heatley, Bill Deacon, Gary Smith, Tony Kriletich. Replacements: John Greengrass and Lummy Graham.

GREAT BRITAIN 11 ....**AUSTRALIA 4**
At Headingley, Leeds, Saturday, October 24, 1970
Attendance: 15,084; **Referee:** Fred Lindop (Great Britain)
Great Britain: T - Hynes; G - Dutton; FG - Hynes
Australia: FG - Simms, Fulton
Great Britain: Ray Dutton, Alan Smith, Frank Myler (c), Syd Hynes, John Atkinson, Mick Shoebottom, Keith Hepworth, Cliff Watson, Tony Fisher, Dennis Hartley, Jim Thompson, Doug Laughton, Mal Reilly.
Australia: Eric Simms, Mark Harris, Ray Branighan, Bob Fulton, Lionel Williamson, Denis Pittard, Billy Smith, Bob O'Reilly, Elwyn Walters, John O'Neill. Pail Sait, Bob McCarthy, Gary Sullivan. Replacement: Ron Turner.

FRANCE 15 ....**NEW ZEALAND 16**
At The Boulevard, Hull, Sunday, October 25, 1970
Attendance: 3,824; **Referee:** Billy Thompson (Great Britain)
France: T - Marsolan 2, Bonal; G - Capdouze 3
New Zealand: T - Brereton, Cooksley; G - Ladner 5
France: Jean-Pierre Cros, Serge Marsolan, Michel Molinier, Andre Ruiz, Elie Bonal, Jean Capdouze, Roger Garrigue, Floreal Bonet, Jacques Cabero, Christian Sabatie, Roger Biffi, Herve Mazard, Jean-Pierre Clar (c). Replacement: Francis De Nadai.
New Zealand: Don Ladner, John Whittaker, Roy Christian (c), Bernie Lowther, Mocky Brereton, Gary Woollard, Graham Cooksley, Doug Gailey, Colin O'Neil, John Greengrass, Elliot Kereopa, Gary Smith, Tony Kriletich. Replacements: Lummy Graham and Bill Deacon.

GREAT BRITAIN 6 ....**FRANCE 0**
At Wheldon Road, Castleford, Wednesday, October 28, 1970
Attendance: 8,958; **Referee:** Fred Lindop (Great Britain)
Great Britain: G - Dutton 3
Great Britain: Ray Dutton, Keri Jones, Frank Myler (c), Syd Hynes, John Atkinson, Mick Shoebottom, Keith Hepworth, Cliff Watson, Kevin Ashcroft, Dennis Hartley, Jim Thompson, Doug Laughton, Mal Reilly.
France: Jean-Pierre Cros, Serge Marsolan, Michel Molinier, Andre Ruiz, Elie Bonal, Jean Capdouze, Germain Guiraud, Francis De Nadai, Jacques Cabero, Christian Sabatie, Gerard Cremoux, Herve Mazard, Jean-Pierre Clar (c). Replacements: Daniel Pellerin and Floreal Bonet.

GREAT BRITAIN 27 ....**NEW ZEALAND 17**
At Station Road, Swinton, Saturday, October 31, 1970
Attendance: 5,609; **Referee:** Fred Lindop (Great Britain)
Great Britain: T - Hesketh, Watson, Hynes, Laughton, Atkinson; G - Dutton 6
New Zealand: T - Kriletich, Christian, Smith; G - Ladner 4
Great Britain: Ray Dutton, Keri Jones, Chris Hesketh, Syd Hynes, John Atkinson, Mick Shoebottom, Keith Hepworth, Cliff Watson, Kevin Ashcroft, Dave Chisnall, Jim Thompson, Bob Haigh, Doug Laughton. Replacement: Paul Charlton.
New Zealand: Don Ladner, John Whittaker, Roy Christian (c), Bernie Lowther, Mocky Brereton, Gary Woollard, Graham Cooksley, Elliot Kereopa, Colin O'Neil, John Greengrass, Gary Smith, Eddie Heatley, Tony Kriletich. Replacement: Lummy Graham.

FRANCE 17 ....**AUSTRALIA 15**
At Odsal Stadium, Bradford, Sunday, November 1, 1970
Attendance: 6,215; **Referee:** Billy Thompson (Great Britain)
France: T - Marsolan 2, Capdouze; G - Capdouze 3; FG - Garrigue
Australia: T - Cootes 2, Fulton; G - Simms 3
France: Jean-Pierre Cros, Serge Marsolan, Michel Molinier,

Jacques Gruppi, Daniel Pellerin, Jean Capdouze, Roger Garrigue, Floreal Bonet, Jacques Cabero, Christian Sabatie, Roger Biffi, Francis De Nadai , Jean-Pierre Clar (c).
Australia: Eric Simms, Ray Branighan, John Cootes, Bob Fulton, Lionel Williamson, Denis Pittard, Billy Smith, Bob O'Reilly, Elwyn Walters, Barry McTaggart. Pail Sait, Bob McCarthy, Ron Coote (c). Replacements: Ron Turner (for McTaggart), Gary Sullivan (for Pittard).

FINAL TABLE

	P	W	D	L	F	A	Pts
Great Britain	3	3	0	0	44	21	6
Australia	3	1	0	2	66	39	2
France	3	1	0	2	32	37	2
New Zealand	3	1	0	2	44	89	2

FINAL

GREAT BRITAIN 7 ....**AUSTRALIA 12**
At Headingley, Leeds, Saturday, November 7, 1970
Attendance: 18,776; **Referee:** Fred Lindop (Great Britain)
Great Britain: T - Atkinson; G - Dutton; FG - Hynes
Australia: T - Cootes, Williamson; G - Simms 2; FG - Simms
Great Britain: Ray Dutton, Alan Smith, Frank Myler (c), Syd Hynes, John Atkinson, Mick Shoebottom, Keith Hepworth, Cliff Watson, Tony Fisher, Dennis Hartley. Jim Thompson, Doug Laughton, Mal Reilly. Replacements: Bob Haigh, Chris Hesketh.
Australia: Eric Simms, Mark Harris, John Cootes, Paul Sait, Lionel Williamson, Bob Fulton, Billy Smith, Bob O'Reilly, Ron Turner, John O'Neill, Bob McCarthy, Ron Costello, Ron Coote (c). Replacements: Ray Branighan, Elwyn Walters.

THE 1970 SQUADS

AUSTRALIA *(Coach: Harry Bath)*

	M	T	G	Pts
Ray Branighan (South Sydney)	4	1	-	3
Johnny Brown (Brisbane Norths)	-	-	-	-
Ron Coote (South Sydney) (c)	3	1	-	3
John Cootes (Newcastle)	3	5	-	15
Ron Costello (Canterbury-Bankstown)	1	-	-	-
Bob Fulton (Manly-Warringah)	4	2	1	8
Mark Harris (Eastern Suburbs)	2	-	-	-
Bob McCarthy (South Sydney)	4	1	-	3
Barry McTaggart (Balmain)	1	-	-	-
John O'Neill (South Sydney)	3	-	-	-
Bob O'Reilly (Parramatta)	4	-	-	-
Dennis Pittard (South Sydney)	3	-	-	-
Paul Sait (South Sydney)	4	-	-	-
Eric Simms (South Sydney)	4	1	17	37
Billy Smith (St George)	4	1	-	3
Gary Sullivan (Newtown)	2	-	-	-
Ron Turner (Cronulla-Sutherland)	4	1	-	3
Elwyn Walters (South Sydney)	4	-	-	-
Lionel Williamson (Newtown)	4	1	-	3

FRANCE *(Coach: Jean Lacoste)*

	M	T	G	Pts
Roger Biffi (Saint-Gaudens)	2	-	-	-
Jean-Marie Bonal (Carcassonne)	2	1	-	3
Floreal Bonet (Saint-Esteve)	3	-	-	-
Jacques Cabero (XIII Catalan)	3	-	-	-
Jean Capdouze (XIII Catalan)	3	1	6	15
Jean-Pierre Clar (Villeneuve) (c)	3	-	-	-
Gerard Cremoux (Villeneuve)	1	-	-	-
Jean-Pierre Cros (Albi)	3	-	-	-
Francis De Nadai (Villeneuve)	3	-	-	-
Roger Garrigue (Saint-Gaudens)	2	-	1	2
Jacques Gruppi (Limoux)	1	-	-	-
Germain Guiraud (Limoux)	1	-	-	-
Serge Marsolan (Saint-Gaudens)	3	4	-	12
Herve Mazard (Lezignan)	2	-	-	-
Michel Molinier (Saint-Gaudens)	3	-	-	-
Daniel Pellerin (Villeneuve)	2	-	-	-
Andre Ruiz (Carcassonne)	2	-	-	-
Christian Sabatie (Villeneuve)	3	-	-	-

GREAT BRITAIN *(Coach: Johnny Whiteley)*

	M	T	G	Pts
Kevin Ashcroft (Leigh)	2	-	-	-
John Atkinson (Leeds)	4	2	-	6
Paul Charlton (Salford)	1	-	-	-
Dave Chisnall (Leigh)	1	-	-	-
Ray Dutton (Widnes)	4	-	11	22
Tony Fisher (Leeds)	2	-	-	-
Bob Haigh (Leeds)	2	-	-	-
Dennis Hartley (Castleford)	3	-	-	-
Keith Hepworth (Castleford)	4	-	-	-
Syd Hynes (Leeds)	4	2	2	10
Keri Jones (Wigan)	2	-	-	-
Doug Laughton (Wigan)	4	1	-	3
Frank Myler (St Helens) (c)	3	-	-	-
Mal Reilly (Leeds)	3	-	-	-
Mick Shoebottom (Leeds)	4	-	-	-
Alan Smith (Leeds)	2	-	-	-

| Jim Thompson (Featherstone Rovers) | 4 | - | - | - |
| Cliff Watson (St Helens) | 4 | 1 | - | 3 |

NEW ZEALAND *(Coach: Lory Blanchard)*

	M	T	G	Pts
Mocky Brereton (West Coast)	3	1	-	3
Bill Burgoyne (Auckland)	-	-	-	-
Eric Carson (Auckland)	-	-	-	-
Roy Christian (Auckland) (c)	3	1	-	3
Graham Cooksley (Canterbury)	3	1	-	3
Bill Deacon (Waikato)	2	-	-	-
Doug Gailey (Auckland)	2	-	-	-
Lummy Graham (Auckland)	3	-	-	-
John Greengrass (Canterbury)	3	-	-	-
Eddie Heatley (Auckland)	2	-	-	-
Elliott Kereopa (Midlands)	2	-	-	-
Tony Kriletich (Auckland)	3	1	-	3
Don Ladner (West Coast)	3	-	13	26
Bernie Lowther (Auckland)	3	-	-	-
Bob McGuinn (Auckland)	1	-	-	-
Colin O'Neil (Wellington)	3	-	-	-
Gary Smith (Wellington)	3	2	-	6
John Whittaker (Wellington)	2	-	-	-
Gary Woollard (Auckland)	3	-	-	-

FRIENDLIES BY WORLD CUP SQUADS

AUSTRALIA

ST HELENS 37 ....**AUSTRALIA 10**

FRANCE 4 ....**AUSTRALIA 7**
France: G - J Capdouze
Australia: T - J Cootes; G - E Simms 2

FRANCE B 8 ....**AUSTRALIA 36**
France B: T - J Managnin; G - J Saurat; FG - Pere
Australia: T - M Harris 2, W Smith 2, E Simms, E Walters, R Branighan, R McCarthy; G - E Simms 6

NEW ZEALAND

BARROW 10 ....**NEW ZEALAND 14**

BRADFORD NORTHERN 17 ....**NEW ZEALAND 28**

SALFORD 7 ....**NEW ZEALAND 8**

FRANCE 16 ....**NEW ZEALAND 2**
France: T - M Molinier, F De Nadai, J Gruppi, S Marsolan; G - J Capdouze 2
New Zealand: G - G Smith

FRANCE B 8 ....**NEW ZEALAND 28**
France B: T - J Calle, V Serrano; G - V Serrano
New Zealand: T - C O'Neil, R Christian, G Cooksley, B Deacon, J Whittaker, B Lowther; G - B Deacon 5

1972

FRANCE 20 ....**NEW ZEALAND 9**
At Stade Municipal, Marseille, Saturday, October 28, 1972
Attendance: 20,748; **Referee:** George Jameau (France)
France: T - Bonal 2, Ruiz; G - Guilhem 4, Bonal; FG - Frattini
New Zealand: T - Orchard 2, Brereton
France: Raymond Toujas, Serge Marsolan, Michel Molinier, Andre Ruiz, Jean-Marie Bonal, Bernard Guilhem, Marius Frattini, Francis De Nadai (c), Jacques Franc, Jacques Garzino, Nestor Serrano, Serge Gleyzes, Michel Anglade. Replacement: Charles Zalduendo (for Garzino).
New Zealand: John Whittaker, Phil Orchard, John O'Sullivan, Roy Christian (c), Mocky Brereton, Dennis Williams, Brian Tracey, Mita Mohi, Bill Burgoyne, Bob Paul, Doug Gailey, Peter Gurnick, Murray Eade. Replacements: Graeme Cooksley (for Tracey), Tony Coll (for Paul).

GREAT BRITAIN 27 ....**AUSTRALIA 21**
At Stade Gilbert Brutus, Perpignan, Sunday, October 29, 1972
Attendance: 6,324; **Referee:** Claude Tissiere (France)
Great Britain: T - Sullivan, Lowe, Atkinson, O'Neill, Stephenson; G - Clawson 6
Australia: T - Fulton 3, Raudonikis; G - Langlands 4; FG - McCarthy
Great Britain: Paul Charlton, Clive Sullivan (c), Chris Hesketh, John Walsh, John Atkinson, Dennis O'Neill, Steve Nash, David Jeanes, Mike Stephenson, Terry Clawson, Phil Lowe, George Nicholls. Replacement: John Holmes (for Walsh).
Australia: Graeme Langlands (c), Stephen Knight, Geoff Starling, Ray Branighan, Mark Harris, Bob Fulton, Tom Raudonikis, Arthur Beetson, Elwyn Walters, John O'Neill, John Elford, Bob McCarthy, Gary Sullivan. Replacements: Dennis Ward (for Beetson), Paul Sait (for Branighan).

AUSTRALIA 9 ....**NEW ZEALAND 5**
At Parc de Princes, Paris, Wednesday, November 1, 1972

Attendance: 8,000; **Referee:** Mick Naughton (Great Britain)
Australia: T - Ward, Fulton; G - Branighan; FG - Fulton
New Zealand: T - Whittaker; G - Wilson
Australia: Graeme Langlands (c), Stephen Knight, Geoff Starling, Ray Branighan, John Grant, Bob Fulton, Dennis Ward, Bob O'Reilly, Elwyn Walters, John O'Neill, John Elford, Gary Sullivan, Paul Sait. Replacement: Gary Stevens (for Sait).
New Zealand: John Wilson, Phil Orchard, Mocky Brereton, Roy Christian (c), John Whittaker, Dennis Williams, Brian Tracey, Doug Gailey, Bill Burgoyne, Don Mann, Bob Paul, Murray Eade, Peter Gurnick. Replacement: Rodney Walker (for Paul).

FRANCE 4 ....GREAT BRITAIN 13
At Stade Municipal, Grenoble, Wednesday, November 1, 1972
Attendance: 5,321; **Referee:** Francois Gril (France)
France: G - Bonal, Serrano
Great Britain: T - Lowe 2, Sullivan; G - Clawson 2
France: Raymond Toujas, Serge Marsolan, Michel Molinier, Andre Ruiz, Jean-Marie Bonal, Bernard Guilhem, Jean-Marie Imbert, Francis De Nadai (c), Jacques Franc, Jean-Pierre Sauret, Nestor Serrano, Serge Gleyzes, Guy Rodriguez. Replacement: Charles Zalduendo (for Sauret).
Great Britain: Paul Charlton, Clive Sullivan (c), Chris Hesketh, John Walsh, John Atkinson, Dennis O'Neill, Steve Nash, David Jeanes, Mike Stephenson, Brian Lockwood, Phil Lowe, Colin Dixon, George Nicholls.

GREAT BRITAIN 53 ....NEW ZEALAND 19
At Stade du Hameau, Pau, Saturday, November 4, 1972
Attendance: 7,500; **Referee:** Georges Jameau (France)
Great Britain: T - Holmes 2, Atkinson 2, Nicholls, Sullivan, Charlton, Hesketh, Stephenson, Jeanes, Nash; G - Holmes 10
New Zealand: T - Whittaker, Coll, Williams, Burgoyne, Eade; G - Wilson 2
Great Britain: Paul Charlton, Clive Sullivan (c), Chris Hesketh, John Walsh, John Atkinson, John Holmes, Steve Nash, David Jeanes, Mike Stephenson, Brian Lockwood, Phil Lowe, Bob Irving, George Nicholls. Replacements: David Redfearn (for Sullivan), Tony Karalius (for Stephenson).
New Zealand: John Wilson, Phil Orchard, Mocky Brereton, Roy Christian (c), John Whittaker, Dennis Williams, Brian Tracey, Doug Gailey, Bill Burgoyne, Don Mann, Murray Eade, Tony Coll, Peter Gurnick. Replacements: Rodney Walker (for Gurnick), Warren Collicoat (for Wilson).

FRANCE 9 ....AUSTRALIA 31
At Stade de Minimes, Toulouse, Sunday, November 5, 1972
Attendance: 10,332; **Referee:** Mick Naughton (Great Britain)
France: T - Ruiz; G - Bonal 3
Australia: T - Harris 2, Sait 2, Fulton, O'Neill, Walters; G - Branighan 5
France: Raymond Toujas, Serge Marsolan, Michel Molinier, Andre Ruiz, Jean-Marie Bonal, Michel Mazare, Marius Frattini, Serge Gleyzes, Francis De Nadai (c), Nestor Serrano, Jacques Garzino, Jacques Franc, Charles Zalduendo. Replacements: Bernard Guilhem (for Toujas) Michel Anglade (for Zalduendo).
Australia: Graeme Langlands (c), Ray Branighan, Mark Harris, Geoff Starling, John Grant, Bob Fulton, Dennis Ward, Bob O'Reilly, Elwyn Walters, John O'Neill, Arthur Beetson, Gary Stevens, Paul Sait.

FINAL TABLE

	P	W	D	L	F	A	Pts
Great Britain	3	3	0	0	93	44	6
Australia	3	2	0	1	61	41	4
France	3	1	0	2	33	53	2
New Zealand	3	0	0	3	33	83	0

FINAL

GREAT BRITAIN 10 ....AUSTRALIA 10
At Stade de Gerland, Lyon, Saturday, November 11, 1972
Attendance: 4,500; **Referee:** Georges Jameau (France)
Great Britain: T - Sullivan, Stephenson; G - Clawson
Australia: T - O'Neill, Beetson; G - Branighan 2
Great Britain: Paul Charlton, Clive Sullivan (c), Chris Hesketh, John Walsh, John Atkinson, John Holmes, Steve Nash, David Jeanes, Mike Stephenson, Terry Clawson, Brian Lockwood, Phil Lowe, George Nicholls. Replacement: Bob Irving (for Jeanes).
Australia: Graeme Langlands (c), Ray Branighan, Geoff Starling, Mark Harris, John Grant, Bob Fulton, Dennis Ward, Bob O'Reilly, Elwyn Walters, John O'Neill, Gary Stevens, Arthur Beetson, Gary Sullivan.
(There was no further score after extra time - 10 minutes each way - was played. Britain was awarded the World Cup because of its better record in preliminary matches.)

THE 1972 SQUADS

AUSTRALIA (Coach: Harry Bath)

	M	T	G	FG	Pts
Arthur Beetson (Eastern Suburbs)	3	1	-	-	3
Ray Branighan (Manly-Warringah)	4	-	8	-	16
John Elford (Western Suburbs)	2	-	-	-	-
Bob Fulton (Manly-Warringah)	4	5	-	1	16
John Grant (Brisbane Souths)	3	-	-	-	-
Mark Harris (Eastern Suburbs)	3	2	-	-	6
Fred Jones (Manly-Warringah)	-	-	-	-	-
Stephen Knight (Western Suburbs)	2	-	-	-	-
Graeme Langlands (St George) (c)	4	-	4	-	8
Bob McCarthy (South Sydney)	1	-	-	1	1
John O'Neill (Manly-Warringah)	4	2	-	-	6
Bob O'Reilly (Parramatta)	3	-	-	-	-
Tom Raudonikis (Western Suburbs)	1	1	-	-	3
Paul Sait (South Sydney)	3	2	-	-	6
Geoff Starling (Balmain)	4	-	-	-	-
Gary Stevens (South Sydney)	3	-	-	-	-
Gary Sullivan (Newtown)	3	-	-	-	-
Elwyn Walters (South Sydney)	4	1	-	-	3
Dennis Ward (Manly-Warringah)	4	1	-	-	3

FRANCE (Coach: Antoine Jiminez)

	M	T	G	FG	Pts
Michel Anglade (Saint-Gaudens)	2	-	-	-	-
Elie Bonal (Carcassonne)	-	-	-	-	-
Jean-Marie Bonal (Carcassonne)	3	2	5	-	16
Francis De Nadai (Limoux)	3	-	-	-	-
Jacques Franc (Carcassonne)	3	-	-	-	-
Marius Frattini (Avignon)	2	-	-	1	1
Jacques Garzino (Avignon)	2	-	-	-	-
Serge Gleyzes (Carcassonne)	3	-	-	-	-
Bernard Guilhem (Carcassonne)	3	-	4	-	8
Jean-Marie Imbert (Avignon)	1	-	-	-	-
Serge Marsolan (Saint-Gaudens)	3	-	-	-	-
Michael Mazare (Villeneuve)	1	-	-	-	-
Michel Molinier (Saint-Gaudens)	3	-	-	-	-
Guy Rodriguez (Toulouse)	1	-	-	-	-
Andre Ruiz (Carcassonne)	3	2	-	-	6
Jean-Pierre Sauret (XIII Catalan)	1	-	-	-	-
Nestor Serrano (Saint-Gaudens)	3	-	1	-	2
Raymond Toujas (Carcassonne)	3	-	-	-	-
Charles Zalduendo (Toulouse)	3	-	-	-	-

GREAT BRITAIN (Coach: Jim Challinor)

	M	T	G	FG	Pts
John Atkinson (Leeds)	4	3	-	-	9
Paul Charlton (Salford)	4	1	-	-	3
Terry Clawson (Leeds)	3	-	10	-	20
Colin Dixon (Salford)	1	-	-	-	-
Chris Hesketh (Salford)	4	1	-	-	3
John Holmes (Leeds)	3	2	10	-	26
David Jeanes (Leeds)	4	1	-	-	3
Bob Irving (Oldham)	2	-	-	-	-
Tony Karalius (St Helens)	1	-	-	-	-
Brian Lockwood (Castleford)	4	-	-	-	-
Phil Lowe (Hull Kingston Rovers)	4	3	-	-	9
Steve Nash (Featherstone Rovers)	4	1	-	-	3
George Nicholls (Widnes)	4	1	-	-	3
Dennis O'Neill (Widnes)	2	1	-	-	3
David Redfearn (Bradford Northern)	1	-	-	-	-
Mike Stephenson (Dewsbury)	4	3	-	-	9
Clive Sullivan (Hull)	4	4	-	-	12
David Topliss (Wakefield Trinity)	-	-	-	-	-
John Walsh (St Helens)	4	-	-	-	-

NEW ZEALAND (Coach: Des Barchard)

	M	T	G	FG	Pts
Mocky Brereton (Canterbury)	3	1	-	-	3
Bill Burgoyne (Auckland)	3	1	-	-	3
Roy Christian (Auckland) (c)	3	-	-	-	-
Tony Coll (West Coast)	2	1	-	-	3
Warren Collicoat (Auckland)	1	-	-	-	-
Graeme Cooksley (Canterbury)	1	-	-	-	-
Murray Eade (Auckland)	3	1	-	-	3
Doug Gailey (Auckland)	3	-	-	-	-
Peter Gurnick (Auckland)	3	-	-	-	-
Don Mann (Auckland)	2	-	-	-	-
Mita Mohi (Canterbury)	1	-	-	-	-
Phil Orchard (Wellington)	3	2	-	-	6
John O'Sullivan (Auckland)	1	-	-	-	-
Bob Paul (Wellington)	2	-	-	-	-
Brian Tracey (Auckland)	3	-	-	-	-
Rod Walker (Canterbury)	2	-	-	-	-
John Whittaker (Wellington)	3	2	-	-	6
Dennis Williams (Auckland)	3	1	-	-	3
John Wilson (Auckland)	2	-	3	-	6

1975

FRANCE 14 ....WALES 7
At Toulouse, Sunday, March 2, 1975
Attendance: 7,563; **Referee:** Fred Lindop (England)
France: T - Curt, Terrats; G - Serrano 3; FG - Imbert, Lacoste
Wales: T - Wilson; G - Coslett 2
France: Francis Tranier, Elie Bonal, Michel Molinier, Rene Terrats, Bernard Curt, Jean-Pierre Lacoste, Jean-Marie Imbert, Francis De Nadia, Fernand Kaminski, Nestor Serrano, Serge Gleyzes, Didier Hermet, Michel Anglade. Replacement: Michel Anglade.
Wales: Bill Francis, Roy Mathias, David Willicombe, Frank Wilson,

Maurice Richards, David Watkins, Peter Banner, Mick Murphy, Richard Evans, Brian Butler, John Mantle, Colin Dixon, Kel Coslett. Replacement: Richard Wallace (for Watkins).

ENGLAND 20 ....**FRANCE 2**
At Headingley, Leeds, Sunday, March 16, 1975
Attendance: 10,842; **Referee:** Keith Page (Australia), *replaced by H Hunt (England) after 28 minutes.*
England: T - Fielding 2, Millward, Morgan; G - Gray 4
France: G - Serrano
England: Paul Charlton, Keith Fielding, Derek Noonan, Les Dyl, John Atkinson, Ken Gill, Roger Millward, Dave Chisnall, John Gray, Phil Jackson, Tommy Martyn, George Nicholls, Barry Philbin. Replacement: Mick Morgan (for Philbin).
France: Francis Tranier, Elie Bonal, Michel Molinier, Rene Terrats, Bernard Curt, Jean-Pierre Lacoste, Jean-Marie Imbert, Francis De Nadia, Fernand Kaminski, Nestor Serrano, Serge Gleyzes, Didier Hermet, Michel Anglade.

AUSTRALIA 36...**NEW ZEALAND 8**
At Lang Park, Brisbane, Sunday, June 1, 1975
Attendance: 10,000; **Referee:** Francois Escande (France)
Australia: T - Cronin 2, Langlands 2, Fulton, Platz, Randall, Branighan; G - Cronin 6
New Zealand: T - Stirling, Whittaker; G - Collicoat
Australia: Graeme Langlands (c), Chris Anderson, Bob Fulton, Mick Cronin, Terry Fahey, Tim Pickup, Ross Strudwick, Terry Randall, John Lang, David Wright, Gary Stevens, Lew Platz, Ron Coote. Replacements: Paul Sait (for Wright), Ray Branighan (for Fahey)
New Zealand: Warren Collicoat, Mocky Brereton, John O'Sullivan, John Whittaker, Phil Orchard, Dennis Williams, John Kerring, John Hibbs, Tom Conroy, Graeme West, Tony Coll, Ray Baxendale, Murray Eade.

ENGLAND 7 ....**WALES 12**
At Lang Park, Brisbane, Tuesday, June 10, 1975
Attendance: 6,000; **Referee:** Don Lancashire (Australia)
England: T - Martyn; G - Fairbairn 2
Wales: T - Sullivan, Treasure; G - Watkins 3
England: George Fairbairn, Keith Fielding, Derek Noonan, Les Dyl, John Atkinson, Roger Millward, Steve Nash, Dave Chisnall, Mick Morgan, Mike Coulman, Eric Chisnall, , George Nicholls, Steve Norton. Replacements: Ken Gill (for Millward), Tommy Martyn (for Coulman).
Wales: Bill Francis, Roy Mathias, David Watkins, David Willicombe, Clive Sullivan, David Treasure, Peter Banner, Jim Mills, Tony Fisher, Bobby Wanbon, Colin Dixon, Eddie Cunningham, Kel Coslett. Replacements: John Mantle (for Dixon), Frank Wilson (for Banner).

AUSTRALIA 30 ....**WALES 13**
At Sydney Cricket Ground, Saturday, June 14, 1975
Attendance: 25,386; **Referee:** Francois Escande (France)
Australia: T - Harris, Langlands, Raudonikis, Fulton; G - Cronin 9
Wales: T - Fisher; G - Watkins 5
Australia: Graeme Langlands (c), Mark Harris, Bob Fulton, Mick Cronin, John Rhodes, Tim Pickup, Tom Raudonikis, Terry Randall, John Lang, John O'Neill, Gary Stevens, Lew Platz, Paul Sait. Replacements: John Donnelly (for Stevens).
Wales: Bill Francis, Roy Mathias, David Watkins, David Willicombe, Clive Sullivan, Glyn Turner, David Treasure, Jim Mills, Tony Fisher, Bobby Wanbon, John Mantle, Eddie Cunningham, Kel Coslett. Replacements: Frank Wilson (for Sullivan), Peter Rowe (for Treasure).

NEW ZEALAND 27 ....**FRANCE 0**
At Christchurch, Sunday, June 15, 1975
Attendance: 2,500; **Referee:** Laurie Bruyeres (Australia)
New Zealand: T - Jarvis 2, Stirling, Eade, Conroy; G - Sorensen 6
New Zealand: John Whittaker, Don Munro, Dennis Williams, John O'Sullivan, Phil Orchard, Bob Jarvis, Ken Stirling, John Greengrass, Tom Conroy, Dane Sorensen, Tony Coll, Ray Baxendale, Murray Eade. Replacements: Warren Collicoat (for O'Sullivan), Lindsay Proctor (for Greengrass).
France: Francis Tranier, Elie Bonal, Andre Ruiz, Rene Terrats, Andre Dumas, Jose Calle, Jean-Marie Imbert, Francis De Nadia, Antoine Gonzales, Charles Zalduendo, Serge Gleyzes, Michel Cassin, Jean-Claude Mayorgas.

NEW ZEALAND 17 ....**ENGLAND 17**
At Carlaw Park, Auckland, Saturday, June 21, 1975
Attendance: 12,000; **Referee:** Laurie Bruyeres (Australia)
New Zealand: T - Williams 2, Orchard; G - Sorensen 4
England: T - Fairbairn 2, Atkinson; G - Fairbairn 4
New Zealand: John Whittaker, Don Munro, Dennis Williams, John O'Sullivan, Phil Orchard, Bob Jarvis, Ken Stirling, John Greengrass, Tom Conroy, Dane Sorensen, Tony Coll, Ray Baxendale, Murray Eade. Replacements: Warren Collicoat (for Whittaker), Lindsay Proctor (for Greengrass).
England: George Fairbairn, Keith Fielding, John Walsh, Les Dyl, John Atkinson, Ken Gill, Steve Nash, Dave Chisnall, Keith Bridges, Eric Chisnall, George Nicholls, Phil Cookson, Steve Norton. Replacement: Mick Morgan (for Dave Chisnall).

AUSTRALIA 26 ....**FRANCE 6**
At Lang Park, Brisbane, Sunday, June 22, 1975
Attendance: 9,000; **Referee:** John Percival (New Zealand)
Australia: T - Harris 2, Fulton 2, Pickup, Cronin; G - Cronin 4
France: G - Calle 3
Australia: Graeme Langlands (c), Mark Harris, Bob Fulton, Mick Cronin, John Rhodes, Tim Pickup, Tom Raudonikis, John Donnelly, John Lang, Arthur Beetson, Lew Platz, Terry Randall, Ron Coote. Replacements: Chris Anderson, John Quayle.
France: Francis Tranier, Bernard Curt, Andre Ruiz, Rene Terrats, Andre Dumas, Jose Calle, Jean-Marie Imbert, Francis De Nadia, Fernand Kaminski, Michel Cassin, Serge Gleyzes, Michel Maique, Michel Anglade. Replacements: Jean-Claude Mayorgas, Charles Zalduendo.

AUSTRALIA 10..**ENGLAND 10**
At Sydney Cricket Ground, Saturday, June 28, 1975
Attendance: 33,858; **Referee:** John Percival (New Zealand)
Australia: T - Coote, Anderson; G - Cronin 2
England: T - Dunn, Gill; G - Fairbairn 2
Australia: Graeme Langlands (c), Mark Harris, Bob Fulton, Mick Cronin, John Rhodes, Tim Pickup, Tom Raudonikis, Terry Randall, John Lang, Arthur Beetson, Lew Platz, Gary Stevens, Ron Coote. Replacements: Chris Anderson (for Harris), John Donnelly (for Pickup).
England: George Fairbairn, Keith Fielding, John Walsh, Les Dyl, Ged Dunn, Roger Millward, Steve Nash, Mike Coulman, Keith Bridges, Mick Morgan, George Nicholls, Phil Cookson, Steve Norton. Replacements: Eric Chisnall (for Cookson), Ken Gill (for Millward).

NEW ZEALAND 13 ....**WALES 8**
At Carlaw Park, Auckland, Saturday, June 28, 1975
Attendance: 9,368; **Referee:** Laurie Bruyeres (Australia)
New Zealand: T - Orchard; G - Collicoat 5
Wales: T- Mills, Francis; G - Watkins
New Zealand: Warren Collicoat, Don Munro, Dennis Williams, John O'Sullivan, Phil Orchard, Bob Jarvis, Ken Stirling, Lindsay Proctor, Tom Conroy, Dane Sorensen, Tony Coll, Ray Baxendale, Murray Eade.
Wales: Bill Francis, Roy Mathias, David Watkins, David Willicombe, Clive Sullivan, David Treasure, Peter Banner, Jim Mills, Tony Fisher, Bobby Wanbon, John Mantle, Col Dixon, Kel Coslett. Replacements: Brian Butler (for Mantle).

ENGLAND 22 ....**WALES 16**
At Wilderspool, Warrington, Saturday, September 20, 1975
Attendance: 5,034; **Referee:** Marcel Caillol (France)
England: T- Fielding, Holmes, Hughes; G - Fairbairn 6; FG - Bridges
Wales: T - Banner, Coslett; G -Watkins 5
England: George Fairbairn, Keith Fielding, Eric Hughes, John Holmes, John Atkinson, Ken Gill, Roger Millward, Brian Hogan, Keith Bridges, Colin Forsyth, Jeff Grayshon, Bob Irving, Steve Norton. Replacements: Dave Eckersley (for Holmes), George Nicholls (for Gill).
Wales: Bill Francis, John Bevan, David Watkins, Frank Wilson, Clive Sullivan, David Treasure, Peter Banner, Mel James, Tony Fisher, John Mantle, Eddie Cunningham, Brian Gregory, Kel Coslett. Replacements: Glyn Turner (for Treasure), Peter Rowe (for Gregory).

NEW ZEALAND 8...**AUSTRALIA 24**
At Carlaw Park, Auckland, Saturday, September 28, 1975
Attendance: 18,000; **Referee:** Fred Lindop (England)
New Zealand: G - Collicoat 4
Australia: T - Quayle, Higgs, Cronin, Schubert; G - Cronin 6
New Zealand: Warren Collicoat, Phil Orchard, Paul Matete, Dennis Williams, Fred Ah Kuoi, Bob Jarvis, Ken Stirling, John Greengrass, Tom Conroy, Dane Sorensen, Tony Coll, Ray Baxendale, Murray Eade. Replacements: John Smith (for Jarvis), Kurt Sorensen (for Coll).
Australia: Graham Eadie, John Rhodes, Mick Cronin, John Brass (c), Ian Schubert, John Peard, Johnny Mayes, Greg Veivers, George Piggins, Ian Mackay, Lou Platz, Ray Higgs, John Quayle. Replacements: Tom Raudonikis (for Eadie), Denis Fitzgerald (for Platz).

FRANCE 2 ....**ENGLAND 48**
At Bordeaux, Saturday, October 11, 1975
Attendance: 1,581; **Referee:** John Percival (New Zealand)
France: G - Calle
England: T - Fielding 4, Dunn 2, Holmes 2, Hogan, Forsyth, Gill, Hughes; G - Fairbairn 4, Millward 2
France: Maurice De Matos, Jean-Francois Grechi, Andre Ruiz, Rene Terrats, Michel Lafargue, Jose Calle, Jean-Marie Imbert, Guy Garcia, Francis Duthil, Michel Gonzales, Jean-Pierre Tremouille, Guy Buchi. Replacements: Guy Vigouroux (for Bosc), Charles Thenegal (for Garcia).
England: George Fairbairn, Keith Fielding, Eric Hughes, John Holmes, Ged Dunn, Ken Gill, Roger Millward, Brian Hogan, Keith Bridges, Colin Forsyth, Jeff Grayshon, Bob Irving, Steve Norton.

FRANCE 12 ....**NEW ZEALAND 12**
At Marseille, Friday, October 17, 1975
Attendance: 8,000; **Referee:** Billy Thompson (England)
France: T - Chauvet 2; G - Guilhem 3
New Zealand: T - Jarvis, Proctor; G - Collicoat 3
France: Marcel Pillon, Jean-Francois Grechi, Andre Ruiz, Bernard Guilhem, Patrick Chauvet, Jose Calle, Jean-Marie Imbert, Charles Zalduendo, Antoine Gonzales, Charles Thenegal , Jean-Pierre Tremouille, Jean-Pierre Sauret, Rene Terrats. Replacement: Michel Moussard (for Thenegal).
New Zealand: Warren Collicoat, Phil Orchard, Bl Dickison, Bob Jarvis, John Smith, Dennis Williams, Ken Stirling, John Greengrass, Tom Conroy, Lindsay Proctor, Ray Baxendale, Tony Coll, Peter Gurnick. Replacement: Tony Gordon (for Dickison).

WALES 6 ....**AUSTRALIA 18**
At Vetch Field, Swansea, Sunday, October 19, 1975
Attendance: 11,112; **Referee:** John Percival (New Zealand)
Wales: G - Watkins 3
Australia: T - Schubert 3, Peard; G - Cronin 3
Wales: David Watkins, Roy Mathias, Bill Francis, Frank Wilson, John Bevan, Glyn Turner, Peter Banner, Jim Mills, Tony Fisher, John Mantle, Eddie Cunningham, Col Dixon, Kel Coslett. Replacement: Peter Rowe (for Dixon).
Australia: Graham Eadie, Allan McMahon, Mick Cronin, Steve Rogers, Ian Schubert, John Peard, Johnny Mayes, Greg Veivers, George Piggins, Arthur Beetson (c), Terry Randall, Ray Higgs, John Quayle. Replacements: Ian Mackay (for Quayle), Jim Porter (for Mayes).

ENGLAND 27 ....**NEW ZEALAND 12**
At Odsal Stadium, Bradford, Saturday, October 25, 1975
Attendance: 5,937; **Referee:** Andre Lacaze (France)
England: T - Gill 3, Norton, Wright, Dunn, Hughes; G - Fairbairn 3
New Zealand: T - Gordon, Smith; T - Collicoat 2, Gordon
England: George Fairbairn, Stuart Wright, Eric Hughes, John Holmes, Ged Dunn, Ken Gill, Roger Millward, Brian Hogan, Keith Bridges, Colin Forsyth, Mick Adams, Jeff Grayshon, Steve Norton. Replacements: George Nicholls (for Adams), Les Dyl (for Wright).
New Zealand: Warren Collicoat, Phil Orchard, John Smith, Dennis Williams, Bruce Dickison, Bob Jarvis, Ken Stirling, John Greengrass, Tom Conroy, Lindsay Proctor, Ray Baxendale, Tony Coll, Murray Eade. Replacements: Tony Gordon (for Stirling), Peter Gurnick (for Baxendale).

FRANCE 2 ....**AUSTRALIA 41**
At Perpignan, Sunday, October 26, 1975
Attendance: 10,440; **Referee:** Bill Thompson (England)
France: G - Guilhem
Australia: T - Rogers 2, Rhodes, Peard, Platz, Higgs, Randall, Raudonikis, Eadie; G - Eadie 7
France: Marcel Pillon, Jean-Francois Grechi, Andre Ruiz, Bernard Guilhem, Patrick Chauvet, Jose Calle, Jean-Marie Imbert, Charles Zalduendo, Antoine Gonzales, Charles Thenegal, Jean-Pierre Tremouille, Jean-Pierre Sauret, Rene Terrats. Replacements: Philippe Clergeau (for Ruiz), Michel Moussard (for Zalduendo).
Australia: Graham Eadie, John Rhodes, Steve Rogers, John Brass, Jim Porter, John Peard, Tom Raudonikis, Arthur Beetson (c), John Lang, Terry Randall, Lew Platz, Ray Higgs, Greg Pierce. Replacement: Ian Schubert (for Rhodes)

ENGLAND 16 ....**AUSTRALIA 13**
At Central Park, Wigan, Saturday, November 1, 1975
Attendance: 9,393; **Referee:** John Percival (New Zealand)
England: T - Grayshon, Holmes; G - Fairbairn 5
Australia: T - Schubert 3; G - Cronin 2
England: George Fairbairn, Dave Redfearn, John Holmes, Les Dyl, Ged Dunn, Ken Gill, Roger Millward, Brian Hogan, Keith Bridges, Jimmy Thompson, Bob Irving, Jeff Grayshon, Steve Norton. Replacements: Mick Adams (for Bridges), Eric Hughes.
Australia: Graham Eadie, John Rhodes, Mick Cronin, John Brass, Ian Schubert, John Peard, Johnny Mayes, Ian Mackay, George Piggins, Arthur Beetson (c), Terry Randall, Ray Higgs, Greg Pierce. Replacement: Steve Rogers (for Peard).

WALES 25 ....**NEW ZEALAND 24**
At Vetch Field, Swansea, Sunday, November 2, 1975
Attendance: 2,645; **Referee:** Georges Jameau (France)
Wales: T - Francis 2, Bevan, Willicombe, Mantle; G - Watkins 5
New Zealand: T - Coll, Orchard, Gordon, Greengrass; G - Gordon 5, Collicoat
Wales: David Watkins, Roy Mathias, Roy Mathias, Frank Wilson, David Willicombe, John Bevan, Bill Francis, Peter Banner, Jim Mills, Tony Fisher, Mick Murphy, John Mantle, Stuart Gallacher, Brian Gregory. Replacement: Clive Jones (for Gregory).
New Zealand: Warren Collicoat, Phil Orchard, Fred Ah Kuoi, Dennis Williams, Tony Gordon, Bob Jarvis, John Smith, John Greengrass, Tom Conroy, Dane Sorensen, Kurt Sorensen, Tony Coll, Peter Gurnick. Replacements: Bruce Dickison (for Collicoat), Lindsay Proctor (for Jarvis).

WALES 23 ....**FRANCE 2**
At The Willows, Salford, Thursday, November 6, 1975
Attendance: 2,247; **Referee:** Fred Lindop (England)

Wales: T - Francis, Gregory, Willicombe, Bevan, Banner; G - Watkins 4
France: G - Guilhem
Wales: David Watkins, Roy Mathias, Frank Wilson, David Willicombe, John Bevan, Bill Francis, Peter Banner, John Mantle, Graham Evans, Mick Murphy, Stuart Gallacher, Brian Gregory, Clive Jones. Replacements: Glyn Turner (for Francis), John Butler (for Mantle).
France: Jose Calle, Jean-Francois Grechi, Rene Terrats, Bernard Guilhem, Bernard Curt, Jean-Pierre Lacoste, Jean-Marie Imbert, Yves Alvernhe, Antoine Gonzales, Michel Moussard, Jean-Pierre Tremouille, Jean-Pierre Sauret, Jean-Claude Mayorgas. Replacement: Michel Maique (for Tremouille).

FINAL TABLE

	P	W	D	L	F	A	Pts
Australia	8	6	1	1	198	69	13
England	8	5	2	1	167	84	12
Wales	8	3	0	5	110	130	6
New Zealand	8	2	2	4	121	149	6
France	8	1	1	6	40	204	3

No Final required. Australia won the Cup.

CHALLENGE MATCH *(Held after World Championship)*

ENGLAND 0 ....**AUSTRALIA 25**
At Headingley, Leeds, Wednesday, November 12, 1975
Attendance: 7,727; **Referee:** Fred Lindop (England)
Australia: T - Lang 2, Peard, Randall, Cronin; G - Eadie 5
England: Ray Dutton, Mike Smith, Nigel Stephenson, Eric Hughes, Ged Dunn, Ken Gill, Roger Millward, Harry Beverley, Keith Bridges, Jimmy Thompson, Jeff Grayshon, Mick Adams, Stanley Fearnley. Replacements: David Topliss (for Fearnley), Richard Stone (for Adams).
Australia: Graham Eadie, John Rhodes, Mick Cronin, Steve Rogers, Ian Schubert, John Peard, Tom Raudonikis, Greg Veivers, John Lang, Arthur Beetson (c), Terry Randall, Ray Higgs, Greg Pierce.

THE 1975 SQUADS

AUSTRALIA *(Captain-coach: Graeme Langlands)*

	M	T	G	FG	Pts
Chris Anderson (Canterbury-Bankstown)	3	1	-	-	3
Arthur Beetson (Eastern Suburbs)	5	-	-	-	-
Ray Branighan (Manly-Warringah)	1	1	-	-	3
John Brass (Eastern Suburbs)	3	-	-	-	-
Ron Coote (Eastern Suburbs)	3	1	-	-	3
Mick Cronin (Gerringong)	7	4	32	-	76
John Donnelly (Western Suburbs)	3	-	-	-	-
Graham Eadie (Manly-Warringah)	4	1	7	-	17
Terry Fahey (Wellington)	1	-	-	-	-
Denis Fitzgerald (Parramatta)	1	-	-	-	-
Bob Fulton (Manly-Warringah)	4	4	-	-	12
Mark Harris (Eastern Suburbs)	3	3	-	-	9
Ray Higgs (Parramatta)	4	2	-	-	6
John Lang (Brisbane Easts)	5	-	-	-	-
Graeme Langlands (St George)	4	3	-	-	9
Ian Mackay (Eastern Suburbs)	3	-	-	-	-
Allan McMahon (Balmain)	1	-	-	-	-
Johnny Mayes (Eastern Suburbs)	3	-	-	-	-
John O'Neill (South Sydney)	1	-	-	-	-
Tim Pickup (Canterbury-Bankstown)	4	1	-	-	3
Lew Platz (Wynnum-Manly)	6	2	-	-	6
John Peard (Eastern Suburbs)	4	2	-	-	6
Greg Pierce (Cronulla-Sutherland)	2	-	-	-	-
George Piggins (South Sydney)	3	-	-	-	-
Jim Porter (Parramatta)	2	-	-	-	-
John Quayle (Parramatta)	3	1	-	-	3
Terry Randall (Manly-Warringah)	7	2	-	-	6
Tom Raudonikis (Western Suburbs)	5	2	-	-	6
John Rhodes (Wynnum-Manly)	6	1	-	-	3
Steve Rogers (Cronulla-Sutherland)	3	2	-	-	6
Paul Sait (South Sydney)	2	-	-	-	-
Ian Schubert (Eastern Suburbs)	4	7	-	-	21
Gary Stevens (South Sydney)	3	-	-	-	-
Ross Strudwick (Brisbane Easts)	1	-	-	-	-
Greg Veivers (Brisbane Souths)	2	-	-	-	-
David Wright (Brisbane Brothers)	1	-	-	-	-

ENGLAND *(Coach: Alex Murphy)*

	M	T	G	FG	Pts
Mick Adams (Widnes)	2	-	-	-	-
John Atkinson (Leeds)	4	1	-	-	3
Keith Bridges (Featherstone Rovers)	6	-	-	1	1
Paul Charlton (Salford)	1	-	-	-	-
Dave Chisnall (Warrington)	3	-	-	-	-
Eric Chisnall (St Helens)	3	-	-	-	-
Phil Cookson (Leeds)	2	-	-	-	-
Mike Coulman (Salford)	2	-	-	-	-
Ged Dunn (Hull Kingston Rovers)	4	4	-	-	12
Les Dyl (Leeds)	6	-	-	-	-
Dave Eckersley (St Helens)	1	-	-	-	-
George Fairbairn (Wigan)	7	2	26	-	58

163

Player	M	T	G	FG	Pts
Keith Fielding (Salford)	6	7	-	-	21
Colin Forsyth (Bradford Northern)	3	1	-	-	3
Ken Gill (Salford)	8	5	-	-	15
Parry Gordon (Warrington)	-	-	-	-	-
John Gray (Wigan)	1	-	4	-	8
Jeff Grayshon (Dewsbury)	4	1	-	-	3
Brian Hogan (Wigan)	4	1	-	-	3
John Holmes (Leeds)	4	3	-	-	9
Eric Hughes (Widnes)	4	5	-	-	15
Bob Irving (Wigan)	3	-	-	-	-
Phil Jackson (Bradford Northern)	1	-	-	-	-
Tommy Martyn (Warrington)	2	1	-	-	-
Roger Millward (Hull Kingston Rovers)	7	1	2	-	7
Mick Morgan (Wakefield Trinity)	4	1	-	-	3
Steve Nash ((Featherstone Rovers)	3	-	-	-	-
George Nicholls (St Helens)	6	-	-	-	-
Derek Noonan (Warrington)	2	-	-	-	-
Steve Norton (Castleford)	6	1	-	-	3
Barry Philbin (Warrington)	1	-	-	-	-
Dave Redfearn (Bradford Northern)	1	-	-	-	-
Jimmy Thompson (Featherstone Rovers)	1	-	-	-	-
John Walsh (St Helens)	2	-	-	-	-
Stuart Wright (Wigan)	1	1	-	-	3

FRANCE *(Coach: Puig Aubert)*

Player	M	T	G	FG	Pts
Michel Anglade (Saint-Gaudens)	3	-	-	-	-
Yves Alvernhe (Albi)	1	-	-	-	-
Elie Bonal (Carcassonne)	3	-	-	-	-
Jean-Marie Bosc (Saint-Esteve)	1	-	-	-	-
Guy Bucchi (Marseille)	1	-	-	-	-
Jose Calle (Saint-Esteve)	6	-	4	-	8
Michel Cassin (Tonneins)	2	-	-	-	-
Jean-Louis Castel (Albi)	-	-	-	-	-
Patrick Chauvet (Carcassonne)	2	2	-	-	6
Philippe Clergeau (Bordeaux)	1	-	-	-	-
Bernard Curt (Bordeaux)	4	1	-	-	3
Maurice De Matos (Toulouse)	1	-	-	-	-
Francis De Nadia (Limoux)	4	-	-	-	-
Andre Dumas (Lezignan)	2	-	-	-	-
Francis Duthil (Bordeaux)	1	-	-	-	-
Guy Garcia (Carcassonne)	1	-	-	-	-
Serge Gleyzes (Carcassonne)	4	-	-	-	-
Antoine Gonzales (Pamiers)	4	-	-	-	-
Michel Gonzales (Pamiers)	1	-	-	-	-
Jean-Francois Grechi (Limoux)	4	-	-	-	-
Bernard Guilhem (Carcassonne)	3	-	5	-	10
Didier Hermet (Villeneuve)	2	-	-	-	-
Jean-Marie Imbert (Avignon)	8	-	-	1	1
Fernand Kaminski (Albi)	3	-	-	-	-
Jean-Pierre Lacoste (Villeneuve)	3	-	-	1	1
Michel Lafargue (Tonneins)	1	-	-	-	-
Gabriel Laskawiec (Albi)	-	-	-	-	-
Michel Maique (Lezignan)	2	-	-	-	-
Jean-Claude Mayorgas (Toulouse)	3	-	-	-	-
Michel Molinier (Saint-Gaudens)	2	-	-	-	-
Michel Moussard (Albi)	3	-	-	-	-
Marcel Pillon (Saint-Esteve)	2	-	-	-	-
Andre Ruiz (Pau)	5	-	-	-	-
Jean-Pierre Sauret (XIII Catalan)	1	-	-	-	-
Nestor Serrano (Saint-Gaudens)	2	-	4	-	8
Rene Terrats (Saint-Esteve)	8	1	-	-	3
Charles Thenegal (Toulouse)	3	-	-	-	-
Francis Tranier (Villefranche)	4	-	-	-	-
Jean-Pierre Tremouille (Tonneins)	4	-	-	-	-
Guy Vigouroux (Tonneins)	1	-	-	-	-
Charles Zalduendo (Toulouse)	4	-	-	-	-

NEW ZEALAND *(Coach: George Menzies)*

Player	M	T	G	FG	Pts
Fred Ah Kuoi (Auckland)	2	-	-	-	-
Ray Baxendale (West Coast)	7	-	-	-	-
Mocky Brereton (Auckland)	1	-	-	-	-
Warren Collicoat (Auckland)	8	-	16	-	32
Tony Coll (West Coast)	8	1	-	-	3
Tom Conroy (Auckland)	8	1	-	-	3
Bl Dickison (Canterbury)	3	-	-	-	-
Murray Eade (Auckland)	6	1	-	-	3
Tony Gordon (Auckland)	3	2	6	-	18
John Greengrass (Canterbury)	6	1	-	-	3
Peter Gurnick (Auckland)	3	-	-	-	-
John Hibbs (Wellington)	1	-	-	-	-
Bob Jarvis (Auckland)	7	3	-	-	9
Paul Matete (Auckland)	1	-	-	-	-
Don Munro (Wellington)	4	-	-	-	-
Phil Orchard (Wellington)	8	3	-	-	9
John O'Sullivan (Auckland)	4	-	-	-	-
Lindsay Proctor (Auckland)	6	1	-	-	3
John Smith (Auckland)	7	1	-	-	3
Dane Sorensen (Auckland)	5	-	10	-	20
Kurt Sorensen (Auckland)	2	-	-	-	-
Ken Stirling (Auckland)	7	2	-	-	6
Graeme West (Taranaki)	1	-	-	-	-
John Whittaker (Wellington)	3	1	-	-	3
Dennis Williams (Auckland)	8	2	-	-	6

WALES *(Coach: Les Pearce)*

Player	M	T	G	FG	Pts
Peter Banner (Salford)	7	2	-	-	6
John Bevan (Warrington)	4	2	-	-	6
Brian Butler (Swinton)	2	-	-	-	-
Kel Coslett (St Helens)	6	1	2	-	7
Eddie Cunningham (St Helens)	4	-	-	-	-
Colin Dixon (Salford)	4	-	-	-	-
Richard Evans (Swinton)	2	-	-	-	-
Tony Fisher (Leeds)	6	1	-	-	3
Bill Francis (Wigan)	8	4	-	-	12
Stuart Gallacher (Keighley)	2	-	-	-	-
Brian Gregory (Wigan)	3	1	-	-	3
Mel James (St Helens)	1	-	-	-	-
John Mantle (St Helens)	8	1	-	-	3
Roy Mathias (St Helens)	7	-	-	-	-
Jim Mills (Widnes)	5	1	-	-	3
Mick Murphy (Bradford Northern)	3	-	-	-	-
Mike Nicholas (Warrington)	-	-	-	-	-
Maurice Richards (Salford)	1	-	-	-	-
Peter Rowe (Blackpool Borough)	3	-	-	-	-
Clive Sullivan (Hull Kingston Rovers)	4	1	-	-	3
David Treasure (Oldham)	4	1	-	-	3
Glyn Turner (Hull Kingston Rovers)	4	-	-	-	-
Richard Wallace (York)	1	-	-	-	-
Bobby Wanbon (Warrington)	3	-	-	-	-
David Watkins (Salford)	8	-	26	-	52
David Willicombe (Wigan)	6	2	-	-	6
Frank Wilson (St Helens)	7	1	-	-	3

FRIENDLIES WHILE ON TOUR

AUSTRALIA

AUCKLAND 6 ....AUSTRALIA 17
Auckland: G - Collicoat 3
Australia: T - Raudonikis, Cronin, McMahon; G - Cronin 4

SALFORD 6 ....AUSTRALIA 44
Salford: T - Fiddler, Mayor
Australia: T - Rhodes 3, Quayle 2, Cronin, Brass, McMahon, Mayes, Platz; G - Cronin 7

ST HELENS 7 ....AUSTRALIA 32
St Helens: T - Hull; G - Pimblett 2
Australia: T - Pierce 2, Schubert 2, Brass, Rogers; G - Eadie 7

OLDHAM 10 ....AUSTRALIA 20
Oldham: T - Murphy, Brown; G - Larder 2
Australia: T - Rogers 2, Rhodes, Raudonikis; G - Eadie 4

YORK 4 ....AUSTRALIA 45
York: G - Hetherington 2
Australia: T - McMahon 2, Rogers 2, Raudonikis 2, Schubert, Lang, Porter, Mackay; G - Cronin 6

ENGLAND

WESTERN AUSTRALIA 2 ....ENGLAND 40
WA: G - Gush
England: T - Atkinson 2, Fielding 2, Dyl 2, Gill, Millward, Walsh; G - Fairbairn 6; FG - Nash

TOOWOOMBA 16 ....ENGLAND 25
Toowoomba: T - Connell, Smith, Collins, Crisp; G - Collins 2
England: T - Fielding 2, Norton, Millward, Noonan; G - Fairbairn 5

SOUTHERN DIVISION 8 ....ENGLAND 19
Sthn Division: T - Harris, Stuart; G - Cronin
England: T - Dyl, Martyn, Cookson; G - Walsh 5

WAIKATO 2 ....ENGLAND 40
Waikato: G - Moru
England: T - Dyl 3, Fielding 3, Atkinson 2, Gill, Fairbairn; G - Walsh 3, Fairbairn 2

ILLAWARRA 15 ....ENGLAND 12
Illawarra: T - Fitzgibbon, Fogarty, Renno; G - Ayliffe 3, Milthorpe
England: T - E Chisnall, Dyl; G - Fairbairn 3

BRISBANE 21 ....ENGLAND 10
Brisbane: T - Richardson, Smith, Veivers; G - Stewart 6
England: T - Dyl, Noonan; G - Fairbairn 2

PAPUA NEW GUINEA 12 ....ENGLAND 40
PNG: T - Eko, Patalui; G - Wartove 3
England: T - Fairbairn 2, Fielding 2, Coulman, Nash, D Chisnall; G - Fairbairn 8

FRANCE

AUCKLAND 9 ....FRANCE 3
Auckland: T - Dyer; G - Jordan 3
France: T - Bonal

NEW ZEALAND

SOUTH-WEST FRANCE 4...................................**NEW ZEALAND 39**
SW France: G - Cazadei
NZ: T - Dickison 3, Ah Kuoi 2, Williams, Smith, Greengrass, Proctor; G - Collicoat 4, Gordon 2

BARROW 0 ....**NEW ZEALAND 24**
NZ: T - Ah Kuoi 2, Smith 2, D Sorensen, Gordon; G - D Sorensen 2, Gordon

KEIGHLEY 8 ....**NEW ZEALAND 20**
Keighley: T - Roe; G - Moncrieff 2; FG - Moncrieff
NZ: T - Dickison 2, Ah Kuoi, Orchard: G - Gordon 4

WALES

IPSWICH 13 ....**WALES 35**
Ipswich: T - Richards 2, Dionysius; G - Dionysius 2
Wales: T - Mathias 4, Francis, Coslett, Fisher, Mills, Watkins; G - Coslett 2, Watkins, Treasure

WELLINGTON 8 ....**WALES 52**
Wellington: T - Farrel, Whare Henry; G - Fox
Wales: T - Cunningham 2, Dixon 2, Mathias 2, Sullivan 2, Treasure, Rowe, Nicholas; G - Watkins 8

WEST COAST 5 ....**WALES 35**
West Coast: T - Low; G - Crestani
Wales: T - Sullivan 3, Wanbon, Mantle, Turner, Mathias; G - Coslett 7

CANTERBURY 18 ....**WALES 25**
Canterbury: Cooksley, Dickison; G - Brereton 5, Lawrence
Wales: Mathias 2, Willicombe, Rowe, Nicholas; G - Watkins 5

AUCKLAND 31 ....**WALES 5**
Auckland: T - Hansen 2, Collicoat, O'Sullivan, Ah Kuoi; G - Collicoat 8
Wales: T - Dixon; G - Coslett

MAORIS 12 ....**WALES 18**
Maoris: T - P Orchard, Williams; G - Wilson 3
Wales: Wilson 2, Banner, Mathias; G - Watkins 3

1977

NEW ZEALAND 12..................................**AUSTRALIA 27**
At Carlaw Park, Sunday, May 29, 1977
Attendance: 20,019; **Referee:** Billy Thompson (England)
New Zealand: T - Smith, Rushton; G - Collicoat 3
Australia: T - Harris, Thomas, McMahon 2, Peard; G - Cronin 6
New Zealand: Warren Collicoat, Dane O'Hara, Olsen Filipaina, Chris Jordan, Kevin Fisher, Dennis Williams, John Smith, Whetu Henry, Alan Rushton, Dane Sorensen, Kurt Sorensen, Tony Coll, Whare Henry. Replacements: John Whittaker (for Jordan), Ray Baxendale (for Whare Henry).
Australia: Graham Eadie, Mark Harris, Mick Cronin, Mark Thomas, Allan McMahon; John Peard, Tommy Raudonikis, Greg Veivers (c), Nick Geiger, Denis Fitzgerald, Terry Randall, Ray Higgs, Greg Pierce

GREAT BRITAIN 23 ....**FRANCE 4**
At Carlaw Park, Auckland, Sunday, June 5, 1977
Attendance: 10,000; **Referee:** Bob Cooper (New Zealand)
Great Britain: T - Wright, Millward, Dyl; G - Fairbairn 7
France: G - Calle 2
Great Britain: George Fairbairn, Keith Fielding, John Holmes, Les Dyl, Stuart Wright, Roger Millward (c), Steve Nash, Steve Pitchford, David Ward, Jim Thompson, Eddie Bowman, George Nicholls, Phil Hogan. Replacements: Ken Gill (for Millward), Len Casey (for Hogan).
France: Jacques Guigue, Jose Moya, Christian Laskawiec, Andre Ruiz, Patrick Chauvet, Jose Calle (c), Guy Alard, Michel Cassin, Herve Bonnet, Henri Daniel, Jean-Pierre Sauret, Jean-Jaques Cologni, Joel Roosebrouck. Replacement: Guy Rodriguez (for Bonnet).

AUSTRALIA 21 ....**FRANCE 9**
At Sydney Cricket Ground, Saturday, June 11, 1977
Attendance: 13,231; **Referee:** Billy Thompson (England)
Australia: T - Eadie 2, McMahon, Fitzgerald, Veivers; G - Cronin 3
France: T - Moya; G - Calle 3
Australia: Graham Eadie, Terry Fahey, Mick Cronin, Mark Thomas, Allan McMahon, John Peard, Tom Raudonikis, Denis Fitzgerald, Nick Geiger, Greg Veivers, Terry Randall, Arthur Beetson (c), Rod Reddy. Replacements: Ray Higgs (for Beetson), Russel Gartner (for Thomas).
France: Jacques Guigue, Jose Moya, Jean-Marc Bourret, Rene Terrats, Christian Laskawiec, Jose Calle (c), Guy Alard, Michel Cassin, Guy Garcia, Max Chantal, Jean-Pierre Sauret, Manuel Caravaca, Joel Roosebrouck. Replacements: Jean-Marie Imbert (for Bourret), Guy Rodriguez (for Caravaca).

NEW ZEALAND 12 ....**GREAT BRITAIN 30**
At Addington Showgrounds, Christchurch, Sunday, June 12, 1977
Attendance: 5,342; **Referee:** Marcel Caillot (France)
New Zealand: T - Fisher, Whittaker; G - Collicoat 3
Great Britain: T - Wright 2, Francis, Nicholls, Bowman, Millward; G - Fairbairn 6
New Zealand: Warren Collicoat, John Whittaker, Olsen Filipaina, Fred Ah Kuoi, Kevin Fisher, Dennis Williams, John Smith, Whetu Henry, Alan Rushton, Lindsay Proctor, Tony Coll (c), Kurt Sorensen, Whare Henry. Replacements: Chris Jordan, Mark Graham.
Great Britain: George Fairbairn, Bill Francis, John Holmes, Les Dyl, Stuart Wright, Roger Millward (c), Steve Nash, Steve Pitchford, David Ward, Jim Thompson, Eddie Bowman, George Nicholls, Phil Hogan. Replacements: Ken Gill, Len Casey.

AUSTRALIA 19 ....**GREAT BRITAIN 5**
At Lang Park, Saturday, June 18, 1977
Attendance: 25,200; **Referee:** Marcel Caillol (France)
Australia: T - Eadie 2, Randall; G - Cronin 5
Great Britain: T - Millward; G - Fairbairn
Australia: Graham Eadie, Terry Fahey, Mick Cronin, Mark Thomas, Allan McMahon, John Peard, Tom Raudonikis, Denis Fitzgerald, Nick Geiger, Greg Veivers, Terry Randall, Arthur Beetson (c), Greg Pierce. Replacements: Ray Higgs (for Raudonikis).
Great Britain: George Fairbairn, Keith Fielding, Bill Francis, Les Dyl, Stuart Wright, Roger Millward (c), Steve Nash, Steve Pitchford, David Ward, Jim Thompson, Eddie Bowman, George Nicholls, Phil Hogan. Replacements: John Holmes (for Fielding), Peter Smith(for Ward).

NEW ZEALAND 28 ....**FRANCE 20**
At Carlaw Park, Auckland, Sunday, July 19, 1977
Attendance: 8,000; **Referee:** Billy Thompson (England)
New Zealand: T - Fisher, Jordan, Smith, Graham; G - Jordan 8
France: T - Cologni 2, Roosebrouck, Guigue; G - Moya 4
New Zealand: Michael O'Donnell, John Whittaker, Dennis Williams, Fred Ah Kuoi, Kevin Fisher, Chris Jordan, John Smith, Whetu Henry, Alan Rushton, Lindsay Proctor, Tony Coll (c), Kurt Sorensen, Mark Graham. Replacements: Olsen Filipaina, Ray Baxendale.
France: Jose Calle (c), Jacques Guigue, Rene Terrats, Andre Ruiz, Jose Moya, Guy Alard, Jean-Marie Imbert, Michel Cassin, Guy Garcia, Jean-Pierre Sauret, Manuel Caravaca, Jean-Jacques Cologni, Joel Roosebrouck. Replacements: Jackie Imbert, Michel Moussard.

FINAL TABLE

	P	W	D	L	F	A	Pts
Australia	3	3	0	0	67	26	6
Great Britain	3	2	0	1	58	35	4
New Zealand	3	1	0	2	52	77	2
France	3	0	0	3	33	72	0

FINAL

AUSTRALIA 13 ....**GREAT BRITAIN 12**
At Sydney Cricket Ground, Saturday, June 25, 1977
Attendance: 24,457; **Referee:** Billy Thompson (England)
Australia: T - McMahon, Gartner, Kolc; G - Cronin 2
Great Britain: T - Pitchford, Gill; G - Fairbairn 3
Australia: Graham Eadie, Mark Harris, Mick Cronin, Russel Gartner, Allan McMahon, John Peard, John Kolc, Terry Randall, Nick Geiger, Greg Veivers, Arthur Beetson (c), Ray Higgs, Greg Pierce. Replacement: Denis Fitzgerald (for Veivers).
Great Britain: George Fairbairn, Bill Francis, John Holmes, Les Dyl, Stuart Wright, Roger Millward (c), Steve Nash, Steve Pitchford, Keith Elwell, Jim Thompson, Eddie Bowman, George Nicholls, Phil Hogan. Replacements: Ken Gill (for Wright), Len Casey (for Hogan).

THE 1977 SQUADS

AUSTRALIA *(Coach: Terry Fearnley)*

	M	T	G	FG	Pts
Arthur Beetson (Eastern Suburbs) (c)	3	-	-	-	-
Steve Crear (Brisbane Wests)	-	-	-	-	-
Mick Cronin (Parramatta)	4	-	16	-	32
Graham Eadie (Manly-Warringah)	4	4	-	-	12
Terry Fahey (South Sydney)	2	-	-	-	-
Denis Fitzgerald (Parramatta)	4	1	-	-	3
Russel Gartner (Manly-Warringah)	2	1	-	-	3
Nick Geiger (Brisbane Norths)	4	-	-	-	-
Mark Harris (Eastern Suburbs)	2	1	-	-	3
Ray Higgs (Parramatta)	4	-	-	-	-
John Kolc (Parramatta)	1	1	-	-	3
Allan McMahon (Balmain)	4	4	-	-	12
Rod Morris (Brisbane Easts)	-	-	-	-	-
Graham Olling (Parramatta)	-	-	-	-	-
John Peard (Parramatta)	4	1	-	-	3
Greg Pierce (Cronulla-Sutherland)	3	-	-	-	-
Terry Randall (Manly-Warringah)	4	1	-	-	3
Tom Raudonikis (Western Suburbs)	3	-	-	-	-
Rod Reddy (St George)	1	-	-	-	-

Mark Thomas (Brisbane Brothers)	3	1	-	-	3
Greg Veivers (Brisbane Souths)	4	1	-	-	3

FRANCE *(Coach: Yves Begou)*

	M	T	G	FG	Pts
Guy Alard (Carcassonne)	3	-	-	-	-
Christian Baile (Carcassonne)	-	-	-	-	-
Herve Bonnet (Saint-Esteve)	1	-	-	-	-
Jean-Marc Bourret (XIII Catalan)	1	-	-	-	-
Jean-Louis Brial (XIII Catalan)	-	-	-	-	-
Jose Calle (Saint-Esteve) (c)	3	-	5	-	10
Manuel Caravaca (Carcassonne)	2	-	-	-	-
Michel Cassin (Toulouse)	3	-	-	-	-
Max Chantal (Villeneuve)	1	-	-	-	-
Patrick Chauvet (Carcassonne)	1	-	-	-	-
Jean-Jacques Cologni (XIII Catalan)	2	2	-	-	6
Henri Daniel (XIII Catalan)	1	-	-	-	-
Guy Garcia (Carcassonne)	2	-	-	-	-
Jacques Guigue (Avignon)	3	1	-	-	3
Jackie Imbert (Avignon)	1	-	-	-	-
Jean-Marie Imbert (Avignon)	2	-	-	-	-
Christian Laskawiec (Albi)	2	-	-	-	-
Gerard Lepine (Bordeaux)	-	-	-	-	-
Jean-Claude Mayorgas (Toulouse)	-	-	-	-	-
Michel Moussard (Albi)	1	-	-	-	-
Jose Moya (Carcassonne)	3	1	4	-	11
Guy Rodriguez (Toulouse)	2	-	-	-	-
Joel Roosebrouck (Villeneuve)	3	1	-	-	3
Andre Ruiz (Carcassonne)	2	-	-	-	-
Pierre Saboureau (XIII Catalan)	-	-	-	-	-
Jean-Pierre Sauret (XIII Catalan)	3	-	-	-	-
Rene Terrats (Saint-Esteve)	-	-	-	-	-

GREAT BRITAIN *(Coach: David Watkins)*

	M	T	G	FG	Pts
Eddie Bowman (Workington Town)	4	1	-	-	3
Len Casey (Hull Kingston Rovers)	3	-	-	-	-
Les Dyl (Leeds)	4	1	-	-	3
Keith Elwell (Widnes)	1	-	-	-	-
George Fairbairn (Wigan)	4	-	17	-	34
Keith Fielding (Salford)	2	-	-	-	-
Bill Francis (Wigan)	3	1	-	-	3
Ken Gill (Salford)	3	1	-	-	3
Alan Hodgkinson (Rochdale Hornets)	-	-	-	-	-
Phil Hogan (Barrow)	4	-	-	-	-
John Holmes (Leeds)	4	-	-	-	-
Sammy Lloyd (Castleford)	-	-	-	-	-
Roger Millward (Hull Kingston Rovers) (c)	4	3	-	-	9
Steve Nash (Salford)	4	-	-	-	-
George Nicholls (St Helens)	4	1	-	-	3
Steve Pitchford (Leeds)	4	1	-	-	3
Peter Smith (Featherstone Rovers)	1	-	-	-	-
Jim Thompson (Featherstone Rovers)	4	-	-	-	-
David Ward (Leeds)	3	-	-	-	-
Stuart Wright (Widnes)	4	3	-	-	9

Chosen to tour but withdrew: Eddie Cunningham (St Helens) (replaced by Thompson); Phil Lowe (Hull Kingston Rovers) (Hogan) ; Tommy Martyn (Warrington) (Pitchford); Jim Mills (Widnes)

NEW ZEALAND *(Coach: Ron Ackland)*

	M	T	G	FG	Pts
Fred Ah Kuoi (Auckland)	2	-	-	-	-
Ray Baxendale (West Coast)	2	-	-	-	-
Tony Coll (West Coast) (c)	3	-	-	-	-
Warren Collicoat (Wellington)	2	-	6	-	12
Tom Conroy (Auckland)	-	-	-	-	-
Olsen Filipaina (Auckland)	3	-	-	-	-
Kevin Fisher (Waikato)	3	2	-	-	6
Mark Graham (Auckland)	2	1	-	-	3
Whare Henry (Wellington)	2	-	-	-	-
Whetu Henry (Wellington)	3	-	-	-	-
Chris Jordan (Auckland)	3	1	8	-	19
Michael O'Donnell (Canterbury)	1	-	-	-	-
Dane O'Hara (Auckland)	1	-	-	-	-
Lindsay Proctor (Auckland)	2	-	-	-	-
Alan Rushton (Canterbury)	3	1	-	-	3
John Smith (Auckland)	3	2	-	-	6
Dane Sorensen (Cronulla-Sutherland)	1	-	-	-	-
Kurt Sorensen (Auckland)	3	-	-	-	-
John Whittaker (Wellington)	3	1	-	-	3
Dennis Williams (Auckland)	3	-	-	-	-

FRIENDLIES

AUSTRALIA

SOUTH ISLAND 5 ....**AUSTRALIA 68**

AUCKLAND 19...**AUSTRALIA 15**

FRANCE

PAPUA NEW GUINEA 37 ....**FRANCE 6**
At Boroko Oval, Port Moresby, Sunday, May 29, 1975
Attendance: 14,000

PNG: T - P Tore, D Boge, P Pais, J Meta, G Kora, B Karavu, A Rero; G - J Lenix 7, D Boge
France: T- C Baile, J-M Bourret

BRISBANE 14 ....**FRANCE 12**

WELLINGTON 0 ....**FRANCE 8**

NEWCASTLE 19 ....**FRANCE 12**

TOOWOOMBA 14...**FRANCE 10**

GREAT BRITAIN

NORTHERN MAORIS 14 ....**GREAT BRITAIN 18**

AUCKLAND 14 ....**GREAT BRITAIN 10**

MONARO 33 ....**GREAT BRITAIN 12**

NORTH QUEENSLAND 17 ....**GREAT BRITAIN 14**

QUEENSLAND 13 ....**GREAT BRITAIN 18**
Queensland: T - J Ribot 2, B Gardiner; G - J Ribot, D Brohman
Gt Britain: T - K Fielding 2, B Francis, P Hogan; G - G Fairbairn 3

NEW SOUTH WALES 35 ....**GREAT BRITAIN 5**
At Sydney Cricket Ground, Saturday, July 2, 1977
Attendance: 7,244
NSW: B Hetherington 2, R McGregor, R Reddy, M Krilich; G - Cronin 9, Rogers
Gt Britain: T - Millward; G - D Watkins

1985-88

NEW ZEALAND 18...**AUSTRALIA 0**
At Carlaw Park, Auckland, Sunday, July 7, 1985
Attendance: 15,327; **Referee:** Julien Rascagneres (France)
New Zealand: T - Friend 2, Leuluai; G - Filipaina 3
New Zealand: Gary Kemble, Dean Bell, Gary Prohm, James Leuluai, Dane O'Hara, Olsen Filipaina, Clayton Friend, Owen Wright, Howie Tamati, Kevin Tamati, Mark Graham (c), Kurt Sorensen, Hugh McGahan. Replacements: Joe Ropati, Ricky Cowan.
Australia: Garry Jack, John Ribot, Mal Meninga, Steve Ella, John Ferguson, Wally Lewis (c), Des Hasler, Peter Tunks, Ben Elias, Steve Roach, Paul Vautin, Peter Wynn, Wayne Pearce. Replacements: Chris Close, Greg Dowling.

GREAT BRITAIN 6 ....**NEW ZEALAND 6**
At Elland Road, Leeds, Sunday, November 9, 1985
Attendance: 22,209; **Referee:** Barry Gomersall (Australia)
Great Britain: G - Crooks 3
New Zealand: T - Graham; G - Dane Sorensen
Great Britain: Mick Burke, Des Drummond, Garry Schofield, Shaun Edwards, Joe Lydon, Ellery Hanley, Deryck Fox, Jeff Grayshon, David Watkinson, John Fieldhouse, Andy Goodway, Ian Potter, Harry Pinner (c). Replacements: Chris Arkwright, Lee Crooks.
New Zealand: Gary Kemble, Darrell Williams, Dean Bell, James Leuluai, Dane O'Hara), Fred Ah Kuoi, Clayton Friend, Kevin Tamati, Wayne Wallace, Dane Sorensen, Mark Graham (c), Kurt Sorensen, Gary Prohm. Replacements: Olsen Filipaina, Hugh McGahan.

FRANCE 0 ....**NEW ZEALAND 22**
At Stade Gilbert Brutus, Perpignan, Saturday, December 7, 1985
Attendance: 5,000; **Referee:** Ronnie Campbell (Great Britain)
New Zealand: T - McGahan 2, Kemble, Kurt Sorensen; G - Filipaina 3
France: Serge Pallares, Hugues Ratier, Denis Berge, Roger Palisses, Didier Couston, Dominique Espugna, Bruno Guasch, Max Chantal, Thierry Bernabe, Serge Titeux, Pierre Montgaillard, Marc Palanque, Guy Laforgue (c). Replacements: Andre Perez, Jean-Luc Rabot.
New Zealand: Gary Kemble, Dean Bell, James Leuluai, Fred Ah Kuoi, Dane O'Hara, Olsen Filipaina, Clayton Friend, Kurt Sorensen, Wayne Wallace, Dane Sorensen, Hugh McGahan (c), Owen Wright, Ron O'Regan. Replacements: Mark Elia, Brent Todd.

FRANCE 10 ....**GREAT BRITAIN 10**
At Parc de Sports, Avignon, Sunday, February 16, 1986
Attendance: 6,000; **Referee:** Kevin Roberts (Australia)
France: T - Dumas; G - Dumas 3
Great Britain: T - Hanley; G - Crooks 3
France: Gilles Dumas, Pascal Laroche, Philippe Fourquet, Alain Maury, Didier Couston, Dominique Espugna, Patrick Entat, Max Chantal, Patrick Baco, Serge Titeux, Marc Palanque, Guy Laforgue (c), Thierry Bernabe. Replacements: Denis Berge (for Laroche), Jean-Luc Rabot (for Titeux).
Great Britain: Mick Burke, Des Drummond, Garry Schofield, Ellery Hanley, Henderson Gill, Tony Myler, Deryck Fox, Lee Crooks, David Watkinson, Shaun Wane, John Fieldhouse, Ian Potter, Harry Pinner (c).

AUSTRALIA 32...**NEW ZEALAND 12**
At Lang Park, Brisbane, Tuesday, July 29, 1986
Attendance: 22,811; **Referee:** Robin Whitfield (England)
Australia: T - Kenny 2, Sterling, Lewis, Miles, O'Connor;
G - O'Connor 4
New Zealand: T - Williams 2; G - Filipaina 2
Australia: Garry Jack, Michael O'Connor, Gene Miles, Brett Kenny,
Les Kiss, Wally Lewis (c), Peter Sterling, Steve Roach, Royce
Simmons, Peter Tunks, Noel Cleal, Steve Folkes, Wayne Pearce.
Replacements: Terry Lamb, Bryan Niebling.
New Zealand: Gary Kemble, Darrell Williams, Joe Ropati, Gary
Prohm, Dane O'Hara, Olsen Filipaina, Gary Freeman, Brent Todd,
Barry Harvey, Kurt Sorensen, Mark Graham (c), Hugh McGahan,
Ron O'Regan. Replacements: Shane Cooper, Owen Wright.

PAPUA NEW GUINEA 24 ....**NEW ZEALAND 22**
At Lloyd Robson Oval, Port Moresby, Sunday, August 17, 1986
Attendance: 15,000; **Referee:** Kevin Roberts (Australia)
Papua New Guinea: T - Haili 2, Ako, Atoi; G - Kovae 4
New Zealand: T - Brown, Wallace, McGahan, Ropati; G - Brown 3
Papua New Guinea: Dairi Kovae, J Katsir, Lauta Atoi, Bal
Nupampo, M Kerekere, Darius Haili, Tony Kila (c), Joe Tep, Roy
Heni, Ati Lomutopa, Bobby Ako, Bernard Waketsi, Arebo Taumaku.
Replacements: Kepi Saea, Nick Andy.
New Zealand: Gary Kemble, Marty Crequer, Darrell Williams, Joe
Ropati, Dane O'Hara, Shane Cooper, Gary Freeman, Adrian
Shelford, Wayne Wallace, Peter Brown, Owen Wright, Hugh
McGahan (c), Ron O'Regan. Replacements: James Leuluai, Sam
Stewart.

PAPUA NEW GUINEA 12 ....**AUSTRALIA 62**
At Lloyd Robson Oval, Port Moresby, October 4, 1986
Attendance: 17,000; **Referee:** Neville Kesha (New Zealand)
Papua New Guinea: T - Numapo 2; G - Kovae 2
Australia: T - Kiss 2, O'Connor 2, Cleal 2, Mortimer, Jack, Lindner,
Roach, Hasler, Lewis; G - O'Connor 7
Papua New Guinea: Dairi Kovae, J Katsir, Lauta Atoi, Bal
Nupampo, M Kerekere, Darius Haili, Tony Kila (c), Joe Tep, Roy
Heni, Ati Lomutopa, Bobby Ako, Bernard Waketsi, Arebo Taumaku.
Replacements: Kepi Saea, Nick Andy.
Australia: Garry Jack, Michael O'Connor, Gene Miles, Chris
Mortimer, Les Kiss, Wally Lewis (c), Des Hasler, Steve Roach,
Royce Simmons, Bryan Niebling, Noel Cleal, Paul Dunn, Bob
Lindner. Replacements: Mal Meninga, Paul Sironen.

GREAT BRITAIN 15 ....**AUSTRALIA 24**
At Central Park, Wigan, Saturday, November 22, 1986
Attendance: 20,169; **Referee:** Julien Rascagneres (France)
Great Britain: T - Schofield 2; G - Lydon2, Gill; FG - Schofield
Australia: T - Miles, Lindner, Shearer, Lewis; G - O'Connor 4
Great Britain: Joe Lydon, Henderson Gill, Garry Schofield, David
Stephenson, John Basnett, Tony Myler, Andy Gregory, Kevin Ward,
David Watkinson (c), Lee Crooks, Chris Burton, Andy Goodway
(Wigan), Harry Pinner (Widnes). Replacements: Ian Potter (for
Burton).
Australia: Garry Jack, Dale Shearer, Brett Kenny, Gene Miles,
Michael O'Connor, Wally Lewis (c), Peter Sterling, Greg Dowling,
Royce Simmons, Paul Dunn, Mal Meninga, Bryan Niebling, Bob
Lindner. Replacements: Terry Lamb (for Meninga), Les Davidson
(for Dunn).

FRANCE 0 ....**AUSTRALIA 52**
At Stade Albert Domec, Carcassonne, Saturday, December 13, 1986
Attendance: 3,000; **Referee:** Fred Lindop (Great Britain)
Australia: T - Shearer 4, Jack 3, Folkes, Niebling, O'Connor; G -
O'Connor 6
France: Patrick Wozniack, Sebastien Rodriguez, Phillipe Fourquet,
Francis Laforgue, Hughes Ratier, Roger Palisses, Christian
Scicchitano, Max Chantal, Thierry Bernabe, Serge Titeux, Guy
Laforgue (c), Daniel Verdes, Philippe Gestas. Replacements: Gilles
Dumas (for Rodriguez), Yves Storer (for Chantal).
Australia: Garry Jack, Dale Shearer, Brett Kenny, Gene Miles,
Michael O'Connor, Wally Lewis (c), Peter Sterling, Greg Dowling,
Royce Simmons, Paul Dunn, Steve Folkes, Bryan Niebling, Bob
Lindner. Replacements: Terry Lamb (for Dowling), Les Davidson
(for Folkes).

GREAT BRITAIN 52 ....**FRANCE 4**
At Headingley, Leeds, Saturday, January 24, 1987
Attendance: 6,567; **Referee:** Mick Stone (Australia)
Great Britain: T - Edwards 2, Hanley 2, Gregory 2, Lydon, Forster,
Goodway; G - Lydon 8
France: G - Perez 2
Great Britain: Joe Lydon, Mark Forster, Garry Schofield, David
Stephenson, Henderson Gill, Ellery Hanley (c), Shaun Edwards,
David Hobbs, Kevin Beardmore, Lee Crooks, Andy Goodway, Roy
Haggerty, Mike Gregory. Replacements: David Creasser, Keith
England.
France: Andre Perez, Didier Couston, Roger Palisses, Hugues
Ratier, Cyrille Pons, Dominique Espugna, Gilles Dumas, Yves
Storer, Yannik Mantese, Jean-Luc Rabot, Daniel Verdes, Marc
Pallanque (c), Thierry Bernabe. Replacements: Patrick Rocci,
Serge Titeux.

GREAT BRITAIN 42 ....**PAPUA NEW GUINEA 0**
At Central Park, Wigan, Saturday. October 24, 1987
Attendance: 9,121; **Referee:** Francis Desplas (France)
Great Britain: T - Edwards 2, Ford, Medley, Hanley, Lydon,
Gregory; G - Stephenson 7
Great Britain: Steve Hampson, Des Drummond, David
Stephenson, Joe Lydon, Phil Ford, Shaun Edwards, Andy Gregory,
Kevin Ward, Paul Groves, Brian Case, Andy Goodway, Paul
Medley, Ellery Hanley (c). Replacements: John Woods, Karl
Fairbank.
Papua New Guinea: Dairi Kovae, Arnold Krewanty, Lauta Atoi, Bal
Numapo (c), Kepi Saea, Darius Haili, Tony Kila, Joe Tep, Roy Heni,
Ati Lomutopa, Mathius Kombra, Bernard Waketsi, Arebo Taumaku.
Replacements: Mathius Kitimon, David Gaius.

FRANCE 21 ....**PAPUA NEW GUINEA 4**
At Stade Albert Domec, Carcassonne, Sunday, November 15, 1987
Attendance: 3,500; **Referee:** John Holdsworth (Great Britain)
France: T - Fraisse 2, Pons, Ratier: G - Bourrel 2; FG - Bourrel
Papua New Guinea: T - Kovae
France: Jean-Philippe Pougeau, Hugues Ratier (c), Guy Delaunay,
David Fraisse, Cyrille Pons, Jacques Moliner, Frederic Bourrel,
Jean -Luc Rabot, Matthieu Khedimi, Pierre Alleres, Pierre
Montgaillard, Daniel Divet, Guy Laforgue. Replacements: Daniel
Verdes, Gilles Dumas.
Papua New Guinea: Dairi Kovae, Arnold Krewanty, Lauta Atoi,
Kepi Saea, Mea Morea, Bal Numapo (c), Tony Kila, Yer Bom,
Taumaku, Roy Heni, Ati Lomutopa, Bernard Waketsi, Bobby Ako,
Gideon Kouoru. Replacements: Darius Haili, Mathius Kombra.

PAPUA NEW GUINEA 22 ....**GREAT BRITAIN 42**
At Lloyd Robson Oval, Port Moresby, Sunday, May 22, 1988
Attendance: 12,107; **Referee:** Greg McCallum (Australia)
Papua New Guinea: T - Kovae 2, Krewanty, Rop; G - Numapo 3
Great Britain: T - Schofield 2, Gill 2, Medley, M Gregory,
Stephenson; G - Loughlin 7
Papua New Guinea: Dairi Kovae, Arnold Krewanty, Mea Morea,
Bal Numapo (c), Kepi Saea, Darius Haili, Tony Kila, Yer Bom,
Michael Matmillo, Isaac Rop, Tuiyo Evei, Mathius Kombra, Haoda
Kouoru. Replacements: Ngala Lapan, Thomas Rombuk.
Great Britain: Paul Loughlin, Phil Ford, Garry Schofield, David
Stephenson, Henderson Gill, Shaun Edwards, Andy Gregory, Kevin
Ward, Kevin Beardmore, Brian Case, Paul Medley, Mike Gregory,
Ellery Hanley (c). Replacements: David Hulme, Paul Dixon.

AUSTRALIA 12 ....**GREAT BRITAIN 26**
At Sydney Football Stadium, Saturday, July 9, 1988
Attendance: 15,994; **Referee:** Francis Desplas (France)
Australia: T - Lewis, Backo; G - O'Connor 2
Great Britain: T - Gill 2, Offiah, Ford, M Gregory; G - Loughlin 3
Australia: Garry Jack, Andrew Ettingshausen, Michael O'Connor,
Peter Jackson, Tony Currie, Wally Lewis (c), Peter Sterling, Martin
Bella, Greg Conescu, Sam Backo, Wally Fullerton Smith, Paul
Vautin, Wayne Pearce. Replacements: Gary Belcher (for Sterling),
Bob Lindner (for Fullerton Smith).
Great Britain: Phil Ford, Henderson Gill, Paul Loughlin, David
Stephenson, Martin Offiah, David Hulme, Andy Gregory, Kevin
Ward, Paul Hulme, Hugh Waddell, Mike Gregory, Roy Powell,
Ellery Hanley (c). Replacements: Brian Case (for Waddell).

NEW ZEALAND 66 ....**PAPUA NEW GUINEA 14**
At Carlaw Park, Auckland, Sunday, July 10, 1988
Attendance: 8,392; **Referee:** Greg McCallum (Australia)
New Zealand: T - S Horo 3, Iro 3, Mercer 2, Graham, Shelford,
Wallace, Williams; G - Brown 9
Papua New Guinea: T - Matmillo, Kovae; G - Numapo 3
New Zealand: Darrell Williams, Shane Horo Dean Bell (c), Kevin
Iro, Gary Mercer, Shane Cooper, Clayton Friend, Peter Brown,
Wayne Wallace, Adrian Shelford, Mark Graham (c), Sam Stewart,
Mark Horo. Replacements: Gary Freeman, Esene Faimalo.
Papua New Guinea: Dairi Kovae, Arnold Krewanty, Bal Numapo
(c), Louta Atoi, Mea Morea, Darius Haili, Tony Kila, Yer Bom,
Michael Matmillo, Daroa Ben Moide, Tuiyo Evei, Mathius Kombra,
Gideon Kouoru. Replacements: Ipisa Wanega, Haoda Kouoru.

NEW ZEALAND 12 ....**GREAT BRITAIN 10**
At Addington Showgrounds, Christchurch, Sunday, July 17, 1988
Attendance: 8,525; **Referee:** Mick Stone (Australia)
New Zealand: T - Freeman 2; Goals: Brown 2
Great Britain: T - Loughlin, D Hulme; G - Loughlin
New Zealand: Darrell Williams, Shane Horo Dean Bell (c), Kevin
Iro, Gary Mercer, Shane Cooper, Clayton Friend, Peter Brown,
Wayne Wallace, Adrian Shelford, Mark Graham (c), Sam Stewart,
Mark Horo. Replacements: Gary Freeman.
Great Britain: Phil Ford, Henderson Gill, Paul Loughlin, David
Stephenson, Martin Offiah, David Hulme, Andy Gregory, Kevin
Ward, Kevin Beardmore, Hugh Waddell, Mike Gregory, Roy Powell,
Ellery Hanley (c). Replacements: Paul Hulme.

AUSTRALIA 70 ....**PAPUA NEW GUINEA 8**
At Eric Weissel Oval, Wagga Wagga, Wednesday, July 20, 1988
Attendance: 11,685; **Referee:** Neville Kesha (New Zealand)
Australia: T - O'Connor 4, Langer 2, Meninga 2, Jack, Currie,
Lewis, Fullerton Smith, Miller, Conescu; G - O'Connor 7

Papua New Guinea: T - Morea; G - Numapo 2
Australia: Garry Jack, Michael O'Connor, Mal Meninga, Peter Jackson, Tony Currie, Wally Lewis (c), Allan Langer, Paul Dunn, Greg Conescu, Phil Daley, Wally Fullerton Smith, Gavin Miller, Wayne Pearce. Replacements: Des Hasler (for Lewis), Paul Vautin (for Fullerton Smith).
Papua New Guinea: Ipisa Wanega, Arnold Krewanty, Darai Kovae, Bal Numapo (c), Mea Morea, Lauto Atoi, Darius Haili, Thomas Rombuk, Michael Matmillo, Daroa Ben Moide, Mathius Kombra, Tuiyo Evei, Joe Gispe. Replacements: Sam Karara (for Gispe), Andrew Kuno (for Kombra).

FINAL TABLE

	P	W	D	L	F	A	Pts
Australia ●	7	5	0	2	252	91	12
New Zealand ●	7	4	1	2	158	86	11
Great Britain	8	4	2	2	203	90	10
Papua New Guinea ●	7	1	0	6	84	325	4
France	5	1	1	3	35	140	3

(● Australia, New Zealand and Papua New Guinea each received two points when France forfeited its Southern Hemisphere away games)

FINAL

AUSTRALIA 25 .... **NEW ZEALAND 12**
At Eden Park, Auckland, Sunday, October 9, 1988
Attendance: 46,000; **Referee:** Graham Ainui (Papua New Guinea)
Australia: T - Langer 2, Miller, Shearer; G - O'Connor 4; FG - Elias
New Zealand: T - T Iron, K Iro; G - Brown
Australia: Garry Jack, Dale Shearer, Andrew Farrar, Mark McGaw, Michael O'Connor, Wally Lewis (c), Allan Langer, Paul Dunn, Ben Elias, Steve Roach, Paul Sironen, Gavin Miller, Wayne Pearce. Replacements: Terry Lamb (for Lewis), David Gillespie (for Roach).
New Zealand: Gary Mercer, Tony Iro, Kevin Iro, Dean Bell (c), Mark Elia, Gary Freeman, Clayton Friend, Adrian Shelford, Wayne Wallace, Peter Brown, Kurt Sorenson, Mark Graham (c), Mark Horo. Replacements: Shane Cooper (for Mercer), Sam Stewart (for Shelford).

THOSE WHO PLAYED (1985-88)

AUSTRALIA

	M	T	G	FG	Pts
Sam Backo (Canberra)	1	1	-	-	4
Gary Belcher (Canberra)	1	-	-	-	-
Martin Bella (North Sydney)	1	-	-	-	-
Chris Close (Manly-Warringah)	1	-	-	-	-
Noel Cleal (Manly-Warringah)	2	2	-	-	8
Greg Conescu (Brisbane)	2	1	-	-	4
Tony Currie (Canterbury-Bankstown)	2	1	-	-	4
Phil Daley (Manly-Warringah)	1	-	-	-	-
Les Davidson (South Sydney)	2	-	-	-	-
Greg Dowling (Wynnum-Manly)	3	-	-	-	-
Paul Dunn (Canterbury-Bankstown)	5	-	-	-	-
Ben Elias (Balmain)	2	-	-	1	1
Steve Ella (Parramatta)	1	-	-	-	-
Andrew Ettingshausen (Cronulla-Sutherland)	1	-	-	-	-
Andrew Farrar (Canterbury-Bankstown)	1	-	-	-	-
John Ferguson (Eastern Suburbs)	1	-	-	-	-
Steve Folkes (Canterbury-Bankstown)	2	1	-	-	4
Wally Fullerton Smith (St George)	2	1	-	-	4
David Gillespie (Canterbury-Bankstown)	1	-	-	-	-
Des Hasler (Manly-Warringah)	3	1	-	-	4
Garry Jack (Balmain)	8	5	-	-	20
Peter Jackson (Canberra)	2	-	-	-	-
Brett Kenny (Parramatta)	3	2	-	-	8
Les Kiss (North Sydney)	2	2	-	-	8
Terry Lamb (Canterbury-Bankstown)	4	-	-	-	-
Allan Langer (Brisbane)	2	4	-	-	16
Wally Lewis (Wynnum-Manly)	8	5	-	-	20
Bob Lindner (Wynnum-Manly)	4	2	-	-	8
Mark McGaw (Cronulla-Sutherland)	1	-	-	-	-
Mal Meninga (Canberra)	4	2	-	-	8
Gene Miles (Wynnum-Manly)	4	2	-	-	8
Gavin Miller (Cronulla-Sutherland)	2	2	-	-	8
Chris Mortimer (Canterbury-Bankstown)	1	1	-	-	4
Bryan Niebling (Redcliffe)	4	1	-	-	4
Michael O'Connor (St George, Manly-Warringah)	7	8	34	-	100
Wayne Pearce (Balmain)	5	-	-	-	-
John Ribot (Manly-Warringah)	1	-	-	-	-
Steve Roach (Balmain)	5	1	-	-	4
Dale Shearer (Manly-Warringah)	3	6	-	-	24
Royce Simmons (Penrith)	4	-	-	-	-
Paul Sironen (Balmain)	2	-	-	-	-
Peter Sterling (Parramatta)	4	1	-	-	4
Peter Tunks (Canterbury-Bankstown)	2	-	-	-	-
Paul Vautin (Manly-Warringah)	3	-	-	-	-
Peter Wynn (Parramatta)	1	-	-	-	-

FRANCE

	M	T	G	FG	Pts
Pierre Ailleres (Toulouse)	1	-	-	-	-
Patrick Baco (XIII Catalan)	1	-	-	-	-
Denis Berge (Le Pontet)	2	-	-	-	-
Thierry Bernabe (Le Pontet)	4	-	-	-	-
Frederic Bourrel (Limoux)	1	-	2	1	5
Max Chantal (Villeneuve)	3	-	-	-	-
Didier Couston (Le Pontet)	3	-	-	-	-
Guy Delaunay (Saint-Esteve)	1	-	-	-	-
Daniel Divet (Limoux)	1	-	-	-	-
Gilles Dumas (Saint-Gaudens)	4	1	3	-	10
Patrick Entat (Avignon)	1	-	-	-	-
Dominique Espugna (Lezignan)	3	-	-	-	-
David Fraisse (Le Pontet)	1	2	-	-	8
Philippe Fourquet (Toulouse)	2	-	-	-	-
Philippe Gestas (Saint-Gaudens)	1	-	-	-	-
Bruno Guasch (Saint-Esteve)	1	-	-	-	-
Matthieu Khedimi (Saint-Esteve)	1	-	-	-	-
Francis Laforgue (XIII Catalan)	1	-	-	-	-
Guy Laforgue (XIII Catalan)	4	-	-	-	-
Pascal Laroche (Villeneuve)	1	-	-	-	-
Yannik Mantese (Albi)	1	-	-	-	-
Alain Maury (Villeneuve)	1	-	-	-	-
Jacques Moliner (Lezignan)	1	-	-	-	-
Pierre Montgaillard (XIII Catalan)	2	-	-	-	-
Marc Palanque (Le Pontet)	3	-	-	-	-
Roger Palisses (Saint-Esteve)	3	-	-	-	-
Roger Palisses (Saint-Esteve)	3	-	-	-	-
Serge Pallares (Saint-Esteve)	1	-	-	-	-
Andre Perez (XIII Catalan)	2	-	2	-	4
Cyrille Pons (Saint-Gaudens)	2	1	-	-	4
Jean-Philippe Pougeau (Saint-Esteve)	1	-	-	-	-
Jean-Luc Rabot (Villeneuve)	4	-	-	-	-
Hugues Ratier (Lezignan)	4	1	-	-	4
Patrick Rocci (Le Pontet)	1	-	-	-	-
Sebastien Rodriguez (XIII Catalan)	1	-	-	-	-
Christian Scicchitano (Carpentras)	1	-	-	-	-
Yves Storer (Saint-Gaudens)	2	-	-	-	-
Serge Titeux (Le Pontet)	4	-	-	-	-
Daniel Verdes (Villeneuve)	3	-	-	-	-
Patrick Wozniack (Villeneuve)	1	-	-	-	-

GREAT BRITAIN

	M	T	G	FG	Pts
Chris Arkwright (St Helens)	1	-	-	-	-
John Basnett (Widnes)	1	-	-	-	-
Kevin Beardmore (Castleford)	3	-	-	-	-
Chris Burton (Hull Kingston Rovers)	1	-	-	-	-
Mick Burke (Widnes)	2	-	-	-	-
Brian Case (Wigan)	3	-	-	-	-
David Creasser (Leeds)	1	-	-	-	-
Lee Crooks (Hull)	5	-	6	-	12
Paul Dixon (Halifax)	1	-	-	-	-
Des Drummond (Leigh, Warrington)	3	-	-	-	-
Shaun Edwards (Wigan)	4	4	-	-	16
Keith England (Castleford)	1	-	-	-	-
Karl Fairbank (Halifax)	1	-	-	-	-
John Fieldhouse (Widnes)	2	-	-	-	-
Phil Ford (Bradford Northern)	3	2	-	-	8
Mark Forster (Warrington)	1	1	-	-	4
Deryck Fox (Featherstone Rovers)	2	-	-	-	-
Henderson Gill (Wigan)	6	4	1	-	18
Andy Gregory (Warrington)	5	3	-	-	12
Mike Gregory (Warrington)	4	2	-	-	8
Andy Goodway (Oldham)	5	1	-	-	4
Jeff Grayshon (Leeds)	1	-	-	-	-
Paul Groves (St Helens)	1	-	-	-	-
Roy Haggerty (St Helens)	1	-	-	-	-
Steve Hampson (Wigan)	1	-	-	-	-
Ellery Hanley (Bradford Northern)	7	4	-	-	16
David Hobbs (Oldham)	1	-	-	-	-
David Hulme (Widnes)	3	1	-	-	4
Paul Hulme (Widnes)	2	-	-	-	-
Paul Loughlin (St Helens)	3	1	11	-	26
Joe Lydon (Widnes)	4	2	10	-	28
Paul Medley (Leeds)	2	2	-	-	8
Tony Myler (Widnes)	2	-	-	-	-
Martin Offiah (Widnes)	2	1	-	-	4
Harry Pinner (St Helens)	2	-	-	-	-
Ian Potter (Wigan)	2	-	-	-	-
Roy Powell (Leeds)	2	-	-	-	-
Garry Schofield (Hull)	5	4	-	1	17
David Stephenson (Wigan)	6	1	7	-	18
Hugh Waddell (Oldham)	2	-	-	-	-
Shaun Wane (Wigan)	1	-	-	-	-
Kevin Ward (Castleford)	5	-	-	-	-
David Watkinson (Hull Kingston Rovers)	3	-	-	-	-
John Woods (Warrington)	1	-	-	-	-

PAPUA NEW GUINEA

	M	T	G	FG	Pts
Bobby Ako (Mt Hagen)	3	1	-	-	4
Nick Andy (Port Moresby)	2	-	-	-	-
Lauta Atoi (Bouganville)	6	1	-	-	4
Daroa Ben Moide	2	-	-	-	-
Yer Bom	3	-	-	-	-

	M	T	G	FG	Pts
Tuiyo Evei (Goroka)	3	-	-	-	-
David Gaius (Rabaul)	1	-	-	-	-
Joe Gispe (Rabaul)	1	-	-	-	-
Darius Haili (Kimbe)	7	2	-	-	8
Roy Heni (Port Moresby)	4	-	-	-	-
Sam Karara	1	-	-	-	-
Joe Katsir (Lae)	2	-	-	-	-
Mofu Kerekere (Port Moresby)	2	-	-	-	-
Tony Kila (Port Moresby)	6	-	-	-	-
Mathius Kitimon (Port Moresby)	1	-	-	-	-
Mathius Kombra (Mendi)	4	-	-	-	-
Gideon Kouoru (Port Moresby)	2	-	-	-	-
Haoda Kouoru (Port Moresby)	2	-	-	-	-
Dairi Kovae (Port Moresby)	7	4	6	-	28
Arnold Krewanty (Port Moresby)	5	1	-	-	4
Andrew Kuno	1	-	-	-	-
Ngala Lapan (Lae)	1	-	-	-	-
Ati Lomutopa (Goroka)	3	-	-	-	-
Michael Matmillo (Port Moresby)	3	1	-	-	4
Mea Morea (Port Moresby)	4	1	-	-	4
Bal Numapo (Kundiawa)	7	2	8	-	24
Thomas Rombuk (Lae)	2	-	-	-	-
Isaac Rop	1	-	-	-	4
Kepi Saea (Port Moresby)	6	-	-	-	-
Arebo Taumaku (Port Moresby)	5	-	-	-	-
Joe Tep (Port Moresby)	3	-	-	-	-
Bernard Waketsi (Port Moresby)	5	-	-	-	-
Ipisa Wanega (Kundiawa)	2	-	-	-	-

NEW ZEALAND

	M	T	G	FG	Pts
Fred Ah Kuoi (Hull)	1	-	-	-	-
Dean Bell (Eastern Suburbs)	6	-	-	-	-
Peter Brown (Auckland)	4	1	16	-	36
Shane Cooper (Auckland)	5	-	-	-	-
Ricky Cowan (Auckland)	1	-	-	-	-
Marty Crequer (Auckland)	1	-	-	-	-
Mark Elia (Auckland)	2	-	-	-	-
Esene Faimalo (Canterbury)	1	-	-	-	-
Olsen Filipaina					
(Eastern Suburbs, North Sydney)	4	-	8	-	16
Gary Freeman (Auckland)	5	2	-	-	8
Clayton Friend (Auckland)	6	2	-	-	8
Mark Graham (North Sydney)	6	2	-	-	8
Barry Harvey (Taranaki)	1	-	-	-	-
Mark Horo (Auckland)	3	-	-	-	-
Shane Horo (Waikato)	2	3	-	-	12
Kevin Iro (Wigan)	3	4	-	-	16
Tony Iro (Wigan)	1	1	-	-	4
Gary Kemble (Hull)	5	1	-	-	4
James Leuluai (Hull)	3	1	-	-	4
Hugh McGahan (Eastern Suburbs)	5	4	-	-	16
Gary Mercer (Bradford Northern)	4	2	-	-	8
Dane O'Hara (Hull)	5	-	-	-	-
Ron O'Regan (Auckland)	3	-	-	-	-
Gary Prohm (Hull Kingston Rovers)	3	-	-	-	-
Joe Ropati (Auckland)	3	1	-	-	4
Adrian Shelford (Canterbury)	4	-	-	-	-
Dane Sorensen (Cronulla-Sutherland)	2	1	-	-	4
Kurt Sorensen (Cronulla-Sutherland, Widnes)	5	1	-	-	4
Sam Stewart (Wellington)	4	-	-	-	-
Howie Tamati (Taranaki)	1	-	-	-	-
Kevin Tamati (Warrington)	2	-	-	-	-
Brent Todd (Canterbury)	2	-	-	-	-
Wayne Wallace (Canterbury)	6	2	-	-	8
Darrell Williams (Auckland)	5	4	-	-	16
Owen Wright (Auckland)	4	-	-	-	-

1989-92

NEW ZEALAND 14...**AUSTRALIA 22**
At Mt Smart Stadium, Auckland, Sunday, July 23, 1989
Attendance: 15,000; **Referee:** Robin Whitfield (Great Britain)
New Zealand: T - Elia, Mercer; G - Shelford 3
Australia: T - Shearer, O'Connor, Meninga, Clyde; G - O'Connor 2, Meninga
New Zealand: Darrell Williams, Gary Mercer, Kevin Iro, Tony Kemp, Mark Elia, Kelly Shelford, Shane Cooper, Gary Freeman, Brent Todd, Duane Mann, James Goulding, Sam Stewart, Mark Horo, Hugh McGahan (c). Replacements: Kurt Sherlock (for Kemp), Brendon Tuuta (for Horo).
Australia: Gary Belcher, Michael Hancock, Dale Shearer, Tony Currie, Michael O'Connor, Wally Lewis, Des Hasler, Sam Backo, Kerrod Walters, Steve Roach, Mal Meninga, Bradley Clyde. Replacement: Bruce McGuire (for Backo).

GREAT BRITAIN 10...**NEW ZEALAND 6**
At Central Park, Wigan, Saturday, November 11, 1989
Attendance: 20,346; **Referee:** Greg McCallum (Australia)
Great Britain: T - Offiah, Tait; G - Loughlin
New Zealand: T - Shelford; G - Shelford
Great Britain: Alan Tait, Phil Ford, Paul Newlove, Paul Loughlin, Martin Offiah, Shaun Edwards, David Hulme, Kelvin Skerrett, Paul Hulme, Andy Platt, Andy Goodway, Roy Powell, Mike Gregory (c).

Replacements: Joe Lydon (for Newlove), Keith England (for Skerrett).
New Zealand: Tony Kemp, Kevin Iro, Dean Bell, Darrell Williams, Gary Mercer, Kelly Shelford, Gary Freeman, Brent Todd, Duane Mann, Esene Family, Kurt Sorensen, Sam Stewart, Hugh McGahan (c). Replacements: Dean Clark (for Shelford), Francis Leota (for Family).

FRANCE 0 ....**NEW ZEALAND 34**
At Stade Albert Domec, Sunday, December 3, 1989
Attendance: 4,208; **Referee:** Robin Whitfield (Great Britain)
New Zealand: T - Watson 3, Kemp, Williams, Kuiti, Bell; G - Sherlock 3
France: Jean-Philippe Pougeau, Philippe Chiron, Philippe Fourquet, David Fraisse, Cyrille Pons, Gilles Dumas (c), Patrick Entat, Jean-Luc Rabot, Mathieu Khedimi, Yves Storer, Daniel Divet, Didier Cabestany, Thierry Bernabe. Replacements: Denis Bienes (for Storer), Regis Courty (for Chiron).
New Zealand: Tony Kemp, David Watson, Dean Bell, Darrell Williams, Gary Mercer, Dean Clark, Gary Freeman, Brent Todd, Duane Mann, George Mann, Mike Kuiti, Sam Stewart, Hugh McGahan (c). Replacements: Kurt Sherlock (for Mercer), Kelly Shelford (for Clark).

PAPUA NEW GUINEA 8 ....**GREAT BRITAIN 40**
At Lloyd Robson Oval, Port Moresby, Saturday, June 2, 1990.
Attendance: 7,837; **Referee:** Dennis Hale (New Zealand)
Papua New Guinea: T - Ongogo; G - Numapo 2
Great Britain: T - Gibson 2, Eastwood, Goulding, Dixon, D Powell, Schofield; G - J Davies 6
Papua New Guinea: Ipisa Wanega, Arnold Krewanty, Philip Boge, Bal Numapo, Mea Morea, Stanley Haru, Gigmai Ongogo, Ati Lomutopa, Tuiyo Evei, Michael Matmillo, Michael Angra, Arebo Taumaku (c), Joe Gispe. Replacements: Max Tiri (for Lomutopa), Chris Itam (for Morea)
Great Britain: Alan Tait, Paul Eastwood, Daryl Powell, Jonathan Davies, Carl Gibson, Garry Schofield, Bobbie Goulding, Roy Powell, Lee Jackson, Keith England, Denis Betts, Paul Dixon, Mike Gregory (c). Replacements: Deryck Fox (for Jackson), Phil Clarke (for Gregory).

AUSTRALIA 34 ....**FRANCE 2**
At Pioneer Oval, Parkes, Wednesday, June 28, 1990.
Attendance: 12,384 *(Ground record)*
Referee: Graham Ainui (Papua New Guinea)
Australia: T - Mackay 3, McGaw 2, Daley, Meninga, Shearer; G - Belcher
France: G - Dumas
Australia: Gary Belcher, Michael O'Connor, Mal Meninga (c), Mark McGaw, Dale Shearer, Laurie Daley, Allan Langer, Martin Bella, Kerrod Walters, Steve Roach, Paul Sironen, David Gillespie, Brad Mackay. Replacements: Mark Carroll (for Sironen), Andrew Ettingshausen (for McGaw).
France: Eric Castel, Hugues Ratier (c), Jean-Bernard Saumitou, Guy Delaunay, Cyrille Pons, Gilles Dumas, Patrick Entat, Jean-Luc Rabot, Francis Lope, Thierry Buttignol, Didier Cabestany, Daniel Divet, Thierry Valero. Replacement: Jean Ruiz (for Buttignol)

NEW ZEALAND 21 ....**GREAT BRITAIN 18**
At Queen Elizabeth II Stadium, Christchurch, Sunday, July 15, 1990.
Attendance: 3,133; **Referee:** Bill Harrigan (Australia)
New Zealand: T - Kemp, Nikau; G - Ridge 6; FG - McGahan
Great Britain: T - Schofield, Roy Powell, Offiah; G - Davies 3
New Zealand: Matthew Ridge, Sam Panapa, Kevin Iro, Darrell Williams, Tony Iro, Tony Kemp, Gary Freeman, Brent Todd, Duane Mann, Peter Brown, Mark Horo, Tawera Nikau, Hugh McGahan (c). Replacements: Morvin Edwards (for Kevin Iro), Dean Lonergan (for Todd).
Great Britain: Joe Lydon, Jonathan Davies, Daryl Powell, Carl Gibson, Martin Offiah, Garry Schofield, Bobbie Goulding, Kelvin Skerrett, Martin Dermott5, Keith England, Denis Betts, Roy Powell, Mike Gregory (c). Replacements: Shaun Irwin, Paul Dixon.

PAPUA NEW GUINEA 10 ....**NEW ZEALAND 18**
At Lloyd Robson Oval, Port Moresby, Saturday, August 11, 1990.
Attendance: 4,478; **Referee:** Bill Harrigan (Australia)
Papua New Guinea: T - Waine, Soga; G - Numapo
New Zealand: T - Lonergan, Panapa, Watson; G - Ridge 3
Papua New Guinea: Ipisa Wanega, Arnold Krewanty, Philip Boge, Bal Numapo (c), Goie Waine, Stanley Haru, Kes Paglipari, Bobby Ako, Tuiyo Evei, Michael Matmillo, Matthew Elara, Opai Soga. Replacements: Max Tiri, Gigmai Ongogo.
New Zealand: Matthew Ridge, Tony Iro, David Watson, Paddy Tuimavave, Sam Panapa, Tony Kemp, Gary Freeman, Peter Brown, Duane Mann, Brent Todd, Dean Lonergan, Tawera Nikau, Mark Horo. Replacements: Mike Kuiti, Morvin Edwards, Mark Nixon, George Mann.

GREAT BRITAIN 0 ....**AUSTRALIA 14**
At Elland Road, Leeds, Saturday, November 24, 1990.
Attendance: 32,500; **Referee:** Alain Sablayrolles (France)
Australia: T - Ettingshausen, Meninga, Elias; G - Meninga
Great Britain: Steve Hampson, Martin Offiah, Daryl Powell, Carl Gibson, Paul Eastwood, Garry Schofield, Andy Gregory, Karl

Harrison, Lee Jackson, Andy Platt, Denis Betts, Paul Dixon, Ellery Hanley (c). Replacements: Jonathan Davies (for Gibson), Mike Gregory (for Dixon), Roy Powell (for Harrison).
Australia: Gary Belcher, Andrew Ettingshausen, Mal Meninga (c), Laurie Daley, Dale Shearer, Cliff Lyons, Ricky Stuart, Glenn Lazarus, Ben Elias, Steve Roach, Paul Sironen, Bob Lindner, Brad Mackay. Replacements: David Gillespie (for Lazarus), Greg Alexander (for Shearer), Des Hasler (for Mackay), Mark Sargent (for Sironen).

FRANCE 10 ....AUSTRALIA 34
At Stade Gilbert Brutus, Perpignan, Sunday, December 9, 1990.
Attendance: 3,428; **Referee:** John Holdsworth (Great Britain)
France: T - Pons, Entat; G - Tisseyre
Australia: T - Mackay 2, Shearer, Alexander, Ettingshausen, Meninga, Roach; G - Alexander 3
France: David Fraisse, Cyrille Pons, Serge Bret, Guy Delaunay, Alain Bouzer, Jacques Moliner, Patrick Entat (c), Thierry Buttignol, Thierry Valero, Marc Tisseyre, Francis Lope, Daniel Divet, Daniel Verdes. Replacements: Denis Bienes (for Bret), Patrick Marginet (for Fraisse).
Australia: Gary Belcher, Greg Alexander, Dale Shearer, Mal Meninga (c), Andrew Ettingshausen, Cliff Lyons, Ricky Stuart, Glenn Lazarus, Ben Elias, Steve Roach, Paul Sironen, Bob Lindner, Brad Mackay. Replacements: David Gillespie (for Lindner), Chris Johns (for Alexander), Des Hasler (for Stuart), Mark Sargent (for Lazarus).

FRANCE 10 ....GREAT BRITAIN 45
At Stade Gilbert Brutus, Perpignan, Sunday, January 27, 1991.
Attendance: 3,965; **Referee:** Greg McCallum (Australia)
France: T - Auroy, Fraisse; G - Tisseyre
Great Britain: T - Schofield 2, Offiah 2, Edwards 2, Betts, Platt; G - Eastwood 6; FG - Schofield
France: Christophe Auroy, Eric Remirez, David Fraisse, Guy Delaunay, Cyrille Pons, Gilles Dumas (c), Patrick Entat, Marc Tisseyre, Thierry Valero, Thierry Buttignol, Jean-Pierre Magnac, Daniel Verdes, Jacques Moliner. Replacements: Denis Bienes (for Dumas), Pierre Chamorin (for Verdes), Abderazach Baba (for Valero).
Great Britain: Steve Hampson, Paul Eastwood, Carl Gibson, Daryl Powell, Martin Offiah, Garry Schofield, Shaun Edwards, Ian Lucas, Lee Jackson, Andy Platt, Denis Betts, Les Holliday, Ellery Hanley (c). Replacements: Mark Aston (for Schofield), St John Ellis (for Hampson), Richie Eyres (for Jackson), Karl Fairbank (for Holliday).

NEW ZEALAND 32 ....FRANCE 10
At Addington Showgrounds, Christchurch, Sunday, June 23, 1991.
Attendance: 2,000; **Referee:** Graham Ainui (Papua New Guinea)
New Zealand: T - Shelford, Blackmore, Watson, Friend, Panapa; G - Botica 6
France: T - Verdes; G - Dumas 3
New Zealand: Frano Botica, Sam Panapa, Jarrod McCracken, David Watson, Richie Blackmore, Kelly Shelford, Gary Freeman (c), Peter Brown, Duane Mann, Brent Todd, Emosi Koloto, Dean Lonergan, Tawera Nikau. Replacements: Clayton Friend, George Mann, Mike Patton, Gary Mercer.
France: Pascal Fages, Jean-Marc Garcia, David Despin, Denis Bienes, Cyrille Pons, Gilles Dumas (c), Patrick Entat, Thierry Buttignol, Thierry Valero, Yves Storer, Didier Cabestany, Gerard Boyals, Daniel Verdes. Replacements: Robert Viscay, Franck Romano, Roger Palisses, Thierry Bernabe.

PAPUA NEW GUINEA 18 ....FRANCE 20
At Danny Leahy Oval, Goroka, Sunday, July 7, 1991.
Attendance: 11,485; **Referee:** Colin Morris (Great Britain)
Papua New Guinea: T - Gela, Naipao; G - Wanega 5
France: T - Despin 2, Garcia; G - Torreilles 4
Papua New Guinea: Ipisa Wanega, Arnold Krewanty, Paul Gela, Elias Kamiak, Joe Rema, Stanley Haru (c); Gigmai Ongogo, James Naipao, Bernard Bate, John Unagi, Thomas Daki, Max Tiri, Joe Gispe. Replacements: Joshua Kouoru, Johannes Kola, Opai Soga, Kes Paglipari.
France: Christophe Auroy, Jean-Marc Garcia, David Despin, Denis Bienes, Cyrille Pons, Pascal Fages, Patrick Entat, Gerard Boyals, Patrick Torreilles, Thierry Buttignol (c), Bertrand Plante, Didier Cabestany, Daniel Verdes. Replacements: Robert Viscay, Marc Tisseyre, Guy Delpeche, Pierre Chamorin.

AUSTRALIA 40..NEW ZEALAND 12
At Lang Park, Brisbane, Wednesday, July 31, 1991
Attendance: 29,139; **Referee:** John Holdsworth (Great Britain)
Australia: T - Carne, Meninga, Walters, Wishart, Clyde, Ettingshausen, Daley; G - Meninga 6
New Zealand: T - McCracken, Blackmore; G - Botica 2
Australia: Andrew Ettingshausen, Willie Carne, Mal Meninga (c), Laurie Daley, Rod Wishart, Peter Jackson, Allan Langer, Martin Bella, Steve Walters, Craig Salvatori, Mark Geyer, David Gillespie, Bradley Clyde. Replacements: Chris Johns (for Jackson), Ian Roberts (for Bella), John Cartwright (for Gillespie), Des Hasler (for Clyde).
New Zealand: Frano Botica, David Watson, Jarrod McCracken, Kevin Iro, Richie Blackmore, Gary Freeman (c), Clayton Friend, Peter Brown, Duane Mann, Brent Todd, George Mann, Gary

Mercer, Tawera Nikau. Replacements: Emosi Koloto (for Mercer), Esene Faimalo (for Brown), Jason Williams (for McCracken), Mike Patton (for George Mann).

PAPUA NEW GUINEA 6 ....AUSTRALIA 40
At Lloyd Robson Oval, Port Moresby, Sunday, October 31, 1991.
Attendance: 14,500; **Referee:** Denis Hale (New Zealand)
Papua New Guinea: T - Haru; G - Boge
Australia: T - Carne 3, Belcher, Ettingshausen, Jackson, Meninga, Wishart, Clyde; G - Meninga 2
Papua New Guinea: Pillip Boge, Lipirin Palangat, Korul Sinemau, Richard Wagambie, Joshua Kouoru, Stanley Haru (c), Sam Karara, John Unagi, Danny Moi, James Naipao, Thomas Daki, Kes Paglipari, Joe Gispe. Replacements: Kera Ngaffin (for Moi), Jack Uradok (for Palangat), Ngala Lapan (for Daki), Leslee Hoffman (for Gispe).
Australia: Gary Belcher, Rod Wishart, Andrew Ettingshausen, Mal Meninga (c), Willie Carne, Peter Jackson, Geoff Toovey, Martin Bella, Kerrod Walters, Glenn Lazarus, Bradley Clyde, Ian Roberts, Brad Fittler. Replacements: Gary Coyne (for Bella), Chris Johns (for Wishart), Cliff Lyons (for Jackson), Kevin Walters (for Kerrod Walters).

GREAT BRITAIN 56 ....PAPUA NEW GUINEA 4
At Central Park, Wigan, Saturday, November 9, 1991.
Attendance: 4,193; **Referee:** Bill Harrigan (Australia)
Great Britain: T - Schofield, 2, Moriarty 2, Jackson 2, Sullivan, Newlove, Betts, Harrison; G - Davies 8
Papua New Guinea: T - Karu
Great Britain: Steve Hampson, Paul Newlove, Jonathan Davies, Daryl Powell, Anthony Sullivan, Garry Schofield (c), Shaun Edwards, Karl Harrison, Martin Dermott, Andy Platt, Paul Moriarty, Denis Betts, Michael Jackson. Replacements: Gary Connolly (for Hampson), Karl Fairbank for Platt), Deryck Fox (for Edwards), Gary Price (for Moriarty).
Papua New Guinea: Ipisa Wanega, Joshua Kouoru, Richard Wagambie, Philip Boge, Chris Itam, Tuksy Karu, Stanley Haru (c), John Unagi, Kes Paglipari, Kera Ngaffin, James Naipo, Leslee Hoffman, Joe Gispe. Replacements: Max Tiri (for Naipo), Ngala Lapan (for Karu), Thomas Daki (for Ngaffin), Lipirin Palangat (for Wanega).

FRANCE 28 ....PAPUA NEW GUINEA 14
At Stade Albert Domec, Carcassonne, Sunday, November 24, 1991.
Attendance: 1,440; **Referee:** Colin Morris (Great Britain)
France: T - Divet, Bonnafous, Garcia, Pons, Dumas; G - Dumas 4
Papua New Guinea: T - Haru, Itam; G - Karu 2, Haru
France: Marc Balleroy, Jean-Marc Garcia, David Despin, Denis Bienes, Cyrille Pons, Gilles Dumas, Patrick Entat, Yves Villoni, Francis Lope, Pierre Ailleres, Daniel Divet, Pierre Montgaillard, Christophe Bonnafous. Replacements: Pascal Fages (for Balleroy), Yves Storer (for Bonnafous), Abderazach Baba (for Ailleres), Alophe Alesina (for Bienes).
Papua New Guinea: Ipisa Wanega, Joshua Kouoru, Richard Wagambie, Phillip Boge, Chris Itam, Tuksy Karu, Stanley Haru (c), Kera Ngaffin, Michael Matmillo, James Naipao, Kes Pagliari, Max Tiri, Joe Gispe. Replacements: Ngala Lapan (for Karu), Leslee Hoffman (for Naipao), Lipirin Palangat (for Kouoru), Michael Angra (for Pagliari).

GREAT BRITAIN 36 ....FRANCE 0
At The Boulevard, Hull, Saturday, March 7, 1992.
Attendance: 5,250; **Referee:** Eddie Ward (Australia)
Great Britain: T - Holliday, Eastwood, Platt, Hunte, Dermott, Fox; G - Eastwood 6
Great Britain: Graham Steadman, Paul Eastwood, Gary Connolly, Allan Bateman, Alan Hunte, Daryl Powell, Shaun Edwards (c), Lee Crooks, Martin Dermott, Kelvin Skerrett, Denis Betts, Karl Fairbank, Les Holliday. Replacements: Andy Platt (for Skerrett), Deryck Fox (for Bateman), Steve McNamara (for Fairbank).
France: Patrick Limongi, Claude Sirvent, Pierre Chamorin, Pascal Fages, Cyrille Pons, Gilles Dumas (c), Patrick Entat, Yves Villoni, Thierry Valero, Pierre Ailleres, Bernard Llong, Christophe Bonnafous, Jacques Pech. Replacements: Patrick Torreilles (for Bonnafous), Francis Lope (for Llong), Pascal Bomati (for Pons).

AUSTRALIA 16 ....GREAT BRITAIN 10
At Lang Park, Brisbane, Friday, July 3, 1992.
Attendance: 33,313; **Referee:** Dennis Hale (New Zealand)
Australia: T - Daley, Meninga; G - Meninga 4
Great Britain: T - Offiah; G - Eastwood 3
Australia: Andrew Ettingshausen, Willie Carne, Mal Meninga (c), Brad Fittler, Michael Hancock, Laurie Daley, Allan Langer, Glenn Lazarus, Steve Walters, Paul Harragon, Paul Sironen, Bob Lindner, Bradley Clyde. Replacements: David Gillespie (for Sironen), Chris Johns (for Carne), Kevin Walters (for Ettingshausen), John Cartwright (for Lindner).
Great Britain: Graham Steadman, Paul Eastwood, Daryl Powell, Paul Newlove, Martin Offiah, Garry Schofield (c), Shaun Edwards, Kelvin Skerrett, Martin Dermott, Andy Platt, Denis Betts, Billy McGinty, Phil Clarke. Replacements: Paul Hulme (for McGinty), Karl Harrison (for Skerrett), Gary Connolly (for Newlove), Joe Lydon (for Schofield).

NEW ZEALAND 66 ....PAPUA NEW GUINEA 10
At Carlaw Park, Auckland, Sunday July 5, 1992.
Attendance: 3,000; **Referee:** Greg McCallum (Australia)
New Zealand: T - Blackmore 3, Clark 2, Ridge, Hoppe, Iro, Kemp, Freeman, Stuart, Mann, Hill; G - Ridge 4, Halligan 3
Papua New Guinea: T - Uradok 2; G - Boge
New Zealand: Matthew Ridge, Sean Hoppe, Kevin Iro, Tony Kemp, Richie Blackmore, Dean Clark, Gary Freeman (c), Brent Stuart, Duane Mann, Brent Todd, Gavin Hill, Quentin Pongia, Tawera Nikau. Replacements: Daryl Halligan, Brendon Tuuta, Tea Ropati, Mark Woods.
Papua New Guinea: Philip Boge, Kini Tani, August Joseph, Richard Wagambie (c), Jack Uradok, Tuksy Karu, Aquila Emil, Ben Bire, Michael Matmillo, Kera Ngaffin, Nande Yer, James Naipao, Joe Gispe. Replacements: Ngala Lapan, John Piel, Korul Sinemau, Michael Angra.

AUSTRALIA 36 ....PAPUA NEW GUINEA 14
At Townsville Sports Reserve, Wednesday, July 15, 1992.
Attendance: 12,470; **Referee:** Dennis Hale (New Zealand)
Australia: T - G Mackay 2, Carne, Fittler, Daley, Sargent, Johns; G - Meninga 4
Papua New Guinea: T - Joseph, Babago, Emil; G - Boge
Australia: Willie Carne, Graham Mackay, Mal Meninga (c), Brad Fittler, Michael Hancock, Laurie Daley, Allan Langer, Glenn Lazarus, Steve Walters, David Gillespie, Bob Lindner, Paul Sironen, Brad Mackay. Replacements: Kevin Walters, Chris Johns, John Cartwright, Mark Sargent.
Papua New Guinea: Philip Boge, Jack Uradok, August Joseph, Korul Sinemau, Richard Wagambie, Tuksy Karu, Aquila Emil, Ben Bire, Michael Matmillo, Kera Ngaffin (c), James Naipao, Daroa Ben Moide, Joe Gispe. Replacements: Sauna Babago, Nande Yer, James Kapai, Nere Launa.

FINAL TABLE

	P	W	D	L	F	A	Pts
Australia	8	8	0	0	236	68	16
Great Britain	8	5	0	3	215	79	10
New Zealand	8	5	0	3	203	120	10
France	8	2	0	6	80	247	4
Papua New Guinea	8	0	0	8	84	304	0

FINAL

GREAT BRITAIN 6 ....AUSTRALIA 10
At Wembley Stadium, London, Saturday, October 24, 1992.
Attendance: 73,631 *(World record for international match)*
Referee: Dennis Hale (New Zealand)
Great Britain: G - Fox 3
Australia: T - Renouf; G - Meninga 3
Great Britain: Joe Lydon, Alan Hunte, Gary Connolly, Garry Schofield (c), Martin Offiah, Shaun Edwards, Deryck Fox, Kevin Ward, Martin Dermott, Andy Platt, Denis Betts, Phil Clarke, Ellery Hanley. Replacements: John Devereux (for Connolly), Alan Tait (for Lydon), Kelvin Skerrett (for Ward), Richie Eyres (for Hanley).
Australia: Tim Brasher, Michael Hancock, Steve Renouf, Mal Meninga (c), Willie Carne, Brad Fittler, Allan Langer, Glenn Lazarus, Steve Walters, Mark Sargent, Paul Sironen, Bob Lindner, Bradley Clyde. Replacements: David Gillespie (for Sironen), Kevin Walters (for Clyde), John Cartwright (for Sargent).

THOSE WHO PLAYED (1989-92)

AUSTRALIA

	M	T	G	FG	Pts
Greg Alexander (Penrith)	2	1	3	-	10
Sam Backo (Brisbane)	1	-	-	-	-
Martin Bella (Manly-Warringah)	3	-	-	-	-
Gary Belcher (Canberra)	5	1	1	-	6
Tim Brasher (Balmain)	1	-	-	-	-
Willie Carne (Brisbane)	4	5	-	-	20
Mark Carroll (South Sydney)	1	-	-	-	-
John Cartwright (Penrith)	4	-	-	-	-
Bradley Clyde (Canberra)	5	3	-	-	12
Gary Coyne (Canberra)	1	-	-	-	-
Tony Currie (Brisbane)	1	-	-	-	-
Laurie Daley (Canberra)	5	4	-	-	16
Ben Elias (Balmain)	1	1	-	-	4
Andrew Ettingshausen (Cronulla-Sutherland)	6	4	-	-	16
Brad Fittler (Penrith)	4	1	-	-	4
Mark Geyer (Penrith)	1	-	-	-	-
David Gillespie (Canterbury-Bankstown)	7	-	-	-	-
Michael Hancock (Brisbane)	3	-	-	-	-
Paul Harragon (Newcastle)	1	-	-	-	-
Des Hasler (Manly-Warringah)	4	-	-	-	-
Peter Jackson (North Sydney)	2	1	-	-	4
Chris Johns (Brisbane)	5	1	-	-	4
Allan Langer (Brisbane)	5	-	-	-	-
Glenn Lazarus (Canberra)	6	-	-	-	-
Wally Lewis (Brisbane)	1	-	-	-	-
Bob Lindner (Western Suburbs)	5	-	-	-	-
Cliff Lyons (Manly-Warringah)	3	-	-	-	-
Mark McGaw (Cronulla-Sutherland)	1	2	-	-	8
Bruce McGuire (Balmain)	1	-	-	-	-
Brad Mackay (St George)	4	5	-	-	20
Graham Mackay (Penrith)	1	2	-	-	8
Mal Meninga (Canberra)	9	7	21	-	70
Michael O'Connor (Manly-Warringah)	2	1	2	-	8
Steve Renouf (Brisbane)	1	1	-	-	4
Steve Roach (Balmain)	4	1	-	-	4
Ian Roberts (Manly-Warringah)	2	-	-	-	-
Craig Salvatori (Eastern Suburbs)	1	-	-	-	-
Mark Sargent (Newcastle)	4	1	-	-	4
Dale Shearer (Manly-Warringah)	4	3	-	-	12
Paul Sironen (Balmain)	6	-	-	-	-
Ricky Stuart (Canberra)	2	-	-	-	-
Geoff Toovey (Manly-Warringah)	1	-	-	-	-
Kerrod Walters (Brisbane)	3	-	-	-	-
Kevin Walters (Brisbane)	4	-	-	-	-
Steve Walters (Canberra)	4	1	-	-	4
Rod Wishart (Illawarra)	2	2	-	-	8

FRANCE

	M	T	G	FG	Pts
Adolphe Alesina (Pamiers)	1	-	-	-	-
Pierre Ailleres (Toulouse)	1	-	-	-	-
Christophe Auroy (XIII Catalan)	2	1	-	-	4
Abderazach Baba (XIII Catalan)	2	-	-	-	-
Marc Balleroy (Avignon)	1	-	-	-	-
Thierry Bernabe (Carcassonne)	2	-	-	-	-
Denis Bienes (Saint-Gaudens)	4	-	-	-	-
Christophe Bonnafous (Albi)	1	1	-	-	4
Alain Bouzer (Toulouse)	1	-	-	-	-
Gerard Boyals (Saint-Gaudens)	2	-	-	-	-
Serge Bret (XIII Catalan)	1	-	-	-	-
Thierry Buttignol (Avignon)	5	-	-	-	-
Didier Cabestany (Saint-Esteve)	4	-	-	-	-
Eric Castel (Albi)	1	-	-	-	-
Pierre Chamorin (Saint-Esteve)	2	-	-	-	-
Philippe Chiron (Carpentras)	1	-	-	-	-
Regis Courty (XIII Catalan)	1	-	-	-	-
Guy Delaunay (XIII Catalan)	3	-	-	-	-
Guy Delpeche (Pamiers)	1	-	-	-	-
David Despin (Villeneuve)	3	2	-	-	8
Daniel Divet (Carcassonne)	5	1	-	-	4
Gilles Dumas (Saint-Gaudens)	5	1	8	-	20
Pascal Fages (Pia)	3	-	-	-	-
Patrick Entat (Avignon, Hull)	6	1	-	-	4
Philippe Fourquet (Saint-Gaudens)	1	-	-	-	-
David Fraisse (Carcassonne)	1	1	-	-	4
Jean-Marc Garcia (Saint-Esteve)	3	2	-	-	8
Mathieu Khedimi (Saint-Esteve)	1	-	-	-	-
Francis Lope (Toulouse)	3	-	-	-	-
Jean-Pierre Magnac (XIII Catalan)	1	-	-	-	-
Patrick Marginet (Saint-Esteve)	1	-	-	-	-
Jacques Moliner (XIII Catalan)	2	-	-	-	-
Pierre Montgaillard (XIII Catalan)	1	-	-	-	-
Roger Palisses (Saint-Esteve)	1	-	-	-	-
Bertrand Plante (Villeneuve)	1	-	-	-	-
Cyrille Pons (Saint-Gaudens)	6	2	-	-	8
Jean-Philippe Pougeau (Saint-Esteve)	1	-	-	-	-
Jean-Luc Rabot (Villeneuve)	2	-	-	-	-
Hugues Ratier (Lezignan)	1	-	-	-	-
Eric Remirez (Carcassonne)	1	-	-	-	-
Franck Romano (Carpentras)	1	-	-	-	-
Jean Ruiz (Lezignan)	1	-	-	-	-
Jean-Bernard Saumitou (Villeneuve)	1	-	-	-	-
Yves Storer (Saint-Gaudens)	3	-	-	-	-
Marc Tisseyre (Pamiers)	3	2	-	-	4
Patrick Torreilles (Pia)	1	4	-	-	8
Thierry Valero (Lezignan)	4	-	-	-	-
Daniel Verdes (Villeneuve)	4	1	-	-	4
Yves Villoni (Avignon)	1	-	-	-	-
Robert Viscay (Saint-Gaudens)	1	-	-	-	-

GREAT BRITAIN

	M	T	G	FG	Pts
Mark Aston (Sheffield)	1	-	-	-	-
Allan Bateman (Warrington)	1	-	-	-	-
Denis Betts (Wigan)	8	2	-	-	8
Phil Clarke (Wigan)	3	-	-	-	-
Gary Connolly (St Helens)	4	-	-	-	-
Lee Crooks (Castleford)	1	-	-	-	-
Jonathan Davies (Widnes)	4	1	17	-	34
Martin Dermott (Wigan)	5	1	-	-	4
John Devereux (Widnes)	1	-	-	-	-
Paul Dixon (Hull, Leeds)	3	1	-	-	4
Paul Eastwood (Hull)	5	2	15	-	38
Shaun Edwards (Wigan)	6	2	-	-	8
St John Ellis (Castleford)	1	-	-	-	-
Keith England (Castleford)	3	-	-	-	-
Richie Eyres (Widnes)	2	-	-	-	-
Karl Fairbank (Bradford Northern)	3	-	-	-	-
Phil Ford (Leeds)	1	-	-	-	-
Deryck Fox (Featherstone Rovers)	4	1	3	-	10
Carl Gibson (Leeds)	4	2	-	-	8
Andy Goodway (Wigan)	1	-	-	-	-
Bobbie Goulding (Wigan)	2	1	-	-	4
Andy Gregory (Wigan)	1	-	-	-	-
Mike Gregory (Warrington)	4	-	-	-	-

171

	M	T	G	FG	Pts
Steve Hampson (Wigan)	3	-	-	-	-
Ellery Hanley (Wigan)	3	-	-	-	-
Karl Harrison (Hull, Halifax)	2	1	-	-	4
Les Holliday (Widnes)	2	1	-	-	4
David Hulme (Widnes)	1	-	-	-	-
Paul Hulme (Widnes)	2	-	-	-	-
Alan Hunte (St Helens)	2	1	-	-	4
Shaun Irwin (Castleford)	1	-	-	-	-
Lee Jackson (Hull)	3	-	-	-	-
Michael Jackson (Wakefield Trinity)	1	2	-	-	8
Paul Loughlin (St Helens)	1	-	1	-	2
Ian Lucas (Wigan)	1	-	-	-	-
Joe Lydon (Wigan)	4	-	-	-	-
Steve McNamara (Hull)	1	-	-	-	-
Paul Moriarty (Widnes)	1	2	-	-	8
Paul Newlove (Featherstone Rovers)	3	1	-	-	4
Martin Offiah (Widnes, Wigan)	6	5	-	-	20
Andy Platt (Wigan)	2	-	-	-	-
Daryl Powell (Sheffield Eagles)	7	1	-	-	4
Roy Powell (Leeds)	4	1	-	-	4
Gary Price (Wakefield Trinity)	1	-	-	-	-
Garry Schofield (Leeds)	7	6	-	1	25
Kelvin Skerrett (Bradford Northern, Wigan)	5	-	-	-	-
Graham Steadman (Castleford)	2	-	-	-	-
Anthony Sullivan (St Helens)	1	1	-	-	4
Alan Tait (Widnes)	3	1	-	-	4
Kevin Ward (St Helens)	1	-	-	-	-

NEW ZEALAND

	M	T	G	FG	Pts
Dean Bell (Wigan)	2	1	-	-	4
Richie Blackmore (Auckland)	3	5	-	-	20
Frano Botica (Wigan)	2	-	8	-	16
Peter Brown (Auckland, Halifax)	4	-	-	-	-
Dean Clark (Auckland)	3	2	-	-	8
Morvin Edwards (Wellington)	2	-	-	-	-
Mark Elia (Canterbury-Bankstown)	1	1	-	-	4
Esene Family (Canterbury, Widnes)	2	-	-	-	-
Gary Freeman (Balmain)	8	1	-	-	4
Clayton Friend (Carlisle)	2	1	-	-	4
James Goulding (Newcastle)	1	-	-	-	-
Daryl Halligan (North Sydney)	1	-	3	-	6
Gavin Hill (Canterbury-Bankstown)	1	1	-	-	4
Sean Hoppe (Canberra)	1	1	-	-	4
Mark Horo (Parramatta)	3	-	-	-	-
Kevin Iro (Wigan, Manly-Warringah)	4	1	-	-	4
Tony Iro (Manly-Warringah)	2	-	-	-	-
Tony Kemp (Newcastle)	6	3	-	-	12
Emosi Koloto (Widnes)	2	-	-	-	-
Mike Kuiti (Wellington)	1	1	-	-	4
Francis Leota (Auckland)	1	-	-	-	-
Dean Lonergan (Auckland)	3	1	-	-	4
Jarrod McCracken (Canterbury-Bankstown)	2	1	-	-	4
Hugh McGahan (Eastern Suburbs)	4	-	-	1	1
Duane Mann (Auckland, Warrington)	8	1	-	-	4
George Mann (Auckland)	4	-	-	-	-
Gary Mercer (Bay of Plenty, Warrington)	5	1	-	-	4
Tawera Nikau (Canterbury-Bankstown)	5	1	-	-	4
Sam Panapa (Auckland)	3	2	-	-	8
Mike Patton (Auckland)	2	-	-	-	-
Quentin Pongia (Canterbury)	1	-	-	-	-
Matthew Ridge (Manly-Warringah)	3	1	13	-	30
Tea Ropati (Auckland)	1	-	-	-	-
Kelly Shelford (Auckland)	4	2	4	-	16
Kurt Sherlock (Eastern Suburbs)	2	-	3	-	6
Kurt Sorensen (Widnes)	1	-	-	-	-
Sam Stewart (Newcastle)	3	-	-	-	-
Brent Stuart (Canterbury)	1	1	-	-	4
Brent Todd (Canberra)	8	-	-	-	-
Paddy Tuimavave (Auckland)	1	-	-	-	-
Brendon Tuuta (Western Suburbs)	2	-	-	-	-
David Watson (Auckland)	4	5	-	-	20
Darrell Williams (Manly-Warringah)	4	1	-	-	4
Jason Williams (South Sydney)	1	-	-	-	-
Mark Woods (Wellington)	1	-	-	-	-

PAPUA NEW GUINEA

	M	T	G	FG	Pts
Bobby Ako (Mt Hagen Eagles)	1	-	-	-	-
Michael Angra (Mt Hagen Eagles)	3	-	-	-	-
Sauna Babago (Port Moresby Vipers)	1	1	-	-	4
Bernard Bate (Rabaul Island Gurias)	1	-	-	-	-
Daroa Ben Moide	1	-	-	-	-
Ben Bire (Port Moresby Vipers)	2	-	-	-	-
Philip Boge (Port Moresby Vipers)	7	-	3	-	6
Thomas Daki (Lae Bombers)	3	-	-	-	-
Matthew Elara (Lae Bombers)	1	-	-	-	-
Aquila Emil (Port Moresby Vipers)	2	1	-	-	4
Tuiyo Evei (Goroka Lahinis)	2	-	-	-	-
Paul Gela (Goroka Lahinis)	1	1	-	-	4
Joe Gispe (Port Moresby Vipers)	7	-	-	-	-
Stanley Haru (Port Moresby Vipers)	6	2	1	-	10
Leslee Hoffman (Mt Hagen Eagles)	3	-	-	-	-
Chris Itam (Mt Hagen Eagles)	3	1	-	-	4

	M	T	G	FG	Pts
August Joseph (Rabaul Island Gurias)	2	1	-	-	4
Elias Kamiak (Mt Hagen Eagles)	1	-	-	-	-
James Kapai (Rabaul Island Gurias)	1	-	-	-	-
Sam Karara (Kundiawa Warriors)	1	-	-	-	-
Tuksy Karu (Port Moresby Vipers)	5	1	2	-	8
Johannes Kola (Port Moresby Vipers)	1	-	-	-	-
Joshua Kouoru (Port Moresby Vipers)	4	-	-	-	-
Arnold Krewanty (Port Moresby Vipers)	3	-	-	-	-
Ngala Lapan (Lae Bombers)	4	-	-	-	-
Nere Launa (Mt Hagen Eagles)	1	-	-	-	-
Ati Lomutopa (Goroka Lahinis)	1	-	-	-	-
Michael Matmillo (Lae Bombers)	5	-	-	-	-
Danny Moi (Port Moresby Vipers)	1	-	-	-	-
Mea Morea (Port Moresby Vipers)	1	-	-	-	-
James Naipao (Port Moresby Vipers)	6	1	-	-	4
Kera Ngaffin (Port Moresby Vipers)	3	-	-	-	-
Bal Numapo (Kundiawa Warriors)	2	-	3	-	6
Gigmai Ongogo (Mt Hagen Eagles)	3	1	-	-	4
Kes Paglipari (Port Moresby Vipers)	6	-	-	-	-
Lipirin Palangat (Rabaul Island Gurias)	3	-	-	-	-
John Piel (Lae Bombers)	1	-	-	-	-
Joe Rema (Mendi Muruks)	1	-	-	-	-
Korul Sinemau (Lae Bombers)	2	-	-	-	-
Opai Soga (Goroka Lahinis)	3	1	-	-	4
Kini Tani (Port Moresby Vipers)	1	-	-	-	-
Arebo Taumaku (Port Moresby Vipers)	1	-	-	-	-
Max Tiri (Mt Hagen Eagles)	5	-	-	-	-
John Unagi (Kundiawa Warriors)	3	-	-	-	-
Jack Uradok (Port Moresby Vipers)	2	2	-	-	8
Richard Wagambie (Port Moresby Vipers)	5	-	-	-	-
Goie Waine (Kundiawa Warriors)	1	1	-	-	4
Ipisa Wanega (Kundiawa Warriors)	5	-	5	-	10
Nande Yer (Lae Bombers)	2	-	-	-	-

1995

GROUP ONE

ENGLAND 20 ....AUSTRALIA 16
At Wembley, Saturday 7 October 1995
Attendance: 41,271; **Referee:** Stuart Cummings (England)
England: T - Robinson, Newlove, Farrell, Joynt; G - Farrell 2
Australia: T - Menzies 2, Coyne; G - Wishart 2
England: Kris Radlinski, Jason Robinson, Barrie-Jon Mather, Paul Newlove, John Bentley, Daryl Powell, Shaun Edwards, Karl Harrison, Lee Jackson, Andy Platt, Denis Betts, Phil Clarke, Andrew Farrell. Subs: Bobby Goulding, Nick Pinkney, Chris Joynt, Simon Haughton
Australia: Tim Brasher, Rod Wishart, Mark Coyne, Terry Hill, John Hopoate, Brad Fittler, Geoff Toovey, David Gillespie, Wayne Bartrim, Mark Carroll, Steve Menzies, Dean Pay, Jim Dymock. Subs: Robbie O'Davis, Matthew Johns, Jason Smith, Paul Harragon

FIJI 52 .... SOUTH AFRICA 6
At Cougar Park, Keighley, Sunday 8 October 1995
Attendance: 4,845; **Referee:** David Manson (Australia)
Fiji: T - Sovatabua 2, Dakuitoga, Seru 2, Nadruku, Taga, Sagaitu, Marayawa, Nayacakalou 3, Taga 3
South Africa: G - van Wyk 3
Fiji: Waisale Sovatabua, Joe Dakuitoga, Livai Nalagilagi, Filemoni Seru, Noa Nadruku, Noa Nayacakalou, Save Taga, Malakai Yasa, Iane Sagaitu, Pio Nakubuwai, Apisalome Degei, Iliesa Toga, Sam Marayawa. Subs: Kajava Salusalu, George Vatubua, Ulaiasi Wainidroa, Kalaveti Naisoro.
South Africa: Pierre van Wyk, Guy Coombe, Andrew Ballot, Willem Boshoff, Mark Johnson, Francois Cloete, Berend Alkema, Gideon Watts, Kobus van Deventer, Jaco Booysen, Gerald Williams, Tim Fourie, Jaco Alberts. Subs: Ernest Ludick, Eugene Powell, Koot Human, Jaco van Niekerk

AUSTRALIA 86 ....SOUTH AFRICA 6
At Gateshead International Stadium, Tuesday 10 October 1995
Attendance: 9,191; **Referee:** Russell Smith (England)
Australia: T - O'Davis 2, Moore 2, McGregor 2, Hopoate 3, A Johns 2, Raper, Smith, Kosef, Brasher, Dymock; G - A Johns 11
South Africa: T - Watts; G - van Wyk
Australia: Robbie O'Davis, Brett Dallas, Danny Moore, Paul McGregor, John Hopoate, Matthew Johns, Andrew Johns, Adam Muir, Aaron Raper, Paul Harragon, Billy Moore, Jason Smith, Nik Kosef. Subs: Tim Brasher, Jim Dymock, Wayne Bartrim, Mark Carroll
South Africa: Pierre van Wyk, Guy Coombe, Andrew Ballot, Willem Boshoff, Mark Johnson, Berend Alkema, Kobus van Deventer, Gideon Watts, Francois Cloete, Jaco Booysen, Gerald Williams, Koot Human, Tim Fourie. Subs: Ernest Ludick, Eugene Powell, Nico Serfontein, Jaco van Niekerk

ENGLAND 46 ....FIJI 0
At Central Park, Wigan, Wednesday 11 October 1995
Attendance: 26,263; **Referee:** Dennis Hale (New Zealand)
England: T - Radlinski, Robinson 2, Newlove, Bentley, Smith, Broadbent, Haughton; G - Farrell 4, Goulding 3

England: Kris Radlinski, Jason Robinson, Nick Pinkney, Paul Newlove, John Bentley, Tony Smith, Bobbie Goulding, Paul Broadbent, Lee Jackson, Dean Sampson, Denis Betts, Mick Cassidy, Andrew Farrell. Subs: Shaun Edwards, Paul Cook, Simon Haughton, Steve McCurrie
Fiji: Waisale Sovatabua, Joe Dakuitoga, Livai Nalagilagi, Filemoni Seru, Noa Nadruku, Noa Nayacakalou, Save Taga, Malakai Yasa, Iane Sagaitu, Pio Nakubuwai, Apisalome Degei, Iliesa Toga, Sam Marayawa. Subs: Niumaia Korovata, Ulaiasi Wainidroa, George Vatubua, Kalaveti Naisoro

AUSTRALIA 66 ....FIJI 0
At Alfred McAlpine Stadium, Huddersfield,
Saturday 14 October 1995
Attendance: 7,127; **Referee:** Eddie Ward (Australia)
Australia: T - Brasher, Dallas 3, Hill 2, O'Davis 3, Menzies 2, Larson; G - A Johns 9
Australia: Tim Brasher, Brett Dallas, Mark Coyne, Terry Hill, Robbie O'Davis, Brad Fittler, Geoff Toovey, Dean Pay, Andrew Johns, Mark Carroll, Steve Menzies, Gary Larson, Jim Dymock. Subs: Paul McGregor, Matthew Johns, Jason Smith, Nik Kosef
Fiji: Waisale Sovatabua, Orisi Cavuilati, Livai Nalagilagi, Filemoni Seru, Noa Nadruku, Noa Nayacakalou, Save Taga, Malakai Yasa, Iane Sagaitu, Pio Nakubuwai, Joe Dakuitoga, Samuela Davetawalu, Niumaia Korovata. Subs: Kalaveti Naisoro, George Vatubua, Waisake Vatubua, Kini Koroibuleka

ENGLAND 46 ....SOUTH AFRICA 0
At Headingley, Leeds, Saturday 14 October 1995
Attendance: 14,041; **Referee:** David Manson (Australia)
England: T - Pinkney 2, Goulding, Haughton, Radlinski, Broadbent, Smith, Sampson; G - Goulding 7
England: Paul Cook, John Bentley, Nick Pinkney, Barrie-Jon Mather, Martin Offiah, Daryl Powell, Bobbie Goulding, Karl Harrison, Mick Cassidy, Andy Platt, Simon Haughton, Chris Joynt, Phil Clarke. Subs: Kris Radlinski, Paul Broadbent, Tony Smith, Dean Sampson
South Africa: Pierre van Wyk, Guy Coombe, Tim Fourie, Willem Boshoff, Andrew Ballot, Mark Johnson, Berend Alkema, Gideon Watts, Kobus van Deventer, Jaco Booysen, Gerald Williams, Jaco Alberts, John Mudgeway. Subs: Justin Jennings, Elmar Lubbe, Francois Cloete, Jaco Vísser

GROUP ONE TABLE

	P	W	D	L	F	A	Pts
England	3	3	0	0	112	16	6
Australia	3	2	0	1	168	26	4
Fiji	3	1	0	2	52	118	2
South Africa	3	0	0	3	12	184	0

GROUP TWO

NEW ZEALAND 25 ....TONGA 24
At Wilderspool Stadium, Warrington, Sunday 8 October 1995
Attendance: 8,083; **Referee:** David Campbell (England)
New Zealand: T - Hoppe, Blackmore 2, Kemp, Okesene; G - Ridge 2; FG - Ridge
Tonga: T - Taufa, Veikoso, W Wolfgramm, Finau; G - Amone 4
New Zealand: Matthew Ridge, Sean Hoppe, Richard Blackmore, Ruben Wiki, Richard Barnett, Gene Ngamu, Stacey Jones, Quentin Pongia, Syd Eru, Jason Lowrie, Tony Iro, Stephen Kearney, Tony Kemp. Subs: Henry Paul, Hitro Okesene, Kevin Iro, Mark Horo
Tonga: Asa Amone, Una Taufa, Tevita Vaikona, Phil Howlett, Jimmy Veikoso, Angelo Dymock, Willie Wolfgramm, Martin Masella, Duane Mann, Lee Hansen, George Mann, Solomon Haumono, Awen Guttenbeil. Subs: Salesi Finau, Talite Liava'a, Luke Leilua, Taukolo Tonga

PAPUA NEW GUINEA 28 ....TONGA 28
At The Boulevard, Hull, Tuesday 10 October 1995
Attendance: 5,121; **Referee:** Claude Alba (France)
Papua New Guinea: Buko, Gene, Lam, Paiyo, Solbat; G - Paiyo 4
Tonga: T - Taufa, Howlett, W Wolfgramm, Guttenbeil 2, Liku; G - Amone 2
Papua New Guinea: David Buko, James Kops, David Gomia, John Okul, Joshua Kouoru, Stanley Gene, Adrian Lam, Tuiyo Evei, Elias Paiyo, David Westley, Max Tiri, Nande Yer, Bruce Mamando. Subs: Robert Tela, Lucas Solbat, Marcus Bai, David Reeka
Tonga: Asa Amone, Una Taufa, Tevita Vaikona, Phil Howlett, Jimmy Veikoso, Angelo Dymock, Willie Wolfgramm, Martin Masella, Duane Mann, Lee Hansen, George Mann, Solomon Haumono, Awen Guttenbeil. Subs: Salesi Finau, Tau'alupe Liku, Luke Leilua, Taukolo Tonga

NEW ZEALAND 22 ....PAPUA NEW GUINEA 6
At Knowsley Road, St Helens, Friday 13 October 1995
Attendance: 8,679; **Referee:** Stuart Cummings (England)
New Zealand: T - Ridge, Hoppe, Blackmore; G - Ridge 4, Ngamu
Papua New Guinea: T - Bai; G - Paiyo
New Zealand: Matthew Ridge, Sean Hoppe, Richard Blackmore, Ruben Wiki, Jason Williams, Henry Paul, Stacey Jones, Quentin Pongia, Gary Freeman, Jason Lowrie, Stephen Kearney, Mark Horo, Tony Kemp. Subs: Gene Ngamu, Hitro Okesene, Kevin Iro, Tony Iro
Papua New Guinea: David Buko, James Kops, David Gomia, John Okul, Joshua Kouoru, Stanley Gene, Adrian Lam, Nande Yer, Elias

Paiyo, David Westley, Max Tiri, Michael Angra, Bruce Mamando. Subs: Robert Tela, Lucas Solbat, Marcus Bai, Ben Biri

GROUP TWO TABLE

	P	W	D	L	F	A	Pts
New Zealand	2	2	0	0	47	30	4
Tonga	2	0	1	1	52	53	1
Papua New Guinea	2	0	1	1	34	50	1

GROUP THREE

WALES 28 ....FRANCE 6
At Ninian Park, Cardiff, Monday 9 October 1995
Attendance: 10,250; **Referee:** Eddie Ward (Australia)
Wales: T - Harris, Devereux, Sullivan 3; G - Davies 3, Harris
France: T - Torreilles; G - Banquet
Wales: Iestyn Harris, John Devereux, Allan Bateman, Scott Gibbs, Anthony Sullivan, Jonathan Davies, Kevin Ellis, Kelvin Skerrett, Martin Hall, David Young, Paul Moriarty, Mark Perrett, Richie Eyres. Subs: Mark Jones, Adrian Hadley, Keiron Cunningham, Rowland Phillips
France: David Despin, Frederic Banquet, David Fraisse, Pierre Chamorin, Jean-Marc Garcia, Pascal Fages, Patrick Entat, Didier Cabestany, Patrick Torreilles, Frederic Teixido, Gael Tallec, Pascal Jampy, Thierry Valero. Subs: Vincent Banet, Karl Jaavuo, Brian Coles, Lilian Hebert

WESTERN SAMOA 56 ....FRANCE 10
At Ninian Park Cardiff, Thursday 12 October 1995
Attendance: 2,173; **Referee:** Kelvin Jeffs (Australia)
Western Samoa: T - P Tuimavave, Laumatia, Tuigamala 2, W Swann, Tatupu 2, Matautia 2, Perelini; G - Schuster 8
France: T - Chamorin, Cabestany; G - Banquet
Western Samoa: Paki Tuimavave, Brian Laumatia, John Schuster, Va'aiga Tuigamala, Lolani Koko, Tea Ropati, Willie Swann, Se'e Solomona, Willie Poching, Fa'ausu Afoa, Tony Tatupu, Vila Matautia, Tony Tuimavave. Subs: Mark Elia, Sam Panapa, Apollo Perelini, Joe Vagana
France: Frederic Banquet, Brian Coles, Jean-Marc Garcia, Pierre Chamorin, Pascal Mons, Pascal Fages, Patrick Entat, Hadj Boudebza, Patrick Torreilles, Karl Jaavuo, Cyril Baudouin, Didier Cabestany, Thierry Valero. Subs: Vincent Banet, Pascal Jampy, Frederic Teixido, Marc Tisseyre

WALES 22 ....WESTERN SAMOA 10
At Vetch Field, Swansea, Sunday 15 October 1995
Attendance: 15,385; **Referee:** Russell Smith (England)
Wales: T - Harris, Sullivan, Ellis; G - Davies 4; FG - Davies, Harris
Western Samoa: T - Matautia; G - Schuster 3
Wales: Iestyn Harris, Anthony Sullivan, Allan Bateman, John Devereux, Adrian Hadley, Jonathan Davies, Kevin Ellis, Kelvin Skerrett, Martin Hall, David Young, Paul Moriarty, Scott Quinnell, Richie Eyres. Subs: Neil Cowie, Keiron Cunningham, Rowland Phillips, Paul Atcheson
Western Samoa: Paki Tuimavave, John Schuster, Tea Ropati, Va'aiga Tuigamala, Brian Laumatia, Sam Panapa, Willie Swann, Se'e Solomona, Willie Poching, Fa'ausu Afoa, Tony Tatupu, Vila Matautia, Tony Tuimavave. Subs: Mark Elia, Des Maea, Apollo Perelini, Joe Vagana

GROUP THREE TABLE

	P	W	D	L	F	A	Pts
Wales	2	2	0	0	50	16	4
Western Samoa	2	1	0	1	66	32	2
France	2	0	0	2	16	84	0

SEMI-FINALS

ENGLAND 25 ....WALES 10
At Old Trafford, Manchester, Saturday 21 October 1995
Attendance: 30,042; **Referee:** Eddie Ward (Australia)
England: T - Newlove, Offiah 2, Betts, Clarke; G - Goulding, Farrell; FG - Goulding
Wales: T - Phillips; G - Davies 3
England: Kris Radlinski, Jason Robinson, Nick Pinkney, Paul Newlove, Martin Offiah, Tony Smith, Bobbie Goulding, Karl Harrison, Lee Jackson, Andy Platt, Denis Betts, Phil Clarke, Andrew Farrell. Subs: Barrie-Jon Mather, Mick Cassidy, Simon Haughton, Dean Sampson
Wales: Iestyn Harris, John Devereux, Allan Bateman, Scott Gibbs, Anthony Sullivan, Jonathan Davies, Kevin Ellis, Kelvin Skerrett, Martin Hall, David Young, Paul Moriarty, Scott Quinnell, Richie Eyres. Subs: Mark Jones, Keiron Cunningham, Rowland Phillips, Adrian Hadley.

AUSTRALIA 30 ....NEW ZEALAND 20 *(AET)*
At Alfred McAlpine Stadium, Huddersfield,
Sunday 22 October 1995
Attendance: 16,608; **Referee:** Russell Smith (England)
Australia: T - Brasher, Coyne, Hill, Fittler, Menzies 2; G - A Johns 3
New Zealand: T - K Iro, Barnett, T Iro; G - Ridge 4
Australia: Tim Brasher, Rod Wishart, Mark Coyne, Terry Hill, Brett Dallas , Brad Fittler, Geoff Toovey, Dean Pay, Andrew Johns, Mark Carroll, Steve Menzies, Gary Larson, Jim Dymock. Subs: Robbie O'Davis, Matthew Johns, Jason Smith, Nik Kosef

World Cup Records

New Zealand: Matthew Ridge, Sean Hoppe, Kevin Iro, Richard Blackmore, Richard Barnett, Tony Kemp, Stacey Jones, John Lomax, Henry Paul, Jason Lowrie, Stephen Kearney, Quentin Pongia, Mark Horo. Subs: Gene Ngamu, Ruben Wiki, Tony Iro, Hitro Okesene.

CENTENARY WORLD CUP FINAL

ENGLAND 8..AUSTRALIA 16
At Wembley, Saturday 28 October, 1995
Attendance: 66,540; **Referee:** Stuart Cummings (England)
England: T - Newlove; G - Goulding 2
Australia: T - Brasher, Wishart; G - A Johns 4
England: Kris Radlinski, Jason Robinson, Gary Connolly, Paul Newlove, Martin Offiah, Tony Smith, Bobbie Goulding, Karl Harrison, Lee Jackson, Andy Platt, Denis Betts, Phil Clarke, Andrew Farrell. Subs: Mick Cassidy, Chris Joynt, Barrie-Jon Mather, Nick Pinkney
Australia: Tim Brasher, Rod Wishart, Mark Coyne, Terry Hill, Brett Dallas, Geoff Toovey, Dean Pay, Andrew Johns, Mark Carroll, Steve Menzies, Gary Larson, Jim Dymock. Subs: Jason Smith, Robbie O'Davis, Matthew Johns, Nik Kosef.

THE 1995 SQUADS

ENGLAND *(Coach: Phil Larder)*

	M	T	G	FG	Pts
John Bentley (Halifax)	3	1	-	-	4
Denis Betts (Auckland Warriors)	4	-	-	-	-
Paul Broadbent (Sheffield Eagles)	2	2	-	-	8
Mick Cassidy (Wigan)	4	-	-	-	-
Phil Clarke (Sydney City Roosters)	4	-	-	-	-
Gary Connolly (Wigan)	1	-	-	-	-
Paul Cook (Leeds)	2	-	-	-	-
Shaun Edwards (Wigan)	1	-	-	-	-
Andrew Farrell (Wigan)	4	1	6	-	16
Bobbie Goulding (St Helens)	4	1	12	-	28
Karl Harrison (Halifax)	4	-	-	-	-
Simon Haughton (Wigan)	4	2	-	-	8
Lee Jackson (Sheffield Eagles)	4	-	-	-	-
Chris Joynt (St Helens)	3	1	-	-	4
Barrie-Jon Mather (Wigan)	2	-	-	-	-
Steve McCurrie (Widnes)	1	-	-	-	-
Paul Newlove (Bradford Bulls)	4	3	-	-	12
Martin Offiah (Wigan)	3	-	-	-	-
Nick Pinkney (Keighley Cougars)	3	2	-	-	8
Andy Platt (Auckland W./Widnes)	4	-	-	-	-
Daryl Powell (Keighley Cougars)	2	-	-	-	-
Kris Radlinski (Wigan)	5	2	-	-	8
Jason Robinson (Wigan)	4	3	-	-	12
Dean Sampson (Castleford)	3	1	-	-	4
Tony Smith (Castleford)	4	2	-	-	8

WALES *(Coach: Clive Griffiths)*

	M	T	G	FG	Pts
Paul Atcheson (Oldham)	1	-	-	-	-
Allan Bateman (Warrington)	3	-	-	-	-
Dean Busby (St Helens)	-	-	-	-	-
Neil Cowie (Wigan)	1	-	-	-	-
Keiron Cunningham (St Helens)	3	-	-	-	-
Jonathan Davies (Warrington)	3	-	10	1	21
John Devereux (Widnes)	3	1	-	-	4
Kevin Ellis (Warrington)	3	1	-	-	4
Richie Eyres (Leeds)	3	-	-	-	-
Phil Ford (Salford)	-	-	-	-	-
Scott Gibbs (St Helens)	2	-	-	-	-
Jonathan Griffiths (St Helens)	-	-	-	-	-
Adrian Hadley (Widnes)	2	-	-	-	-
Martin Hall (Wigan)	3	-	-	-	-
Iestyn Harris (Warrington)	3	2	1	1	11
Mark Jones (Warrington)	2	-	-	-	-
Paul Moriarty (Halifax)	3	-	-	-	-
Mark Perrett (Halifax)	1	-	-	-	-
Rowland Phillips (Workington T)	3	1	-	-	4
Scott Quinnell (Wigan)	2	-	-	-	-
Kelvin Skerrett (Wigan)	3	-	-	-	-
Gareth Stephens (Castleford)	-	-	-	-	-
Anthony Sullivan (St Helens)	3	4	-	-	16
Richard Webster (Salford)	-	-	-	-	-
David Young (Salford)	3	-	-	-	-

AUSTRALIA *(Coach: Bob Fulton)*

	M	T	G	FG	Pts
Wayne Bartrim (St George)	2	-	-	-	-
Tim Brasher (Sydney Tigers)	5	3	-	-	12
Mark Carroll (Manly)	5	1	-	-	4
Mark Coyne (St George)	4	1	-	-	4
Brett Dallas (Sydney Bulldogs)	4	3	-	-	12
Jim Dymock (Sydney Bulldogs)	5	1	-	-	4
Brad Fittler (Penrith)	4	-	-	-	-
David Gillespie (Manly)	1	-	-	-	-
Paul Harragon (Newcastle Knights)	2	-	-	-	-
Terry Hill (Manly)	4	2	-	-	8
John Hopoate (Manly)	2	3	-	-	12

Andrew Johns (Newcastle Knights)	4	2	-	24	56
Nik Kosef (Manly)	3	1	-	-	4
Gary Larson ● (North Sydney)	3	1	-	-	4
Paul McGregor (Illawarra)	2	2	-	-	8
Steve Menzies (Manly)	4	4	-	-	16
Billy Moore (North Sydney)	1	-	-	-	-
Danny Moore (Manly)	1	2	-	-	8
Adam Muir (Newcastle Knights)	1	-	-	-	-
Robbie O'Davis (Newcastle Knights)	3	5	-	-	20
Dean Pay (Sydney Bulldogs)	4	-	-	-	-
Aaron Raper (Cronulla)	1	1	-	-	4
Jason Smith (Sydney Bulldogs)	5	1	-	-	4
Geoff Toovey (Manly)	4	-	-	-	-
Rod Wishart (Illawarra)	3	1	2	-	12

● *Larson replaced injured Harragon after two matches*

FIJI *(Coach: Graham Murray)*

	M	T	G	FG	Pts
Orisi Cavuilati (Bulldogs)	1	-	-	-	-
Joe Dakuitoga (Penrith)	3	1	-	-	4
Samuela Davetawalu (Fiji Fish Nadi)	1	-	-	-	-
Apisalome Degei (Parramatta)	2	-	-	-	-
Kini Koroibuleka Niumaia Korovata (Yanco)	2	-	-	-	-
Sam Marayawa (Tumbarumba)	2	1	-	-	4
Noa Nadruku (Canberra Raiders)	3	1	-	-	4
Kalaveti Naisoro (Lautoka Foodtown)	3	1	-	-	4
Pio Nakubuwai (Yanco)	3	-	-	-	-
Livai Nalagilagi (Penrith)	3	-	-	-	-
Noa Nayacakalou (Penrith)	3	-	3	-	6
Inoke Ratudina (Carpenters Motors)	-	-	-	-	-
Kiniviliame Ratukana (Fiji Bitter Army)	-	-	-	-	-
Freddie Robarts (Waitakere Raiders)	-	-	-	-	-
Iane Sagaitu (North Sydney)	3	1	-	-	4
Kaiava Salusalu (Lautoka Foodtown)	1	-	-	-	-
Filemoni Seru (S Queensland Crushers)	3	2	-	-	8
Waisale Sovatabua (Carpenters Motors)	3	2	-	-	8
Save Taga (Fiji Fish Nadi)	3	1	3	-	10
Iliesa Toga (Narrabeean)	2	-	-	-	-
Vonivate Toga (Fiji Fish Nadi)	-	-	-	-	-
George Vatubua (Lautoka Foodtown)	3	-	-	-	-
Waisake Vatubua (Hyundai Bulldogs)	-	-	-	-	-
Ulaiasi Wainidroa (Fiji Fish Nadi)	2	-	-	-	-
Malakai Yasa (Lautoka Foodtown)	3	-	-	-	-

FRANCE *(Coach: Ivan Greseque)*

	M	T	G	FG	Pts
Patrick Acroue (Avignon)	-	-	-	-	-
Ezzedine Attia (Cannes)	-	-	-	-	-
Vincent Banet (Limoux)	1	-	-	-	-
Frederic Banquet (Sheffield Eagles)	2	-	2	-	4
Cyril Baudouin (Carpentras)	1	-	-	-	-
Hadj Boudebza (St Esteve)	1	-	-	-	-
Didier Cabestany (Catalan)	2	1	-	-	4
Pierre Chamorin (St Esteve)	2	1	-	-	4
Brian Coles (Catalan)	2	-	-	-	-
David Despin (Villeneuve-sur-Lot)	1	-	-	-	-
Patrick Entat (Avignon)	2	-	-	-	-
Pascal Fages (Pia)	2	-	-	-	-
David Fraisse (Workington Town)	1	-	-	-	-
Jean-Marc Garcia (St Esteve)	2	-	-	-	-
Lilian Hebert (Pia)	1	-	-	-	-
Karl Jaavuo (Pia)	2	-	-	-	-
Pascal Jampy (St Esteve)	2	-	-	-	-
Stephan Millet (St Gaudens)	2	-	-	-	-
Pascal Mons (Carcassonne)	1	-	-	-	-
Gael Tallec (Wigan)	1	-	-	-	-
Frederic Teixido (Limoux)	2	-	-	-	-
Marc Tisseyre (Limoux)	1	-	-	-	-
Patrick Torreilles (Pia)	2	1	-	-	4
Thierry Valero (FC Lezignan)	2	-	-	-	-

NEW ZEALAND *(Coach: Frank Endacott)*

	M	T	G	FG	Pts
Richard Barnett (Cronulla)	2	1	-	-	4
Richard Blackmore (Auckland Warriors)	3	3	-	-	12
Syd Eru (Auckland Warriors)	3	-	-	-	-
Gary Freeman (Penrith)	1	-	-	-	-
Daryl Halligan (Sydney Bulldogs)	-	-	-	-	-
Sean Hoppe (Auckland Warriors)	3	2	-	-	8
Mark Horo (Western Suburbs)	3	-	-	-	-
Kevin Iro (Leeds)	3	1	-	-	4
Tony Iro (Sydney City Roosters)	3	1	-	-	4
Stacey Jones (Auckland Warriors)	3	-	-	-	-
Stephen Kearney (Auckland Warriors)	3	-	-	-	-
Tony Kemp (Leeds)	3	1	-	-	4
John Lomax (Canberra Raiders)	1	-	-	-	-
Jason Lowrie (Sydney City Roosters)	3	-	-	-	-
Gene Ngamu (Auckland Warriors)	3	-	1	-	2
Hitro Okesene (Auckland Warriors)	3	1	-	-	4
Henry Paul (Wigan)	3	-	-	-	-
Quentin Pongia (Canberra Raiders)	3	-	-	-	-
Matthew Ridge (Manly)	3	1	10	1	25
Brent Stuart (Western Suburbs)	-	-	-	-	-
John Timu (Sydney Bulldogs)	-	-	-	-	-
Brendon Tuuta (Castleford)	-	-	-	-	-

Ruben Wiki (Canberra Raiders) 3 - - - -
Jason Williams (Sydney Bulldogs) 1 - - - -

PAPUA NEW GUINEA *(Coach: Joe Tokam)*

	M	T	G	FG	Pts
Michael Angra (Hagen Eagles)	1	-	-	-	-
Marcus Bai (Port Moresby Vipers)	2	1	-	-	4
David Buko (Goroka Lahanis)	2	1	-	-	4
Aquila Emil (Port Moresby Vipers)	-	-	-	-	-
Tuiyo Evei (Goroka Lahanis)	1	-	-	-	-
Stanley Gene (Goroka Lahanis)	2	1	-	-	4
David Gomia (Goroka Lahanis)	2	-	-	-	-
August Joseph (Rabaul Gurias)	-	-	-	-	-
James Kops (Hagen Eagles)	2	-	-	-	-
Joshua Kouoru (Rabaul Gurias)	2	-	-	-	-
Adrian Lam (Sydney City Roosters)	2	1	-	-	4
Bruce Mamando (Canberra Raiders)	2	-	-	-	-
Billy Noi Jnr (Hagen Eagles)	-	-	-	-	-
John Okul (Moorebank Bulldogs)	2	-	-	-	-
Elias Paiyo (Port Moresby Vipers)	2	1	5	-	14
Samuel Pinpin (Mendi Muruks)	-	-	-	-	-
David Reeka (Lae Bombers)	1	-	-	-	-
Lucas Solbat (Rabaul Gurias)	2	1	-	-	4
Robert Tela (Lae Bombers)	2	-	-	-	-
Petrus Thomas (Mendi Muruks)	-	-	-	-	-
Max Tiri (Hagen Eagles)	2	-	-	-	-
David Westley (Canberra Raiders)	2	-	-	-	-
Nande Yer (Mendi Muruks)	2	-	-	-	-

SOUTH AFRICA *(Coach: Tony Fisher)*

	M	T	G	FG	Pts
Jaco Alberts (S Queensland Crushers)	2	-	-	-	-
Berend Alkema	3	-	-	-	-
Andrew Ballot (Bay of Plenty)	3	-	-	-	-
Jaco Booysen (St Helens Devils)	3	-	-	-	-
Willem Boshoff (Eastern Reds)	3	-	-	-	-
Francois Cloete (Barea Students)	3	-	-	-	-
Guy Coombe (Durban Sharks)	3	-	-	-	-
Tim Fourie (City Scorpions)	3	-	-	-	-
Pierre Grobbelaar (Vaal Buffaloes)	-	-	-	-	-
Koot Human (S Queensland Crushers)	2	-	-	-	-
Justin Jennings (S Queensland Crushers)	1	-	-	-	-
Mark Johnson (Workington Town)	3	-	-	-	-
Elmar Lubbe (Eastern Reds)	1	-	-	-	-
Ernest Ludick	2	-	-	-	-
Warren McCann		-	-	-	-
John Mudgeway (Durban Sharks)	1	-	-	-	-
Eugene Powell (City Scorpions)	1	-	-	-	-
Nico Serfontein	1	-	-	-	-
Kobus van Deventer (Germiston Warriors)	3	-	-	-	-
Jaco van Niekerk (Eastern Reds)	2	-	-	-	-
Pierre van Wyk (Eastern Reds)	3	-	4	-	8
Jaco Visser	1	-	-	-	-
Gideon Watts	3	1	-	-	4
Gerald Williams (Durban Sharks)	3	-	-	-	-

TONGA *(Coach: Mike McClennan)*

	M	T	G	FG	Pts
Peri Amato (Mua Saints)		-	-	-	-
Asa Amone (Halifax)	2	-	6	-	12
Angelo Dymock (Moorepark)	2	-	-	-	-
Salesi Finau (Canberra Raiders)	2	1	-	-	4
Awen Guttenbeil (Manly)	2	2	-	-	8
Lee Hansen (Widnes)	2	-	-	-	-
Solomon Haumono (Manly)	2	-	-	-	-
Phil Howlett (Parramatta)	2	1	-	-	4
Luke Leilua (Otahuhu)	-	-	-	-	-
Talite Liava'a (Litchfield)	1	-	-	-	-
Tau'alupe Liku (Leigh)	1	1	-	-	4
Mateaki Mafi (Kolomua)	-	-	-	-	-
Duane Mann (Auckland Warriors)	2	-	-	-	-
George Mann (Leeds)	2	-	-	-	-
Martin Masella (Illawarra)	2	-	-	-	-
Andrew Tangata-Toa (Newcastle Knights)	-	-	-	-	-
Una Taufa (Canberra Raiders)	2	2	-	-	8
Taukolo Tonga (Kolomua Warriors)	1	-	-	-	-
Tevita Vaikona (Hull)	2	-	-	-	-
Jimmy Veikoso (Belconen)	2	1	-	-	4
Frank Watene (Auckland Warriors)	-	-	-	-	-
Willie Wolfgramm (Narrendera)	2	2	-	-	8

WESTERN SAMOA *(Coach: Graham Lowe)*

	M	T	G	FG	Pts
Fa'ausu Afoa (Penrith)	2	-	-	-	-
Mark Elia (Albi)	2	-	-	-	-
Lolani Koko (Narrendera)	1	-	-	-	-
Brian Laumatia (Cronulla)	2	1	-	-	4
Des Maea (Auckland Warriors)	1	-	-	-	-
Gus Malietoa-Brown (Auckland Warriors)	-	-	-	-	-
Vila Matautia (St Helens)	2	3	-	-	12
Sam Panapa (Salford)	2	-	-	-	-
Apollo Perelini (St Helens)	2	1	-	-	4
Robert Piva (Queensland Cowboys)	-	-	-	-	-
Willie Poching (Auckland Warriors)	2	-	-	-	-
Tea Ropati (Auckland Warriors)	2	-	-	-	-
John Schuster (Halifax)	2	-	11	-	22
Mike Setefano (North Harbour)	-	-	-	-	-

Se'e Solomona (Auckland Warriors) 2 - - - -
Henry Suluvale (Sydney City Roosters) - - - - -
Willie Swann (Auckland Warriors) 2 1 - - 4
Tony Tatupu (Auckland Warriors) 2 2 - - 8
Setu Tuilaepa (Narrendera) - - - - -
Va'aiga Tuigamala (Wigan) 2 2 - - 8
Paki Tuimavave (North Harbour) 2 1 - - 4
Tony Tuimavave (Auckland Warriors) 2 - - - -
Earl Va'a (Wellington Dukes) - - - - -
Joe Vagana (Auckland Warriors) 2 - - - -
Nigel Vagana (Auckland Warriors) - - - - -

EMERGING NATIONS 1995

GROUP ONE

COOK ISLANDS 64 ....**USA 6**
At Featherstone, Monday 16 October, 1995; **Attendance:** 3,133
Cook Islands: T - Cuthers 3, Hunter 2, Noovao 2, Johnston 2,
Bowen, Toa; G - Noovao 10
USA: T - Preston; G- Niu

SCOTLAND 34 ....**RUSSIA 9**
At Featherstone, Monday 16 October, 1995; **Attendance:** 3,133
Scotland: T - Blee 2, Tait 2, How, Waddell; G- McAlister 4,
Thompson
Russia: T - Netchaev, Otradnov; FG - Scheglov

COOK ISLANDS 58 ....**RUSSIA 20**
At Leigh, Wednesday 18 October, 1995; **Attendance:** 1,921
Cook Islands: Tariu 4, Cuthers 2, Tuaru 2, Shepherd, Noovao,
Bowen, Toa; G - Noovao 4, Piakura
Russia: T - Kiryakov 2, Sirgeev, Romanov; G - Kozlov, Vinokhodov

SCOTLAND 38 ....**USA 16**
At Northampton, Wednesday 18 October, 1995; **Attendance:** 2,088
Scotland: T - Shelford 3, Thompson, Ketteridge, How, M Smith;
G - Thompson 5
USA: T - Niu 2, Lewis; G - Niu 2

COOK ISLANDS 21 ....**SCOTLAND 10**
At Castleford, Friday 20 October, 1995; **Attendance:** 2,889
Cook Islands: T - Tariu 2, Shepherd 2; G - Noovao 2; FG - Davys
Scotland: T - A Tait 2; G - Thompson

RUSSIA 28 ....**USA 26**
At Warrington, Friday 20 October, 1995; **Attendance:** 1,950
Russia: T- Gavriline 3, Kiryakov, Romanov, Netchaev;
G - Scheglov, Netchaev
USA: T- Preston 2, Maffie, Wallace, Broussard; G - Niu 3

GROUP TWO

IRELAND 48 ....**MOLDOVA 26**
At Rochdale, Monday 16 October, 1995; **Attendance:** 1,235
Ireland: T - Gordon 3, Crompton, Foy, Casey, Grainey, Smith,
McElhatton; G - Comerford 6
Moldova: T - Piskunov 2, Olar, Krivtsov, Benkowskiy; G - Olar 3

MOLDOVA 24 ....**MORROCCO 19**
At Northampton, Wednesday 18 October, 1995; **Attendance:** 2,008
Moldova: T - Piskunov 3, Strakh, V Sapega; G - Olar, Piskunov
Morocco: T - Katir 2, Mahabi; G - Echalouki 2, Mahabi; FG - Katir

IRELAND 42 ....**MOROCCO 6**
At Dewsbury, Friday 20 October, 1995; **Attendance:** 1,756
Ireland: T - Ricky Smith, Horrigan, Grainey, Gordon, Comerford,
Foy, Browne, Sullivan; G - Comerford 5
Morocco: T - Bibarss; G - Amar

GROUP ONE TABLE

	P	W	D	L	F	A	Pts
Cook Islands	3	3	0	0	143	36	6
Scotland	3	2	0	1	82	46	4
Russia	3	1	0	2	57	118	2
USA	3	0	0	3	48	130	0

GROUP TWO TABLE

	P	W	D	L	F	A	Pts
Ireland	2	2	0	0	90	32	4
Moldova	2	1	0	1	50	67	2
Morocco	2	0	0	2	25	66	0

1995 EMERGING NATIONS FINAL

COOK ISLANDS 22 ....**IRELAND 6**
At Gigg Lane, Bury, Tuesday 24 October, 1995;
Attendance: 4,147; **Referee:** Dennis Hale (New Zealand)
Cook Islands: T - Cuthers, Bowen, Kermonde, Shepherd;
G - Noovao 3
Ireland: T - Comerford; G - Comerford
Cook Islands: Tiri Toa, Sonny Shepherd, Andrew Paita, Allan
Tuaru, Ngere Tariu, Craig Bowen (c), Ali Davys, Bob Hunter, James
Cuthers, Jason Temu, Alex Kermonde, Tama Henry, Meti Noovao,
Subs, Tangi Tangimeta played, Tungane Tini used, Lloyd Matapo
not used, Lefou Jack not used.
Ireland: Gavin Gordon, Phelim Comerford, Richard Smith, Ricky
Smith, Eugene McEntaggert, Craig McElhatton, Martin Crompton,
Bryan Smyth, Seamus McCallion, Leo Casey, Gary Grainey, Tony
Nuttall, Paul Owens, (c), Subs, Conor O'Sullivan played, Des Foy
played, Sean Casey played, Eric Boyle not used.